PRAISE FOR RICHARD B. SCHWARTZ

Proof of Purchase

It's like this guy is just channeling Raymond Chandler on every page. . . . The ending . . . would make Mike Hammer proud.

— Jochem Steen, *Sons of Spade*

In this engaging hard-boiled mystery, one of three in Schwartz's Jack Grant series (Frozen Stare; The Last Voice You Hear), the seasoned California PI looks into the disappearance of an ex-girlfriend at the request of the woman's husband. When her mutilated body turns up in the woods, Grant makes it his mission to track down her murderer. With the assistance of Lt. Diana Craig, an attractive fast-riser in the San Bernardino police department, Grant follows leads that point to his client, as well as to a consortium of underworld bosses who are branching out into a mega-real estate project. The pair find time, between car chases and gun battles, to begin a relationship. . . . Fans of Robert Parker will enjoy encountering Grant . . . .

— *Publishers Weekly*

The Last Voice You Hear

It's not often that an author's second book is as good as the first, and even less frequent are the instances when an author . . . top[s] it with an extraordinary second . . . deliver[ing] a walloping good tale as well. Richard B. Schwartz has done just that. In *The Last Voice You Hear*, Mr. Schwartz places himself on par with our finest contemporary murder-mystery writers. This is a book you won't want to miss. . . .

— Alan Paul Curtis in *Who Dunnit*

The author . . . writes vividly, putting the reader right into the scene. Schwartz explores the meaning of right and wrong, crime and justice.

— Mary Helen Becker in *Mystery News*

The story rockets along . . . a fast-moving, well-told story with a surprising conclusion that blurs the line between crime and justice.
— Joseph Scarpato, Jr. in *Mystery Scene*

Jack Grant, the Vietnam vet and Pasadena-based PI who debuted in Frozen Stare (1989), returns in this engrossing sequel by Schwartz, author of several scholarly studies of Samuel Johnson. Schwartz knows his London, but surprisingly he evokes California with equal ease, mainly with vividly etched strokes. An apparently maniacal killer is on the loose in London, someone strong and very practiced at impalement. So far, so nasty. But when a victim is dispatched in similar fashion in Disneyland, of all places, Jack Grant is called in. He discovers the killer's identity, but there's a problem: there's a method to the killer's madness. Moreover, Grant has an ethical problem of his own: he's plagued by his conscience, since he understands and even sympathizes with the murderer's cause. The cinematic climax takes place high above the floor of the California desert, and Schwartz squeezes every last drop of suspense from his setting. . . . The result is a high-tension thriller awash in sanguinary detail. Paper towels, anyone?
— *Publishers Weekly*

Frozen Stare

I welcome Richard Schwartz to the club. It's been a long time since I've seen two more engaging characters entering the series scene.
— Sandra Scoppettone

Grant and White play nicely off each other and the switch-on-a-switch works well.
— *Kirkus Reviews*

This tale, in the California private eye tradition, has a rousing finish and is an enjoyable read.
— *Publishers Weekly*

A new author devoted to the hard-boiled tradition. . . . Schwartz has the hard-boiled formula down pat. . . . Schwartz does not break any rules in Frozen Stare. . . . He writes crisply. The narrative moves at a slam-bang pace as bodies pile up. . . . As a dedicated student of the hard-boiled school of detective fiction [Schwartz] has learned his lessons well.
— *The Washington Post Book World*

Gives a whole new meaning to the phrase 'cold-blooded murder'. . . . This is a quick read with plenty of action. Schwartz's first novel is a winner!
— *Sarasota, FL Herald Tribune*

This is a delightful tale, full of amusing touches, and the relationship between Grant and his good cop friend, black Frank White, is a joy. I hope that Schwartz can keep this standard up for a long time to come.
— *The Armchair Detective*

Nice and Noir: Contemporary American Crime Fiction

Opinionated but always fascinating, shrewd and smart, but always readable. . . .
— *The Thrilling Detective*

BOOKS BY RICHARD B. SCHWARTZ
FICTION
The Jack Grant Novels
Frozen Stare
The Last Voice You Hear
Proof of Purchase
The Tom Deaton Novels
Into the Dark
The Survivor's Song
Nightmare Man
Death Whispers
Poison Touch
The Gwen Harrison Novels
No Exit
Red City

CRITICISM
Samuel Johnson and the New Science
Samuel Johnson and the Problem of Evil
Boswell's Johnson: A Preface to the Life
Daily Life in Johnson's London
After the Death of Literature
Nice and Noir: Contemporary American Crime Fiction
The Wounds that Heal: Heroism and Human Development
(with Judith A. Schwartz)
ed. The Plays of Arthur Murphy, 4 vols.
ed. Theory and Tradition in Eighteenth-Century Studies

MEMOIRS
The Biggest City in America: A Fifties Boyhood in Ohio
Accidental Soldier: A Reserve Officer at West Point in the Vietnam Era
Postwar Higher Education in America: Just Yesterday

EBOOK
Is a College Education Still Worth the Price? A Dean's Sobering Perspective

A GWEN HARRISON NOVEL

RED CITY

RICHARD B. SCHWARTZ

DARK
HARBOR
BOOKS

RED CITY

Published by Dark Harbor Books
First Edition 2022

Cover design: Jana Rade

ISBN: 979-8-9855721-8-6 Paperback Edition
         979-8-218-09413-3 Hardcover Edition
         979-8-9855721-9-3 Digital Edition

Library of Congress Control Number: 2022920304

Author services by Pedernales Publishing, LLC
www.pedernalespublishing.com

10 9 8 7 6 5 4 3 2 1

Printed in the United States of America

For Those Who Stood Up Against the Voices of Fanaticism

*Hide nothing, for time, which sees all
and hears all, exposes all.*
Sophocles

*At eighteen our convictions are hills
from which we look; at forty-five
they are caves in which we hide.*
F. Scott Fitzgerald

He can run. But he can't hide.
Joe Louis

I

BLEEDOUT

1

MacArthur Park

Terry Rader's future was bright. His associate's degree from Barstow Community College had taken him to Cal State-Northridge and, eventually, a master's degree in Computer Science there. His college loans had been kept to a minimum, Mary Anne Hennessey had accepted his proposal of marriage and his mom and dad--Kathy and Bill Rader--had offered him the family Corolla to kick off their son and his bride's new life together. When times and the economy changed and Terry's eight-year job in the software systems industry suddenly evaporated, Mary Anne recommended he turn to something more stable. "What will people always need?" she asked, and, after thinking about it for a week, Terry began the process of securing a loan from the Small Business Administration, a loan that—with some personal savings—led to the creation of Rader Sanitary Systems.

He noted his *Master of Science* degree on his business cards and on the company stationery, but left off the 'computer science' specification. His educational credentials, businessman's dress and personable manner engendered confidence in a succession of gratified clients and resulted in a host of steady, lucrative contracts. He now had more port-o-lets than any other dealer in southern California and a sizeable portion of the Los Angeles municipal market. The city itself, as a physical presence, was in a constant state of reinvention and every worksite—whether new construction or a rehab or renovation--required Terry's company's services.

A good portion of his effectiveness was due to his *hands-on* approach, a subject of humor with new clients, but a serious element in his business strategy. "You can't understand the client's needs and assess the client's degree of satisfaction without being in the field and seeing what the client sees and experiencing what the client experiences," he said. Once a week he drove the cleaning truck from site to site, pumping out selected units, checking them for cleanliness and serviceability, and, in the process, monitoring the work of his field staff and sustaining a high level of quality control.

In its way the work was gratifying. Each site was freshened and the results were instantaneous and palpable. The momentary stench was replaced by the strong, antiseptic smell of fresh fluid and what had been an outhouse suddenly exuded the scents and aromas of, well…a greenhouse. The efficiency of the operation was equally gratifying and the smiles of surprise on the faces of the facilities' patrons gave Terry a feeling of accomplishment which, though not a subject for dinner conversation, was nevertheless very real.

And the money didn't hurt at all, particularly after Mary Anne gave birth to the twins and rising fuel costs in 2021 and 2022 eroded the profit margin of every competitive enterprise in the southland dependent on the internal-combustion engine. Rader Sanitary Systems had taken the family to a four-bedroom Spanish revival home in the Antelope Valley and an annual cruise to the Mexican Riviera. The old Corolla had been replaced by a luxury SUV and family van and a set of new investments insured that when the time came for the twins to attend college Terry and Mary Anne would be ready to cover their tuition and related expenses in full.

RSS did more than provide a service; it provided an entire range of installations, from simple single-stall units to the trailer-sized models termed "Crowd Pleasers". The latter could include elaborate hand washing stations as well as complete, air-conditioned comfort.

The single stalls also offered attractive conveniences. Terry's personal favorite was the Purell sanitizing, no-rinse hand wash. The Purell system killed 99.9% of most common germs without the use of towels or running water. Purell's moisturizers (their brochure stated) left hands feeling soft and refreshed even after repeated use. The Purell product was dermatologist-tested and dye free. It even came in an aloe formula.

The City of Beverly Hills specified the inclusion of Purell products in all of their RSS contracts. In MacArthur Park the situation was different. A nocturnal battle zone for ethnic gangs and a twenty-four hour drug emporium, the Park had lost most of the charm that had inspired Richard Harris' 1968 hit song. It was now rare to see women in yellow cotton dresses, foaming like waves on the ground around their knees, with birds like tender babies in their hands and old men playing chess or checkers under the local palm trees. Harris had been staying at the nearby Sheraton Townhouse Hotel on the rainy afternoon when inspiration struck, the very same place in which Elizabeth Taylor and Richard Burton had once wed. Its time had passed as well.

The public restrooms in the Park (now under refurbishment) were stark and prison-like. Cinder block compartments, they were designed for effortless (and constant) cleansing and their appointments were minimalist: polished steel mirrors, bolted above sensor-driven faucets, adjoining automatic driers. There were no paper towel dispensers. The containers for the liquid soap were sequestered behind bolted steel plates, to discourage theft or vandalism, and the narrow, physical space of each stall and washup area had been configured to discourage both sexual encounters and full-body bathing.

The RSS port-o-lets that had been installed during the course of the renovation project were barebones facilities. There were no Purell products, since they would be immediately stolen, and the toilet tissue dispensers were equipped with single-rotation blocks, so that no more than three sheets of paper were released with each tug. Enlarged floor drains and special toilet tissue caps were utilized to facilitate the cleaning of each unit. The facilities were purely functional. Their configuration insured that no one would spend more time in them than was absolutely necessary.

Terry had cleaned four of the units and was surprised by their condition. Except for some fecal scrawls in unit #2 (each disappearing with a single application of a stream of 409) and the usual dried urine puddles and scraps of tissue on the floors, the users had been uncommonly careful. "It's *their* environment, after all," Terry would say. "Perhaps they're finally protecting it."

He opened the door to unit #5 and noticed that a recent occupant had done his or her best to wipe the walls and seat area. There were some smears, but the attempt had been made. "Outstanding," he said, audibly. "Maybe this is a part of some new cultural trend."

The final unit was #8. After finishing that, Terry could splash some 409 on his rubber gloves and rubber boots, dry them with paper towels, and head west on Wilshire for breakfast. There was a mom and pop operation called Nell's just beyond the old Bullock's Wilshire building, a handsome landmark he had often visited in his youth. Nell's specialized in omelets. He was imagining his filled with cheese and peppers, side by side with some sausage patties, sliced fruit and homemade hash browns.

It was a promising day all around. The sun was unusually bright and warm. The marine layer had been light and there was some growing pedestrian activity in the Park, with metro riders emerging from the local station, walking toward him, their eyes filled with hope and expectation.

He spritzed the gloved fingers of his left hand with the 409 and turned the handle on the door of the last unit. When the door didn't move he stepped back, fearing that he had disturbed an occupant. He then knocked but there was no response. He knocked a second time, in case the first attempt had been muffled by the sounds of vehicular traffic. He wanted to be certain. There was nothing worse for business than alarming a person under these circumstances, when imaginations always run to darker possibilities than that of the helping hand of an RSS serviceman.

There was still no response, so he tugged the handle a second time. While it was common for teenagers to lock toilet doors and then slip under or climb over them, this could not be done in a port-o-let. He inspected the door further and saw that someone had nailed the door to the roof and flooring of the unit with several large finishing nails. The nails at the top of the door were loose; the plastic roof had not held firmly. The nails at the bottom, however, had penetrated the plastic flooring and lodged in the wooden base.

Terry returned to his truck and secured a claw hammer large enough to remove a 16-penny nail. He also found a piece of 2x4 to place behind the head of the hammer for support, lest he damage the plastic case of the port-o-let in removing the nails. He returned to the bank of port-o-lets and carefully removed the nails. "There," he said. "A little cleaning and we'll be back in business."

He opened the door, expecting to see the results of some other form of mischief. He found something altogether different. As he stood there, trembling and staring in shock and disbelief, hot bitter juices rose up in his throat, and his hands—now suddenly damp with sweat—began to shake within their rubber gloves.

2

MacArthur Park

Her blue nurse's scrubs were streaked with reddish black blood from the center of her chest to her lap and knees. The slick polyester fabric had not been able to absorb all of the flow and a resulting pool had formed on the floor between her white, thick-cushioned sneakers, its edges drying and darkening. The walls of the port-o-let were covered with arterial spurts and spray, the blood forming angry red lines and dribbles. Blood was everywhere. One line of it was smeared with a hand-print, probably from the victim. Terry pulled back his own right hand, clutching it against his chest, in fear and shock. He was light headed, his stomach churning and convulsing, the rancid taste of the fluid in his esophagus preparing him for the onslaught of vomit which, for some reason, never came. He fell back against a berm of grass and earth and fumbled at his belt, trying to release his cell phone from its case.

After three attempts he realized that he was still wearing his rubber gloves. When he pulled them off, his hands were caked with moist talcum powder. He called 911 and in seven minutes heard the sound of a single police siren. Terry had been as explicit as he could be, under the circumstances. The responding officers were a Robbery/Homicide detective named Dearing and a lab tech named Cloke. Dearing introduced himself while Cloke went to work processing the port-o-let unit.

Terry introduced himself, told the detective about RSS, explained that he was the owner and CEO, and tried to reduce any potential skepticism by explaining the reason for his making regular rounds in cleaning the company's units. Dearing seemed impatient. He was tapping the eraser end of his pencil against his notepad. Terry was disappointed; he had expected the detective to write down everything that he had said.

"When did you discover the body, Mr. Rader?"

"About ten minutes ago, Detective Dearing. I called the moment I found her."

"What did you touch?"

"Just the door handle and the nails...the door had been nailed shut...I removed them."

"And do you know if your fingerprints are on file with the department?"

"No, sir, but I didn't use my bare hands; I had my gloves on." He removed them from his pocket and showed them to Dearing. "I had sprayed some 409 on them before I opened the door. I'm sorry...that's our standard procedure. I hope I didn't disturb any evidence..."

Dearing didn't respond. "Did you see anyone else in the area while you were cleaning out the port-o-lets?"

"There was some vehicular traffic and a few people walking through the park, but I didn't notice anyone nearby."

"Anybody sitting down, watching, for example?"

"No, sir, not really."

"You used your own hammer to remove the nails?"

"Yes, sir."

"And you didn't see any tools in the area that could have been used to drive in those nails?"

"No, sir. I mean...I didn't really look around for any, but there weren't any right by the unit."

"Did you touch the body at all?"

"No, sir. She was just sitting that way when I found her. I was kind of in shock. I caught my breath for a second or two and then called 911."

Dearing removed a form from his pocket and handed it to Terry.

"Please take a seat and fill this out for me. It will give us your contact information. At the bottom there's room to summarize what you've already told me. Write down what you just said; we'll be back in touch for a full statement later. I'd also appreciate it if you'd wait here a few minutes to see if Mr. Cloke has any questions after his initial processing."

"Sure, I'll be happy to," Terry said. He took the sheet of paper, sat back on the berm, balanced the form on his knee, removed a pen from his shirt pocket, and started to fill in the blanks. He noticed that his knee was unsteady and his hand was still shaking.

When he finished filling out the form he looked around for Dearing. The wind was blowing in from the coast and the sheet of paper was flapping around in his hand. At first he thought about folding it, but thought that Dearing might not want him to do that.

Dearing was talking to Cloke; they were out of earshot.

"What have we got, Charlie?" Dearing asked.

"Black female, probably early thirties. Multiple stab wounds to the chest and sternum. One showed the remnants of a sucking chest wound; the assailant must have punctured a lung. Two fatal entry wounds to the heart. Two slash marks along the throat."

"Looks like whoever did it wanted to make sure," Dearing said.

"Yes, it wouldn't have taken this many to do it."

"What else?"

"From the body temperature I'd put the time of death at late last night."

"Midnight or so?"

"Later. Maybe 2:00 a.m. That's just an estimate."

"That's too late for a school nurse to be out. Has to be a hospital or emergency health care nurse...don't you think?"

"Best guess, sure."

"How about a name?"

"*Denise.* On her i.d. bracelet. No surname. Just 'Denise' with little roses on either side of the name. She also had an aspirin allergy noted on the back."

"Anything else?"

"Slash and stab wounds on her wrists and the palms of her hands. She resisted, Vince. The hand smear's almost surely her's—either when she tried to block the knife or couldn't stop her body from convulsing. Maybe just reaching out helplessly as she was losing consciousness."

"Couldn't have been very pleasant."

"I wouldn't think so," Cloke said.

"We'll know more when we get her on the coroner's table," Dearing said.

"Pretty girl," Cloke said. "Terrible place to die—left alone like that, propped up in a public toilet."

3

North Mission Road

The Coroner's Office was filled with the bittersweet smell of burned coffee. Dearing could sense it on the street as he approached the building. Somebody forgot to flip the *off* switch, he thought...unless they somehow liked it charred and syrupy.

The Coroner's Office was no longer a dimly-lit basement operation populated by sallow-faced file clerks and old men in brown pants with stained shirt sleeves. It was now a vast bureaucracy with a thriving gift operation, education arm and growing list of community-outreach functions. The people there conduct an array of programs for youthful drunk drivers and they sell tee shirts, polo shirts, sweatshirts and oversized coffee mugs with the California seal on a deputy coroner's badge juxtaposed with the chalk outline of a corpse. The one thing that they have always done and still continue to do is examine the remains of homicide victims.

Dearing was sipping a can of Diet Pepsi while Dr. Annette Li examined the decedent's remains. She said very little as she went about her business. The room was brightly-lit and the smells were of chemicals rather than of bloat and decay.

"Victim fought back," Li said.

"I don't think she had much of a chance," Dearing answered.

"Killed her three or four times," Li said. "Heart...throat..."

"What kind of weapon?"

"Knife. Long. Four inches. Maybe five. Not serrated. Narrow. Probably not kitchen tool. Width of paring knife but much longer."

"Maybe a switchblade or gravity knife?"

"Something like that...possible."

"Regular weapon, not something brought specifically for this purpose."

"Hard to say...but possible."

"Speaks to intent...or could. No premeditation, used on impulse."

"You walk around *that* park you find couple dozen people carrying knives like this. Small timers. Kids."

"Or people who don't have silencers for their guns and don't want to attract attention."

"True. Around that park...you find plenty guns too."

"Anything under her nails?"

"Cloke said he checked."

"Yes, but I thought you might find something that he missed."

"No. Just a little talcum powder. Probably from rubber gloves. Nurse."

"What was in her stomach?"

"Not much: salad, vegetables, I think a little chicken. Hadn't eaten in awhile."

"What about her general health?"

"Heart slightly enlarged. Little tilted. No big deal. Well groomed. Clean hair. Trimmed nails. Slight pinpricks on lower left arm, just above wrist. Not always above veins."

"Diabetic probably. Checking glucose levels. How about her fingertips?"

"No. People avoid that now. More nerve endings there. More sensitive. You see B. B. King commercial?"

"Yes. Did you check her blood sugar level?"

"Ninety-seven. Average morning number."

"So she was taking care of herself."

"Yes. Trying to. Doesn't help when people stick knives in you."

"How about time of death?"

"Cloke thought 2:00 a.m. Good number. Works for me."

"Anything else? Any sign of sexual activity?"

"No. Nothing detectible. No fluid residue. No marks."

"If he wanted something from her it probably wasn't that."

"No. Nothing irregular with clothing. She had plenty—underwear, t-shirt, scrubs…cold in doctor's office, cold in hospital…everything in place; buttons all straight; straps not twisted."

"Maybe what he wanted was her silence," Dearing said.

"Maybe. Some kill for thrill. Twisted, evil. This is sex for them."

"Yes," Dearing said, "but if that was what you were seeking, I don't think you'd look in MacArthur Park."

"Not rational person. You know what you find in MacArthur Park?"

"What's that?" Dearing asked.

"Defenseless people."

"Yes, but not people with money, at least not at night."

"Could have taken her there. Not a place most people go at night."

"Right," Dearing said, "at least not the kind of people who would call the police if they saw anything suspicious."

"Close to everything, but still…remote. Could have been downtown. Could have been on the freeway."

"We've got to get her last name, find out where she worked and who she knew," Dearing said.

"Unless this event random, she knew one very bad person," Dr. Li answered.

4

North Mission Road

Dearing excused himself and went out in the hallway to call Cloke. The smell from the autopsy room clung to his hair and clothing. He caught Cloke on the third ring.

"Anything on the prints yet?" he asked.

"There's some kind of problem, Vince," Cloke answered.

"What do you mean?"

"I don't know. IAFIS never takes longer than two hours."

"That's funny. And it's still too early for the DNA…"

"Maybe by late tomorrow," Cloke said.

"I've got to go to court, Charlie. I'll check back with you later."

"I'll be here," Cloke answered.

IAFIS, the integrated automated fingerprint identification system, is one of the jewels in the FBI's Criminal Justice Information Services Division crown—an outpost in Clarksburg, West Virginia that sits on just under 1,000 acres of land and includes a 500,000 square foot main office building that is slightly shorter than the length of three football fields. Crime is a growth industry. IAFIS is open for business twenty-four hours a day, three hundred and sixty-five days a year--the largest biometric database in the world, with 47,000,000 subjects in the Criminal Master File. The officials there pride themselves on their 24-hour turnaround time for civil fingerprint submissions and 2-hour turnaround for criminal submissions. A request from the LAPD on a homicide case should merit most-favored-nation status; Cloke and Dearing both wondered what the cause of the delay could be.

The surface streets were clogged with traffic, but Dearing reached the metropolitan courthouse on South Hill in nineteen minutes. The case was a straightforward one. A steady repeater by the name of Cal Weber had held up a grocery store in South Central. Fortunately for him, the proprietor—a man named Kim—had survived the head shot which had taken part of an ear in the process. Weber dodged the lethal injection gurney and needle, but the judge was unlikely to be favorably disposed toward an individual who went for the kill shot for seventy-eight dollars and thirteen cents.

Mr. Kim had identified Weber's mugshot and picked him out of a lineup without a moment's pause. This case of theft and attempted murder was the most recent entry for a rap sheet that began when Weber was a thirteen year-old shoplifter in rural Tennessee. In those days he was stealing for beer money; he had since graduated to more expensive substances.

Dearing had caught the case and collared the perp. He now had to close the loop by testifying to the steps that he had taken in locating him and to the results of the GSR test on his right hand and wrist, the fingerprint test on his cheap revolver, and the identification processes involving the victim, Mr. Kim.

The Public Defender would make a legal gesture or two and recite some formulaic requests, but Cal Weber's fate was clear from the get-go. With standard sentencing for robbery, assault, battery, and attempted murder, the likelihood of this repeat offender's being sighted on the streets of the golden state as a free man would turn on his chances of living until the age of 107.

The judge was a hard case by the name of Delaney. If Cal had any hopes of getting a slap on the wrist from him it would be with a sledge hammer or a spiked mace. Dearing saw Delaney's bailiff in the hall outside his courtroom; he told Dearing there would be a brief delay. Dearing thought about calling Cloke again, but decided instead to get a cup of 'freshly-brewed' coffee from the nearest vending machine and take a few minutes to catch his breath and remind himself of the testimony he would be giving.

He later learned that the cause of the delay was a last-minute attempt by the Public Defender to plead his client down to simple assault. The DA laughed out loud, Dearing spent twenty minutes on the stand, and Cal Weber was sent back to jail to await the next scheduled state prison bus to what would surely be his last address of record.

The DA thanked Dearing for his help by patting him on the arm and offering him a friendly nod. As soon as Dearing reached the hallway he pulled out his cell phone and called Cloke.

"I know your question, Vince," he said, "but I still don't have an answer."

"How long has it been since you submitted your request, Charlie?"

"Three hours and…just a second…twenty-seven minutes. No, twenty eight, now."

"The longer we have to wait the colder the trail gets," Dearing said.

"Yep," Cloke answered.

"Have you called them?"

"Three times. They said they'd check on it. They haven't. Or at least if they have, they haven't told me about it. What do you want me to do?"

"Sit tight. I'm going to the Bureau office."

5

The Santa Monica Freeway

The Los Angeles Field Office of the FBI actually has investigative jurisdiction over the entire Central District of California, including Los Angeles, Orange, Riverside, San Bernardino, San Luis Obispo, Santa Barbara, and Ventura Counties. Eighteen million people live within its territory, an area covering 40,000 square miles.

The office is presided over by an Assistant Director in Charge, who in turn has three Special Agents in Charge within his organization: a SAC for the Counterterrorism Division, a SAC for the Criminal Division, and a SAC for the Counterintelligence and Cyber Division. The principal office is on the far west side of town, on Wilshire, just east of the 405. There are ten satellite offices, termed *Resident Agencies*, in Lancaster, Long Beach, Palm Springs, Riverside, Santa Ana, Santa Maria, Ventura, Victorville, West Covina, and at LAX. The L.A. Field Office—a gargantuan bureaucracy--has the third greatest concentration of Special Agents in America.

Dearing would start with the Criminal Division SAC as a courtesy, but move on to the Assistant Director if he had to. The fingerprint request had been routine, but the delay in processing it was not. Phone calls were being dodged and further requests put off. It was time to turn up the volume.

Traffic on the Santa Monica was dense but moving at a steady 30 mph—annoying, but far preferable to the steady red lights and gridlock of surface streets. The 405 was dead stopped heading south, but moving slowly north. Dearing noticed the change in the color of the air. The grayish yellow had been replaced by a light beige, with intermittent clouds and flashes of blue. The L.A. basin was the worst spot on the planet in which to introduce the internal-combustion engine; it had already been significantly polluted by Indian campfires long before the arrival of the Model T and the millions of vehicles which followed in its wake.

The SAC for the Bureau Criminal Division was named McCandless. Bureau-gray in dress, with short salt-and-pepper hair, and lightly-polished black wingtips, his bright blue eyes were his singular feature, like a human structure breaking up a flat horizon. He and Dearing had cooperated on a number of occasions in the past, each knowing the other's value and each placing success above turf or ego.

Bureau executive assistants have long been the industry standard. McCandless' was named Jeanne. She saw Dearing talking to the suite receptionist, got up from her desk behind a pane of eye-level, clear glass, and approached him. She was wearing a wool skirt and a matched sweater/cardigan combination.

"Detective Dearing," she said. "We haven't seen you in awhile."

At the sound of her voice the receptionist ended her mini-interrogation and deferred to her Bureau superior.

"Hello, Jeanne," he answered, "it's been nearly a year…"

"Do you need to see the SAC?"

"Yes. Is he available?"

"They're all with the AD, but he should be back before too long. I just put on a fresh pot of coffee. A double dose."

"Sounds good," he said. She was referring to the fact that she routinely added a second packet to the filter.

"True high test," she added.

When the receptionist reached for her phone to take an incoming call, the SAC's executive assistant invited Dearing to wait in his office. She brought the black coffee in a ceramic Bureau cup. Standard procedure—a proven form of recycling as well as an efficient method for picking up a fingerprint or two, should they be needed later.

First-class treatment, Dearing thought. No time logged on the vinyl chairs in the sparsely-furnished waiting room. Instead: McCandless' leather couch with a mahogany coffee table and a soothing environment of wood paneling with signed photos and miscellaneous Bureau mementos.

The coffee was hot, fresh, and as strong as Jeanne had promised. After three sips Dearing could feel a noticeable increase in his heart rate.

When McCandless appeared, twenty minutes later, there were no exaggerated smiles or strokes.

"Vince," he said, "good to see you. How long has it been…ten, twelve months?"

"Yes," Dearing responded. "The kidnapping case."

"DiBartolo," McCandless said. "Very sad. We got the perp at least."

"Yes."

"What can I do for you today, Vince?"

"Murder in MacArthur Park, this morning, John. A woman stabbed in a port-o-let."

"I saw it on the morning police log," McCandless answered. "Who was she?"

"That's what I hoped you could help me with," Dearing said.

"How?" he asked.

"We sent the prints to IAFIS. It's been over four hours now and there's been no response."

"What do they say when you call back and ask about the delay?"

"They just put us off," Dearing answered. "I thought you might put in a word."

"Case number?"

"Here," Dearing said, sliding a slip of paper across the coffee table.

"I've got a follow up with the Assistant Director in a few minutes,"

McCandless said. "I'll call IAFIS in the meantime and ask them to get on the stick. If you don't have the i.d. by the time you get back downtown, call Jeanne. I like to stay in normal channels with something like this, but a homicide case should always jump to the top of the pile. If we have to, we can up the ante a little bit. You could send the data to us, for example, and we could forward it for identification over the Assistant Director's name."

"I don't want to create any tidal waves, John, but we *do* need the i.d."

"Understood."

Dearing extended his hand. "Always a pleasure doing business with the government," he said.

McCandless smiled and said, "I'm not so sure I'd go that far."

On the way out Dearing thanked Jeanne again. He was on his cell to Cloke before he got in his car. "Try again in ten minutes, Charlie," he said. "The SAC is jerking their chain for us."

"Will do," Cloke answered. "Drive carefully, Vince. Remember: there are thieves and murderers out there along with the sleepy heads, drunks and dopers."

"I know, thanks," Dearing said, as he turned the key in the ignition and looked up, hoping for some broader patches of blue sky between the heavy gray clouds.

6

The Santa Monica Freeway

This time the westbound traffic on the Santa Monica was stopped and the eastbound was skipping along at a brisk forty-five mile an hour pace. L.A. karma.

When Dearing approached the Fairfax exit, his cell phone rang. Cloke, he figured, but when he looked at the display he saw that he was wrong. It was his daughter calling, probably to thank him for her recent birthday present. They talked a little about her job and about the Chicago weather, about her newest boyfriend and about the Bulls and Bears of the market as well as those of the court and field. He thanked her for calling as he approached the four-stack and clicked on his turn signal.

When he got to his desk there was a note from Cloke to see him ASAP. Dearing wondered why he hadn't simply called. Cloke was at his desk, futzing nervously with some swab vials and spray bottles.

"What's up, Charlie?" Dearing asked. "Why the note?"

"Let's get some coffee, Vince."

The coffee urns were in the corner of the oblong suite of offices and work stations that included Cloke's. The table sat next to the window and the sunlight created shadows on the carpet, muting some of the stains from past coffee spills. It was quiet there and when Charlie poured each of them a cup Dearing noticed that he had lowered his voice as if he was about to convey some deep secret.

"What is it, Charlie? Spit it out."

"The i.d. came in, Vince. I didn't even have to ask."

"That's good," Dearing said. "McCandless is strictly standup."

"I don't know what to do, Vince. I wanted to talk to you first."

"What to do about what, Charlie? Who's the vic?"

"Her name is Denise White."

"Yes…?"

"She's the lieutenant's cousin, Vince. Charles White is her uncle."

Lieutenant Frank White was in Washington—actually at a Dulles Airport hotel—for an international conference with officials from Interpol. He would want to be contacted immediately and Dearing did so, through the lieutenant's principal assistant, Officer Jane Foley. Foley had his private cell phone number and would be aware of the scheduling details for the Washington meeting.

Cloke's apprehensions centered on Lieutenant White's uncle. Denise was the daughter of Charles's younger brother, Carl, a retired autoworker in Lansing, Michigan. Frank was the son of Charles's middle brother, Marshall, a master electrician, living with his wife Clara in St. Louis. Carl's wife Dorothy had died five years previously. Denise had been born to them late in life and Carl had always doted on her.

This information had been gathered hastily from local sources. Cloke was a careful man, concerned about steps and processes. He wanted to learn as much as he could about the family dynamics so that he could brief Officer Foley. He already knew Frank and Charles.

Frank had been a lieutenant for eight years and he was frequently mentioned as a likely candidate for promotion to captain. Quiet and measured in manner, he was huge in size: 6'3" or 6'4" Cloke estimated, and at least 265 pounds. His frame and movements were athletic, his demeanor that of a quiet, thoughtful person, a man of few words but one fully capable of swift and violent actions.

His Uncle Charles was his physical opposite. Short in stature and lean and wiry in appearance, he bore a striking resemblance to the 70's and 80's actor Adolph Caesar, though he was clean-shaven and his nose was narrower and his eyes more piercing.

Charles White was the most senior noncom to serve in Vietnam and the first black soldier to receive the Medal of Honor in Korea. It went well with his DSM and Silver Star with three clusters. Charles White's actions were legendary; they rippled and expanded in the constant retelling, like a course of strong waves rearranging a beach. His specialties were silent kills and the eradication of seemingly-inaccessible snipers.

Even in his late eighties he had retained his skills. Hardened retired officers were still deferential to him, particularly those whose lives he had saved. He avoided this kind of attention and routinely turned down offers of media profiles and interviews, the latter multiplying at the approach of each national holiday.

Frank's ex-wife, Marie, who reported the evening news on the L.A. ABC affiliate, had sought him out in particular, but he always declined politely, despite the temptation to help, in his modest way, to advance her career.

His own wife Mary was the executive staff assistant who held the Caltech chemistry department and its assorted faculty together. Though she was approaching 80, she resolutely refused to even consider the possibility of retirement. After years of being moved from one military post to another, she relished the stability of a steady job and the comforts of their quiet home, a small craftsman on a shaded section of Hill in Altadena. When Charles spoke of the snow and ice in Seoul or the heat and humidity in Saigon she sat back in her porch chair and sipped the orange juice or lemonade made from the fruit of their own trees. The avocado had not been as productive as the citrus plantings, but lately it was showing signs of promise.

She had never tried to fully domesticate Charles, but she had taken every opportunity to focus his attention on the joys of the moment—the hummingbirds at the multiple feeders at the corners of the lodge atop Mt.

Wilson or those rare moments in the desert garden at the Huntington when a sudden shower would bring the entire garden to life--the cacti and other succulents all in sudden motion with flowers blossoming and colors appearing as if they were being photographed in stop action.

When she walked across the campus this morning she would have taken note of the olive trees west of the Athenaeum and seen the stains they left on the tiles and walkways. She would have seen the fan palms along the quadrangle and the koi in the carefully-terraced reflecting ponds, the campus a lush monastery of science, insulated from the mundane concerns of the world beyond and the traffic sounds of the nearby boulevards.

She would not yet have known that her niece had been cruelly murdered, bleeding to death in a makeshift toilet in a public park frequented by youth gangs and drug dealers. Her thoughts would not yet have turned to the cupboard in their guest room, with its lock box containing her husband's service automatic, his .44 magnum, his carborundum sharpening stone, his collection of knives, and the simple handmade weapon consisting of oak handles with a single piece of steel piano wire suspended between them.

7

The Pasadena Library, Central Branch

Charles White made a point of staying in touch with the men who had served with him during the thirty-five years of his Army career. He scanned the internet and the collection of military periodicals to which—at his request—the local library subscribed. The saddest fact to him was that men who had survived the bloody hills of Korea and the booby traps and ambushes of Vietnam had fallen to cancer and heart disease, to strokes and to diabetes.

Historically, the everyday threats to health had always taken a greater toll than grape, canister, or musket balls, but it still struck him as a mean fate to befall a survivor of modern combat. When he saw an obituary on one of his corporals from the Central Highlands—an Oklahoma City man named Stokes—he made a note to himself to send the man's widow a personal letter. Returning the computer to its homepage—the online index to the library catalogue—he put the note in the pocket of his gray poplin jacket and walked out onto East Walnut.

He had parked on Euclid, but walking east he saw a group of five boys surrounding a sixth, a boy slight in stature and bookish in appearance. The tallest of the five was pushing the smaller boy, while his friends kept the boy from escaping the circle that they had formed around him. The boys were in their late teens, marked with homemade hand, shoulder, and neck tattoos and wearing purple and gray shirts and jackets. Charles had stopped trying to identify the colors of each of the above-the-freeway gangs, as their numbers continued to increase and multiply.

The boy who was being bullied was doing his best to hold back tears, despite the escalation of the curses and shoves to which he was being subjected. When Charles approached them, the tallest boy—the lead bully—spoke to him.

"What the fuck are you looking at, old man?" he said.

"Cowards, probably," Charles responded.

"Cowards?" the boy answered. "You've got a lot of fucking nerve to say something like that to us."

"Accurate, though," Charles said. "Bullies are almost always cowards. It's their way of trying to convince themselves that they're brave."

"Well, I hope you're feeling brave, nigger, because when we're through with him we'll give you a taste."

Charles smiled, suppressing a laugh.

"You think that's funny?" the boy asked.

Charles continued to smile.

"How funny is this?" he asked, taking a gravity knife from his pocket and flicking it open with a snap of his right wrist.

Two of his friends grabbed the arms of the lone boy. One said, "Stick him, Coop; we'll hold onto this one until you're ready for him."

The one called Coop raised the point of the blade to chin level and said, "Where do you want it, nigger?"

Charles didn't change his stance or adopt some martial arts posture. He simply raised his left hand, extended his index finger, and invited the boy forward. When he lunged, Charles grabbed his right wrist and snapped it, then thrust his right elbow into the center of the boy's face before the nerve endings in his arm could signal his brain that it was time to feel intense pain and let his mouth know that it could begin screaming. As the blood began to flow freely from his nose over his lips and chin and his legs became rubbery, Charles let him fall into the edge of the curb and roll over into the gutter.

By now he *was* screaming. Charles picked up the gravity knife, which had fallen on the sidewalk, closed it, and slipped it into his pocket. The other four boys stared at him; the two holding the lone boy released their grip.

"You might want to call an ambulance," Charles said. "With a fracture like that he will go into shock within a matter of minutes." Turning to the boy they had bullied, he said, "Come along, young man. I think that's enough excitement for them for one day."

As they walked away, the four remaining boys knelt down in the gutter and began arguing among themselves on their next course of action. When Charles and the boy had put enough distance between themselves and the gang members, he told the young man to take care of himself. The boy said, "Thanks," and hurried east toward Los Robles. As Charles opened the door to his car, his cell phone rang.

8

Herndon, VA:
The Hilton Washington Dulles

Frank White was still stunned in disbelief. He had spoken with Officer Foley a few minutes earlier and told her that he wanted to break the news to his Uncle Carl. When he reached him he learned that someone from the FBI had contacted him first, a breach of protocol, but not something that--under the circumstances—Frank was anxious to contest.

He spent most of the conversation urging his uncle to stay in Michigan, assuring him that *he* would make certain that the investigation would be accelerated and that Denise's remains would be treated with all due love and respect. "There really is nothing you can do at this time, Uncle Carl," he said. "Stay with your family and friends. I'll check in with you the instant we learn anything."

Next he called Charles, but Charles's cell was busy, as was his Aunt Mary's work line. He assumed that they were talking to one another, probably about dinner. He knew that Carl had not phoned them, because Frank specifically requested that he not do so. The last thing that he wanted was for Charles to begin his own, private investigation before they had a chance to speak.

As he looked at the keyboard of his cell phone, his right index finger poised above the number 1, he noticed the cup of coffee balanced on the arm of his chair that had now grown cold and oil-slicked. The whole conference routine of coffee and sweet rolls, midmorning and mid-afternoon breaks, bowls of hard candy in the center of the table, conference notepads and hotel pens, lunch buffets with generic pasta salad, cold cuts, and processed cheese, sweating pitchers of ice water and scuffed plastic containers of coffee with widening drip stains beneath the spouts, the mechanical speakers with loud ties and rehashed PowerPoints...the whole world of lost time on the government's nickel...had dissolved in an instant when Officer Foley told him of Denise's death.

Vince Dearing was a good man. Smart, tenacious, focused, his only living family member a stockbroker daughter living in Chicago. What was her name--Sharon? The case was in good hands. Frank's captain, Carl Loram, would keep Dearing on the case. Frank was too close to it. Besides, Loram would need him to maintain the distance between Dearing and Frank's Uncle Charles.

Charles would not rush in, making demands and asking questions, seeking reports and timetables. He would shadow Dearing at a distance and conduct his own investigation, an investigation in which such things as probable cause and Miranda rights would play little or no role.

Charles was not a trained investigator, but he was the best hunter his nephew had ever seen and his ability to take pains—any pains—was clear from the results of his hunts and the circumstances under which they were conducted. He could sit silently in the cold, the dark, or the muck for hours, waiting for his prey to make a single mistake or miscalculation.

The last thing Frank wanted was a second tragedy for his family—the arrest and conviction of his uncle for meting out vigilante justice. He focused on his cell phone again, tapping in Charles's number. He got a cell service message instead of a ring. Charles had turned off his phone. Why--because he had already begun and didn't want his location traced?

Frank returned his phone to its case on his belt and went directly to his room, collecting his things as quickly as he could, then checking out, and taking the Hilton shuttle back to the airport. He was not scheduled to return to Los Angeles for another day and a half. Allowing for check-in and the time before the next flight, he might be in L.A. in six and a half hours: an eternity if Charles had already armed himself and begun his search.

9

Silver Lake Boulevard at Earl

Dearing had secured Denise White's address from her vehicle registration records and was driving north on Silver Lake Boulevard to her apartment building. The newish structure was four stories in height and heavily gated, with security keypads at the entrance to the underground parking structure as well as at the front gate and front door.

Her unit was on the third floor, a small two-bedroom with a kitchen, living room/dining room combination, and a single bathroom. The second bedroom was small, no more than 9' x 12'; she had used it as an office. The appointments were modest: laminate countertops and cabinetry, vinyl floors in the kitchen and bath, and generic wall-to-wall carpeting in the other areas. The landlord had invested in safety rather than style; in this always-changing neighborhood—now largely a haven for young professionals--security was the sought-after luxury, not granite countertops or stainless steel appliances.

The apartment was neat and orderly. There was no clutter to be seen. Indeed there was little of anything to be seen. The kitchen was outfitted like an extended-stay motel: four place settings of everything, saucepans in several sizes, minimal cutlery, and minimal cleaning equipment—some cleanser, hand soap, dishwasher soap, and Windex.

While Cloke checked for prints and any suspicious fluid or fiber evidence, Dearing checked the bedroom. He was immediately struck by the fact that the closet was not filled. For him that was a first. He had never known a woman over the age of 8 who was incapable of filling every inch of closet space at her disposal. There was clothing—including several sets of nurse's scrubs—and shoes of various sorts and sizes, but there was still available room for more.

She had kept her outerwear in the guest closet by the front door, along with some baseball- and other caps, while her underwear and nightshirts were kept in a chest of drawers beside her bed. The linen closet outside the bathroom had exactly four sets each of sheets, pillow cases, towels, hand towels, and wash cloths, all of them white. Dearing wondered if this was the result of nurse's training and a compulsive need to boil and bleach everything for maximum cleanliness.

The medicine chest in the bathroom contained another assortment of predictable items: Crest tooth paste and brush, Arm and Hammer baking soda deodorant, Advil and Aleve, tampons, Robitussin, Coricidin, Q-tips, cotton balls, and two different forms of dental floss.

Her cosmetics were on a shelf within the linen closet. Again, the collection of lotions and polishes was minimal. Perhaps nurses were discouraged from using certain cosmetics. There was a single lipstick, some eye makeup, and a comb and brush set. There was also a lint roller, which Dearing brought to Cloke's attention—a possible treasure trove of fiber evidence.

She kept her vitamins in her pantry cupboard. Everything else enjoyed its own shelf: cereal boxes and other cardboard containers; canned goods; oils, vinegars and other liquids not requiring refrigeration, and a section for sugar, flour, and other bulk items. On the top shelf was an unopened bottle of white wine, resting on its side, and a 6-pack of diet soda.

The freezer contained some leftovers, with dates recorded on the wrappers, packets of frozen vegetables, and reusable ice packs. The refrigerator contained butter, eggs, some milk with four days left on the sell-by date, grapefruit juice, fresh vegetables and lettuce, carrots and onions in the crisper, and, finally, something interesting.

Dearing called to Cloke, who was examining the material clinging to the bathtub drain plug.

"What is it, Vince?"

"I'm not sure. It's in the refrigerator. It looks like a large pen."

"You mean like a ballpoint?"

"No, it's some kind of medical thing."

By then Cloke had appeared at the edge of the kitchen, wiping his hands on a paper towel. "For insulin, maybe?"

"I don't think so. It says *Byetta* on the side."

"Oh," Cloke said, "no big deal. It's a product for diabetics. It mimics the actions of a naturally-occurring hormone. Regulates blood sugar. Helps your body make more of its own insulin."

"But you inject it?"

"Yeah. You get a month's worth in one of those pens. Good thing that she was an orderly person…"

"Why's that?"

"Because you take it right before breakfast and right before dinner. You've got an hour between when you dose yourself and when you have to eat. You can't wait any longer than that, so if you're eating at some place you can't make it to in an hour, you have to take the pen with you and take the shot in the car or bathroom or some place. Plus it has to be refrigerated."

"That's why she had those ice bag things in the freezer."

"Yeah, probably. You get a day or two a month when it can go unrefrigerated—for example, if you've got a long travel time between you and the next refrigerator. It's very complicated. My brother uses the stuff. Swears by it, actually."

"Must be worth all the trouble," Dearing said.

"They say it's one of the only things out there that shows signs that it can actually reverse the effects of diabetes."

"Pity," Dearing said. "It's not doing her any good now."

The building manager showed them to Denise White's vacant parking space.

"No car," Vince said. "Not that I expected one."

"And no purse," Cloke added, "other than the two empty spares in her closet."

"Maybe we'll get lucky," Dearing said, "and find them before somebody in MacArthur Park does."

"She's due some luck," Cloke answered, in a voice that was growing increasingly weary.

10

Midfield Terminal—Dulles Airport

Frank's flight was scheduled for departure in fifty-five minutes. He picked up a large cup of black coffee, searched out an empty gate area, took out his cell phone, and called Dearing, who picked up on the second ring.

"Vince, Frank White."

"How you doing, lieutenant?"

"I'm on my way back, Vince," Frank responded. "What have you got so far?"

"Unfortunately, not very much. Charlie's going over the hard drive on your cousin's computer, but he hasn't found anything of interest yet. We've got both her home phone and cell phone records, but, again, nothing important has jumped out so far. Mostly just calls to family and friends. As you know, she hadn't been in town but a year or so. Much of the information flow seems to involve her orienting herself to the area—a lot of material on weather, traffic, cineplexes, church schedules…she seems like a very nice young lady. Nothing questionable in the paper or cyber trail."

"You don't have to sugar coat anything for me, Vince."

"I know, lieutenant. We're pursuing all of the personal stuff. Our top priority is to find the person who did this to her."

"What about credit card information?"

"MasterCard," Vince said, "all very generic—gas, groceries,

restaurants. She did most of her shopping in Glendale, at the Galleria. Got her groceries from Vons, her gas from Chevron or Shell. She seems to have been very busy with her work."

"Why do you say that?" Frank asked.

"Because there's no real evidence of a social life. Did she ever say anything to you about a boyfriend, for example?"

"No. I didn't ask, but she didn't volunteer anything. She talked about some people at work, but no one in particular. She didn't seem to be thinking much about those kinds of things. She liked to drive up in the mountains and drive up the coast. She visited the Hearst Castle, I know. She also went up to Carmel once. She seemed to be taking her time at settling in—getting the lay of the land, if you know what I mean."

"We still haven't located her car or her purse. Maybe there will be something there, lieutenant."

"The motive doesn't appear to be theft," Frank said. "Too much violence."

"Nothing sexual, lieutenant," Vince said.

"That's a blessing," Frank said. "With all the trauma I doubt that she suffered very much. Whoever did this only had one thing in mind: killing her as quickly and...what?... as *definitively*...as possible."

"I agree. Do you want one of us to meet you at the airport, lieutenant?"

"No, Vince, but thanks. I've got my car in the long-term lot there."

"I'll be here late, lieutenant. Call me any time. If I learn anything in the next couple hours—*anything*—I'll call your cell and leave a message while you're in the air. I'm going to her workplace as soon as I get off the phone."

"Thank Charlie Cloke for me," Frank said. "I know that the two of you are giving this your full attention."

"I will. Just one other thing, lieutenant..."

"What's that, Vince?"

"Have you had a chance to talk to your Uncle Charles?"

"Not yet. He's turned off his cell. My aunt is next on my list. He always checks in with her."

"That's good, lieutenant. I know that the captain's concerned that he might…well, you know…start his own search. Not that he couldn't be helpful…*very* helpful for that matter…but…well…it would be good if he was inside the tent on this one. We know how you all must feel, but…"

"I understand, Vince. You don't want World War III and you don't want him to get hurt in any way."

"Exactly, lieutenant."

"I'll talk to my aunt."

"Thanks very much."

"He already knows," Mary White said to Frank. "Her name hadn't been released yet, but he started putting the facts together and called Carl. Carl admitted to him that he was waiting for you to call him first. I told him not to do anything foolish. He assured me that he wouldn't. He's on his way downtown now, to talk to Captain Loram."

"I'll call the captain," Frank said, "and make sure that Charles and the family are fully informed on the progress of the investigation. Are you OK, Aunt Mary?"

"I still can't believe it. It's so horrible…"

"I know. Do whatever feels best. Stay at work and keep occupied or go home, pull the drapes, and lay down for awhile."

"Charles is picking me up after he's finished downtown," Mary said. "He told me not to go home, that you never know what the person who did this might be up to. I told him that if the person knew anything about our family he wouldn't be stupid enough to come to our home."

"Wait for Charles, Aunt Mary. People who kill other people… they're all stupid in some way."

11

Wilshire at South Commonwealth

Vince passed Lafayette Park and saw the art deco tower of what had once been Bullock's Wilshire come into view on his left. No more than six or seven blocks from MacArthur Park now, the area took on a slightly more upscale feel. What the local merchants termed 'mid-Wilshire' was a long way from what the tourists were likely to understand by that term. Still, it was a place where you could park your car with relative safety and feel the surrounding presence of investment money and the power that accompanied it.

Tracing Denise's social security records, Dearing had learned that she was employed by USC. The directory information on the university's website identified her as a senior staff nurse at something called the 'Community Health Clinic' on Vermont Avenue, near Wilshire.

At first he wondered why the clinic wasn't part of the USC hospital complex, but he also realized that universities were vast and complicated things these days. The clinic was probably part of some research project or outreach activity, possibly both.

The Community Health Clinic was located in what was once a single-screen movie theatre called the Wilshire Plaza. The owner had made a last-ditch attempt at survival from the cineplex onslaught by carving the principal auditorium into three screening rooms, one a sound-insulated balcony used for small-audience art films. When that failed, the building was sold to a discount drug store chain, which functioned for two years before relocating to Alhambra and selling its mid-Wilshire site to USC.

While the architectural details of the building had been maintained, the marquee signage opportunities had not been utilized. Instead, the glass entrance doors had been replaced with more-secure steel and simple lettering had been affixed to them:

University of Southern California
North Campus
Community Health Clinic

There was no real 'campus' beyond the old theatre building, though there was perhaps a quarter-acre of surface parking space on the southern and eastern sides of the structure. Dearing parked in a Visitor space on the side of the building, entered, and approached the receptionist, who sat behind a semicircular desk with built-in slots containing pamphlets, leaflets and other handouts. Beyond the desk on the opposite wall was an outline sketch of the building and an adjoining, alphabetical list of its occupants.

Dearing badged the receptionist and asked to see the official in charge of the clinic.

"That would be Dr. Hinden," she said. "He's in room 112, right at the end of that corridor." She pointed to her left, Dearing's right. He thanked her, walked through the rabbit warren of offices and work stations, and badged the secretary outside of room 112. She phoned Hinden, who was visible through his glass wall, and then told Dearing to go right in. He badged Hinden and asked him if he was familiar with a senior staff nurse named Denise White.

"Of course, officer. She's our senior nurse practitioner."

"I thought she was a staff nurse," Dearing responded.

"That's her title, but she's credentialed as a nurse practitioner. H.R. won't permit that title, since it's not in their official inventory."

"Really? Not that it's that big a deal, but I would have thought that USC's medical facilities would have included a lot of nurse practitioners."

"They do, particularly in their HMO, but they have a separate H.R. office and a separate set of policies. We actually began as part of a research project in the School of Social Work."

"Well, it doesn't make a great deal of difference now, Dr. Hinden," Dearing said. "We found Denise White's body this morning in MacArthur Park. She was murdered."

He said it abruptly in order to assess Hinden's response. Hinden didn't answer instantly. Finally the words spilled out a syllable at a time: "De-nise…is…dead…she… was…mur-dered? This…morn-ing?"

His face drained of blood, his lower lip twitched; he stood up suddenly and said, "You'll have to excuse me," and left his office. A few minutes later he returned. His face was covered in sweat, his left shirt sleeve was soaked and his breath smelled of vomit.

"I'm so sorry," he said, taking a tin of Altoids from his desk drawer and chewing several of them at once. Composing himself, he said, "Who would do such a thing? Denise was a wonderful person. Why would anyone want to hurt someone that sweet, someone who did so much good?"

"I can't answer that yet, Dr. Hinden," Dearing said. "The investigation is still in its early stages. We're just beginning to talk to the people who knew her. That's why I'm here."

Hinden paused, took a sip from the water bottle on his desk, replaced the cap, and took a deep breath before continuing. "She worked with us for about a year," Hinden said. "Her immediate supervisor was Bill Clemmer. He's actually in Seattle today, talking to people at one of the foundations that supports us."

"Who is in the office who worked closely with her?" Dearing asked.

"Jeff Billups is in, I think," Hinden said. "I'll introduce you."

Billups' work station was in the southeast corner of the building, adjoining the clinical space used by the nurse practitioners. Hinden introduced them, volunteered to help later in any way that he could, and then excused himself.

Billups was short, thin, and well-groomed. His dress was youthful but the receding hairline and crow's feet suggested that the onset of middle age had already arrived. His lab coat was heavily starched and his pocket contained a matched, expensive pen and pencil set. His desk was organized down to the point of parallel post-it note pads. From the slight glimmer underneath the overhead lights, Dearing thought he could detect some clear polish on Billups' fingernails. He took the news of Denise's death stoically. Finally he said, "Horrid, that's simply horrid."

"What was your relationship with Miss White?" Dearing asked.

"We were coworkers," Billups said. "I was her junior, but we always worked together closely."

"It would be very helpful if you could tell me about your patients (or *clients*) and give me a sense of just what it is that your part of the Clinic does," Dearing said.

Billups paused, steepled his fingertips, and said, "How can I describe it? I would say that our job is to understand and prevent suicide."

"*Suicide?*" Dearing asked.

"Slow suicide," Billups answered. "Gradual suicide. An immigrant generation comes here, fleeing political and religious oppression or—more commonly—grinding poverty and a life with no foreseeable future. They build a life here that's light years ahead of what they left behind, but still on the bottom rungs of the L.A. ladder. A few of the kids build on their success and move up that ladder. A lot don't. They join gangs, get into trouble with the police, and spiral downward."

"What did you mean by *gradual suicide?*" Dearing asked.

"They practice behaviors that are ultimately deleterious to their health. In some cases the behaviors are *immediately* deleterious to their health. The Clinic was designed to look at the intersection between health and those behaviors. It basically asks the question, why do people do things that they know will harm them? It's not a question of education, though many still want to believe that it is. And it's not a question of hopelessness, since these people see examples of success fairly frequently.

"But why do they have pin and ink tattoos? It's not as if real tattoos are prohibitively expensive. Why do they stick unhygienic pins and needles into their skin? They *see* infections. They know that all you need to do is use a little bleach or boiling water to purify them. Why do they do something so stupid? Why do they have unprotected sex on a regular basis? They know all about illegitimacy and its costs. They know all about AIDS and its results. They all know drug addicts and they know the results of drugs in the lives of the poor. They know they don't have unlimited wealth and unimpeded access to the best medical care. They've seen dead people with syringes hanging from their arms, but still…

"The more subtle stuff is easier to explain. They eat food that's highly caloric and laden with sugar and fat, but they're surrounded by other apparently healthy people who eat it and they see athletes endorsing it. They have a vague sense of cardiovascular disease and they've heard of diabetes, though most of them do not regularly see people who lose their eyesight or their toes and legs to it. While we have a program that deals with healthy nutrition, we recognize that that's more of a long-term issue, with fairly complex medical dimensions. Other things seem much more simple. You see the filth in a gutter; you know that the world is a contaminated place, so you think twice before you take an object and plunge it through your skin and into your bloodstream. How complicated is that?

"In some cases the issues are financial. Proper dental care is expensive. They don't have insurance and if they did they couldn't afford the deductibles. So they're vulnerable. Three hundred years ago one of the principal causes of death was infected teeth. They had cancer and they had strokes and all the things that we have (though the names were sometimes different), but they often *died* from bad teeth. Here it still happens. That's a different issue than dirty needles and diabetes, but it's an important issue for us.

"We even see a high incidence of what are thought of as nineteenth-century diseases, such as thrush. Most are easily cured if you have the medication and some common sense. Thrush sometimes spreads because children get it who are breastfeeding and it persists on their mothers' nipples, so the problem continues if you don't treat the nipples as well as the baby's throat. At least with something like thrush we usually see a prompt response; mothers become upset when they see lesions in their children's mouths and they come to the Clinic right away. However, those same mothers and the men who have fathered their children pursue other practices that lead to results that are not always treated as quickly as they should be."

"So basically you're part nurses, part psychologists, part social workers," Dearing said. "You try to get into peoples' heads to help them make better choices and you provide some primary care to reassure them and attain their confidence, so they can take the necessary steps to turn themselves around."

"Exactly. That's the theory at least, but sometimes—unfortunately--we're simply doing triage."

"I know what you mean," Dearing said. "So are we."

Billups nodded.

"I'd like to see the files on Miss White's patients," Dearing said.

"I can make them available if you secure a warrant," Billups answered. "That's the law, as I understand it. Unfortunately, I can't simply pull out Denise's files, since cases aren't assigned exclusively to a single nurse or nurse practitioner. We each have some specialty areas but people simply walk in and whoever's here at the time treats them."

"How many current files do you have--*approximately*?"

"There they are," Billups said, pointing to a wall of beige metal shelves. "Thousands."

"Thanks," Dearing said, running his eyes over the shelves, dense with color-coded file folders. "I'll be back."

Dearing left the Clinic, walked back into the sunlight, opened his car door, and put on his seatbelt. As he did, his cell phone rang. It was Cloke.

"Vince…Charlie; they've found Denise White's car."

12

Vermont above Wilshire

Dearing slipped his phone into its belt case, turned left on Vermont and then left on Wilshire. The car had been found in the rear of a parking lot on Alvarado, northeast of MacArthur Park. The lot had been built on the site of a demolished building and some of the remnants of the demolition project—scattered bricks and the remains of a cinderblock wall—were still in evidence. The lot was used by an adjoining Texaco station to park cars waiting for or stored after service. There was also a row of spaces for spillover parkers from an adjacent apartment building.

Denise White's car was parked in the rear of the lot, near the spaces reserved for the tenants of the apartment building. Since the lot was privately owned, the LAPD would not monitor or ticket illegal parkers. With the service station closed at night, she may have parked there, knowing that any private patrols would assume that her car was to be serviced or picked up the following day. The neighborhood was dodgy, but not the worst within walking distance of the park.

"Anything yet, Charlie?" Dearing asked. Cloke was dusting the door handles on the two year-old Taurus.

"The prints on the driver's handle and on the trunk match," Cloke said. "They look like the victim's. We haven't started rooting around inside yet. At first blush it looks pretty clean—just about what you'd expect from a person with a neat apartment and a well-organized life. There's nothing obvious to the naked eye—no stains or suspicious marks."

"What about in the trunk?"

"We looked, but we didn't vacuum it yet. Nothing that jumps out at you—a spare tire with tools, a street guide, a miniature copy of the yellow pages…"

"How about a purse?"

"Not in the trunk. I haven't looked in the glove compartment or under the seat yet. That's next."

The Texaco station sold coffee. Dearing took the opportunity to give Cloke some breathing space, bought two cups, and then returned to the lot.

"Guess what," Cloke said, "it was under the driver's seat." He held up a medium-size black purse.

"Anything interesting in it?"

"Yes," Cloke said. "Something very interesting, I think."

Dearing handed him the coffee and Cloke drank it without sipping first. "That's good, Vince, thanks," he said. "First, her full set of keys were in the purse. Since we didn't find any keys or fob on her body, I wonder how she planned to get back into her car."

"The killer probably took it, thinking that her car might be parked nearby."

"Possibly," Cloke said. "He never found it, not if his motive was theft, since there's $80 in the wallet and a MasterCard."

"Driver's license and other things you'd expect to find there?"

"Yes. Plus a lipstick, some nail polish, a small packet of Kleenex, and a separate set of two keys. Each says 'do not duplicate'—probably her keys for the Clinic."

"So what's in it that's interesting, Charlie?"

"Two things. First, the purse is only about half full. How many women use only half of the available space in their purses?"

"Remember her closets, Charlie. This is normal for her."

"Maybe so, but something else in there is *not* normal, Vince."

"What's that?"

"I thought I caught the slightest scent when I opened it…the smell of Hoppe's oil…I sticky-taped the bottom of the purse, applied some chemical, and I got what looks like it could be GSR."

"Are you sure?"

"Yes."

"There's a lot of junk that collects in the bottom of a purse, Charlie."

"I know. We won't be sure until we check it in the lab."

"You're saying that Denise White had room in her purse for a weapon, a weapon that had been recently fired."

"Yes."

"But it's not there now and it was not found at the scene."

"No."

"What about her clothing? Did you check for GSR there?"

"No. There was no reason to."

"Do it," Dearing said. "ASAP."

13

LAX

The moment that Frank White's plane hit the tarmac and the flight attendant announced that cell phones could now be utilized, he checked his messages and saw the call from Vince Dearing. The voice mail simply asked that Frank call Vince as soon as possible. As soon as he left the end of the jetway and could have some privacy, he did.

"Vince…Frank," he said.

"Hi, lieutenant," Vince answered. "No solid leads yet, just an update and a question."

"Go ahead, Vince."

"I visited the USC clinic where your niece worked. I'm getting a warrant to access her clients' records. The problem is that when a person comes in for treatment or advice they're referred to whoever is available at the time. There are thousands of such records. We'll get through them as quickly as possible, but it will still take awhile."

"Good, Vince. What else is happening?"

"We found your niece's car—undisturbed as far as we can see. It was parked in a lot on Alvarado, a few blocks from the park. The lab is evaluating the fiber evidence, but the car looked squeaky clean. This is where it gets more interesting; her purse was in the car, under the front seat."

"Were the car keys in the purse?"

"Yes."

"Is there a keypad on the door handle?" Frank was frustrated that he couldn't remember.

"No, lieutenant."

"Then she must have had a spare key; otherwise she couldn't get back in the car."

"Right, but we didn't find it on her person."

"The perp might have taken it and checked out the area, trying to find the car."

"That's my hunch and, as I said, there's no evidence that he was successful. The purse was under the front seat and there was money and a charge card still in the wallet. There's something else, however…"

"What's that, Vince?"

"When Charlie Cloke inspected the purse he noticed a couple of things. First, the purse was only about half full. Most women would choose a purse large enough to hold whatever they wanted to carry at the time, then they'd fill it up. She had a couple other purses. One was also black, but smaller. For some reason she took the larger one."

"OK…"

"Charlie's wondering if there was something else in the purse that she might have taken with her to the park."

"Like what?"

"When he opened up the purse he thought he detected the smell of some Hoppe's oil."

"Why would she have a weapon?"

"I don't know, lieutenant. He also applied some tape to the inside of the purse, dribbled some chemical and found what he thought looked like GSR."

"A lot of things can look like GSR," Frank said, "and a lot of grit can collect in the bottom of a purse."

"Understood, lieutenant."

"Did he have a dog with him?"

"No, lieutenant."

"A dog would have a more reliable nose than a lab tech."

"Right, lieutenant. Charlie's doing the full lab test now."

"GSR can rub off on anything it comes in contact with, especially fabric," Frank said. "It's possible that *if* she had a handgun and *if* it was recently fired and *if* she then put it in her purse, some GSR could rub off."

"That's my question, lieutenant. Is it at all possible that she could have had a handgun?"

"I don't remember her ever commenting on it. Is there a record of her registering a weapon?"

"No, lieutenant."

"I wouldn't walk into MacArthur Park at night unarmed," Frank said, "but a lot of people do. I can also understand that if you work in a clinic in an edgy part of town and have shelf after shelf of drugs on the premises, you might want to prepare yourself to be robbed from time to time."

"Right, but…"

"But she never said anything to me about it."

"No offense on the next question, lieutenant, but could your uncle have loaned her a weapon if he was worried about her safety?"

"It's possible, but Charles is a stickler for the law. He wouldn't do something like that routinely. He'd have to know that there was an imminent threat of some kind."

"Could you ask him, lieutenant?"

"Of course."

Frank paused before continuing.

"If she did have a weapon the perp must have taken it from her, unless somebody got into the port-o-let before the company guy did… but he said it was nailed shut when he got there."

"Right."

"And if she did have a weapon and if she did take it with her that night she might have known she was in danger."

"Right."

"It wasn't random; she was meeting someone."

"That's what I'm thinking, *if*, of course, Charlie's hunch pans out."

"I'll touch base with my uncle. Let me know the minute the GSR test comes back. And Vince…"

"Yes, lieutenant?"

"Get that warrant and get into those files. If Cloke is right, the murderer now has a handgun as well as a knife and the longer it takes for us to develop a lead the greater the likelihood that time will be on his side rather than ours."

14

MacArthur Park

Charles White sat above the lake at MacArthur Park, watching teenagers in paddle boats, earnest tourists clutching digital cameras, and homeless men rummaging through trash receptacles. He was dressed simply, in old, weathered pants and a shirt that he wore when he did yard work. He had left his poplin jacket in his car, which was parked on a side street, four blocks to the west. He had walked into the park eating a sandwich and carrying a bottle in a brown paper bag. The bottle actually contained tea, but he thought it might draw the attention of one or more of the park regulars.

From his vantage point he could see the location of the port-o-let where Denise's body had been found. It was now encircled by a temporary fence with strips of bright yellow-and-black crime scene tape. A uniformed officer was standing near the site. Charles sat there for an hour and fifteen minutes before he was approached by a local—a homeless man who called himself Chick.

"Never seen you around here before," the man said.

"Came for the sunshine," Charles said. "Nice and warm today."

"Southern exposure, that's what you want," the man replied.

"Had it in my house," Charles said, "until I couldn't make the payments any longer."

"Right," the man answered.

"Looks like you had a crime recently," Charles said.

"That's nothing new, not around here."

"Looks serious though," Charles said, "a fence, tape, the whole deal."

"Glad I missed it," the man said. "I always try to do that."

"What's that?" Charles asked.

"Miss it. Whatever's going down that's bad…I want to avoid it."

"Good practice," Charles said. He thought about asking another question, but he didn't want the man to think that he was an undercover cop or worse. Instead he fabricated a life story that seemed to hold the man's interest. He said that he had been an autoworker who lost his job to foreign competition and lost his home when the values plummeted but the mortgage charges stayed the same. The man sympathized and told his own story of losing his manufacturing job to competition from Mexico.

"The Mexicans still want to come here," he said, "maybe I should have gone there…except that they don't pay there what I made here. Besides, since my wife's gone there's no real need to. I pick up day jobs here and there and somehow seem to get by."

"I understand," Charles said. The man was looking at the neck of the bottle extending above the paper bag next to Charles's side. "Want a drink?" Charles asked.

"Wouldn't say no," the man responded.

Charles reached into his pants pocket and removed a glass flask. "This is better than the stuff in the bottle," he said. "190 proof vodka."

"Christ," the man said, taking the flask from Charles's hand.

"They call it vodka; it's basically straight alcohol. The guy that sold it to me called it 'mother-in-law' vodka. Said you put it in punch. A couple drinks and she falls asleep and stops talking."

"Works for me," the man said, taking a gulp, and swallowing it as if it was ice water.

He took another deep drink and handed the flask back to Charles. "Good stuff," he said.

"Glad you enjoyed it," Charles said, appearing to take a sip himself.

He was hesitant to put his mouth against the rim, but figured that the alcohol probably killed anything that was left there. He let the liquid hit his lips, but didn't swallow any appreciable amount. Then he sat back, as if the vodka had relaxed him. A few minutes later he offered the man another drink and he took two. Charles then waited another minute before he spoke.

"I don't know what happened at the port-a-potty, but I'm glad I wasn't here."

"Yeah, me too," the man answered. "I'll tell you who *would* know: Donnie. He's always here."

"Oh yeah?" Charles said. "A permanent resident, huh?"

"Yeah, something like that. It helps, you know."

"What do you mean?"

"To have somebody here all the time. Somebody who knows the dealers, knows when the gangbangers come around and when they don't, knows the cops and their schedules...sort of like a lookout for the rest of us. Keeps us in the know. Warns us from time to time..."

"Sounds like a valuable man," Charles said. "I guess if I ever come here regularly I should get to know him."

"He's right over there," the man said.

"Oh yeah?" Charles answered.

"Yep. Right by the bandshell. The tall guy."

"Looks pretty well-dressed," Charles said.

"Smart guy. He figures things out," the man said. "Want me to introduce you?"

"Why not?" Charles said. "Maybe he'd like a drink. Maybe he's got some ideas on where I could find some clothes like he has."

"I'll tell him to come over," the man said. He got up and walked toward the bandshell. The seat of his pants and the back of his legs were covered in dust and grass clippings but he didn't bother to brush them off.

15

MacArthur Park

A few minutes later the tall man approached Charles. "How you doing?" he asked.

"Not so bad," Charles said. "A clear day, warm sun, a comfortable seat and nice view. Take a load off."

The man sat down on Charles's left. When he turned slightly and nodded toward him he saw the man's left cheek. Though it was covered by a thin patch of gray and black whiskers Charles could see a massive scar, running from his temple to his throat.

"I'm Donnie," the man said.

"That's what Chick said. Said you were the man around here."

"I don't know about that. I spend a lot of time here. You a first-timer?"

"Yes," Charles said. "Might be coming back though. It's pretty."

"It's not as pretty as it looks," Donnie said.

"I understand," Charles said. "I guess somebody found out the hard way," he added, as he looked in the direction of the port-o-let.

"Yep," Donnie said, "you have to be vigilant. Have to keep your eyes open and your flanks covered. Most of all you've got to have an exit strategy."

"You mean an escape route," Charles said, smiling.

"That's exactly what I mean. The better part of valor," Donnie said.

"Didn't expect to hear Shakespeare quoted today," Charles said.

"A surprise a minute," Donnie said. "You never know who you might meet or what you might learn."

"You've got that right," Charles said. "Thirsty?"

"I'll take a sip," Donnie said.

"Take two," Charles said, handing him the flask. It was a-third full. "Just save me the last one."

"Will do," the man answered. "I'd never take a man's last drink."

After a few minutes Charles broke the silence. "How long you been coming around here?"

"Couple years. Had to get myself right first. Too dangerous otherwise."

"What do you mean?" Charles asked.

"*You've* got to be in full command," Donnie said. "Too many coyotes around."

"Of your senses, you mean."

"Right. No *troops* to command. It's just you and them."

"Don't think I'd like that," Charles said. "Glad to know *you're* keeping an eye out."

"Wondering about the scar, aren't you?" he then said.

"I noticed it," Charles said. "Impolite to ask, and anyway, it's none of my business."

"Right," Donnie said, "but it looks like something out of a horror magazine. I understand."

"Just so it doesn't hurt; that's my motto," Charles said.

"It doesn't. Not now, anyway," Donnie said. "Hurt pretty bad when it happened. Lesson there for all of us."

"Yeah?" Charles asked.

"Yep. Simple lesson too. You shouldn't use PCP as an anesthetic. The docs thought about using it that way once upon a time, but there were too many side effects. It worked for me, though. At least the first couple times. I had this terrible pain…"

Tic douloureux, Charles thought; his aunt's friend, Miss Nancy, suffered from it.

"Had a French name, 'tick de la rue' they call it. Affects the trigeminal nerve; something's leaning on it. Hurts like a four-star son-of-a-bitch."

"Never heard of it," Charles said.

"Usually the dust worked," Donnie said. "Poor man's approach, but what can I say? I *was* a poor man. Then one day it didn't. The pain kept coming and when I upped the dosage I started to hallucinate. Felt like there was something in my cheek. Something with horns all over it. Every time my heart beat it throbbed. I could feel the sharp points coming through my skin. My vision blurred; I started puking my guts out, even began to pass out, but the pain was too intense. It wouldn't let up. By then I was hearing noises. The little dragon in my cheek was screaming, trying to get out. I tried to ease his way, make a little passage with my fingernails. That didn't help so I dug a little deeper, made the exit route longer. I woke up a couple days later. They said I lost a pint and a half of blood and had been in a coma. They stitched me up as best they could.

"Should have gone to a doc in the first place, I guess, except that I couldn't afford one. Had to be far enough gone that they could experiment on me--learn something, you know? You don't have to pay when they can experiment on you. Turned out it was no big deal. A little microsurgery. Moved the vessel that was pressing on the nerve. Suddenly no problemo."

"I've been lucky," Charles said. "Always managed to stay a step ahead of physical things. I saw a guy lose a thumb once; he was working a lathe. He wasn't paying attention and suddenly it was gone. Hell of a shame. Learned a lesson though—whatever it is that you're doing…you always have to pay attention."

"That's my motto," Donnie said. "I live by that. Got a second one too: don't dust yourself to relieve the pain. Whatever that is in your flask is safer."

"Vodka," Charles said, "190 proof."

"Works for me," Donnie said.

Charles looked toward the port-o-let. "I wonder when that went down," he said.

"Last night. Late," Donnie said.

"You were here?"

"Oh yeah. I'm nearly always here."

"But keeping a distance."

"Always."

"Did you see anything?"

"Saw the guy hammer the door shut."

"The door was *nailed* shut?"

"Yep. There was a body inside. I didn't know that at the time, but I saw the cops take the body out this morning."

"Wonder why he would nail it shut," Charles said. "To keep the person inside or keep other people out?"

"Maybe all of the above," Donnie said.

"The person was dead, huh?"

"Oh yeah. Came out feet first."

"And you saw the guy hammer the door shut."

"That I did."

"Anybody from around here?"

"I don't think so. I just saw him from the back, but I don't think he was from around here."

"Why's that?"

"Because he was dressed like a farmer."

16

MacArthur Park

"A *farmer?*"

"Yeah, a farmer."

"You mean like with a straw hat and a piece of hay sticking out of his mouth?"

"Not quite, but something like that. He was wearing…like…a playsuit."

"Overalls."

"Yeah, but not like he was a mechanic or something. And he was wearing a hat, but not a baseball cap kind of thing. A farmer's hat."

Again Charles was concerned that he not appear to be grilling the man, like a cop leaning into a suspect. "I'll be damned," he said. "Wouldn't have expected that. And nailing up a portable toilet…"

"Yep, that's what he was doing. I didn't get too close, of course. I couldn't see how old he was or anything. And I couldn't see his hair color. It was too dark. He did have hair though, not like one of those bald guys or guys who shave their head and then get the 5:00 o'clock shadow around the back of their heads and over their ears. And he wasn't fat or anything. Just Mr. Average."

"Except that he nails up toilets with bodies in them."

"Right," Donnie said.

"Where'd he go after he was finished?"

"Just down to Wilshire. Turned left and kept walking. He never ran or anything. Very nonchalant about it all."

"Maybe he does that sort of thing all the time."

"Wouldn't surprise me," Donnie answered. "I always say, 'if you'll do it once, you'll do it again.'"

Charles took out his flask, pretended to take a sip, and then offered it to Donnie.

"Thanks, don't mind if I do," he said.

Charles paused and fiddled with the cuffs on his shirt. "So you didn't see him until you heard him pounding the nails?"

"Nope. I was actually asleep until then. That's the interesting thing. They mustn't have made much noise before he put the person in the toilet."

"Maybe the person was already in there, minding his own business, having a sit-down. Maybe it was just what they call random violence."

"Could be," Donnie said, "but that late at night...most people wouldn't go out of their way to come here looking for a toilet."

"True," Charles said.

"I figure they walked here together or met here and then something went sour."

"Maybe," Charles said, "except I don't know many people that carry a hammer and nails around with them just in case they might need them."

"I'll give you that," Donnie said. "Maybe he was a carpenter rather than a farmer..."

"You would have noticed a utility belt," Charles said.

"Yep. I try not to miss too many things," Donnie said.

"You should probably talk to the po-lice," Charles said. "I bet they'd be interested in what you saw."

"I don't like to deal with them," Donnie said. "Besides, I didn't see all that much. All I could tell them was that he looked average and dressed like a farmer."

"That might help," Charles said.

"Maybe. I can tell you this…they don't have much else. I walked over after the guy left. I didn't hear anything inside and I didn't see anything on the ground. He didn't leave the hammer or whatever it was he was using to drive the nails. I watched the cops later…you know…when they were trying to find fingerprints and stuff…I didn't hear anybody yell 'Eureka' or suddenly get on the phone, all excited and stuff."

"Weird," Charles said. "Not like a professional killer or anything. I've never heard of somebody being nailed in a toilet. I've heard of people being shot and people being stabbed and people being hit by a piece of pipe or a 2x4, but this one takes the cake."

"Yeah, well you got to remember," Donnie said, "this is your first day in MacArthur Park. Around here weird is normal."

17

Vermont above Wilshire

Dearing had presented his warrant to Stephen Hinden, who, in turn, had informed Jeff Billups that he should open his case files to the LAPD. Hinden had also made a call to Bill Clemmer, who would soon return from Seattle and wonder who the individual was who was going through these confidential records.

Dearing stood before the mountain of files, felt the weight on his heart, and then did a quick count of the number of folders in one running foot, so that he might have a decent estimate of the total number when he requested help from his lieutenant, Dave Carlow. He then did a mental measure of the length of a shelf, ran his eye down the length of the wall, counted the shelves, and estimated the total number of files to be somewhere between 12,000 and 15,000.

He opened a file at random. Inside the jacket was a data sheet stapled to the left and a loose medical log on the right. The data sheet contained the client's name, current address, date of birth, place of employment, eye and hair color, height and weight, ongoing medical conditions, and currently-prescribed medications. On the file in question, the place of employment line contained the notation *N/A*. The medical log sheets were forms that had been Xeroxed hundreds of times. The lines, which were blurred and wavy, contained space for notations concerning the reason(s) for the visit, blood pressure, changes in height and weight, symptoms, and medications and/or therapies prescribed.

The file that Dearing had selected was that of one Luther Voss, age 76, suffering from chronic alcoholism. He had last appeared at the Clinic fourteen months ago, malnourished and experiencing seizures. Nurse Billups had referred him to County Hospital; there were no further notations concerning later visits. "One down, and about 13 or 14 thousand to go," Dearing said to himself.

Dave Carlow authorized the temporary assignment of two officers; he was also able to detail three academy cadets. Dearing would establish the parameters for the scan of the files, eliminating the very young and the very old, the infirm, and the unlikely. Cloke would continue the study of the forensic evidence and follow up on any evidentiary leads. Hinden made a cubicle available to Dearing. While he awaited the arrival of the supporting officers and cadets he called the state, seeking information on Denise White and her vehicle.

Her Taurus had been purchased in Detroit, registered in Virginia, and then in California. There were no bank liens on the title and no co-owners. Her California driver's license carried no points and there were no records of moving violations.

Dearing was about to call Cloke for an update on his progress when a man walked into the office wearing a decent suit and tie, carrying an attaché case and a cup of Starbucks coffee. "Bill Clemmer?" he asked.

"Yes," the man said, "you must be Detective Dearing."

"I am," Dearing said. His surprise must have been visible in his expression, because Clemmer quickly added, "Steve Hinden told me you would be working here."

"How was Seattle?" Dearing asked.

"Productive, I think. We're always beating the bushes for funding."

"I would think so," Dearing said.

"Do you want to come in and chat about Denise?" he asked.

"Yes," Dearing answered. "Do you want to get settled for a minute or two?"

"Just give me five minutes," Clemmer said.

18

Vermont above Wilshire

Clemmer hung up his jacket, took some papers from his attaché case and put them in his in-box, invited Dearing in, took a sip of his coffee, and started right in. "Denise was a wonderful young woman," he said, "all that you could ask for in an organization such as this. She was warm and empathetic, patient, scrupulously professional, knowledge-able...you name it. Her death is a personal tragedy to her family, but it's also a significant loss to the Clinic. I was actually about to promote her, despite the fact that she had been here a relatively brief period of time."

"Did anybody know that?"

"Not really. I was about to mention it to Steve, but so far I hadn't said anything about it to anyone. You think someone would kill her out of professional jealousy?"

"No, not necessarily. I'm just gathering information, trying to get a feel for the office and the organization."

"Everybody loved her," Clemmer said. "Why wouldn't they? This isn't easy work. People burn out quickly. They lose their patience; sometimes they lose their temper. It's enormously frustrating. They see terrible problems that continue and fester even though most of them have fairly straightforward and readily-available solutions. It's one thing to see somebody die of lymphoma, another to see them die of complications from measles. The city is full of children with diabetes who have good insurance, receive good care, and get on with their lives with minimal interruption. Here you see people with type two diabetes that could be controlled by diet, exercise, regular testing, and proper medication. Instead you watch them lose toes and limbs and their eyesight. Denise was diabetic, you know."

"Yes, we did know that."

"Type 2. Usually it doesn't hit people that young. She had it under control."

Dearing was surprised that Clemmer would know that. Again, Clemmer must have seen something in his expression. "I've got it too," he said, "but I earned mine the old-fashioned way. Lost 45 pounds last year and started actually walking on my treadmill instead of just hanging my shirts and pants on it."

"What do you know about her personal life?" Dearing asked.

"I don't think she had one," Clemmer answered. "Janice and I have parties every couple months for the staff; Denise always came alone. She was usually the first person in the office in the morning and the last to leave at night. I didn't pry or anything, but she never mentioned any relationships except professional ones. She pretty much rotated her standard outfits; she wasn't into fashion or anything like that. Not that she was unkempt; far from it. It just wasn't a big thing to her. She drove a simple car...a basic Taurus, I think. Put it this way: she wasn't what you would think of as an L.A. type. She was more of a Midwesterner. I think her family is in Detroit."

Dearing didn't confirm that. "Were there any particular cases that she worked on that we should know about?" he asked.

"You mean involving people who were violent?"

"Right. Or people who seemed to have a problem with her."

"You should also talk to Jeff," Clemmer said, "but I don't know of anyone with whom she came in contact that I could imagine doing her physical harm. Generally they do the harm to themselves. Not that we don't have violent people here; we do...but they come to us for help, not for a fight. They're sometimes belligerent and demanding, but they depend on us to take care of them. They also know, up front, that we absolutely must report any evidence of a stabbing or gunshot wound or evidence of general physical abuse, so the hard core would generally avoid us. They can't come here and receive treatment without questions being asked. If we didn't report evidence of certain forms of activity we'd be shut down in a minute. That doesn't mean that we inform on everybody. If we see symptoms of drug abuse, for example, we don't reach for the phone right away and call the LAPD. If we did, we wouldn't have time to do anything else and neither would the LAPD, but in the case of a stabbing or a shooting or the abuse of a child...we always act immediately."

"How about the abuse of a domestic partner?"

"A matter of degree," Clemmer said. "Anything serious would be reported. Abuse in one form or another is pretty much a constant within this community, especially if you define *abuse* broadly. Denise had a calming influence on these kinds of people and these kinds of situations. I'd say it was her greatest strength. People somehow sensed that she was only interested in helping them and not in judging them. It's hard to believe she's gone; it's even harder to imagine someone wanting to hurt her. Unless it was somehow random..."

Dearing simply nodded in agreement, not wishing to get into the specifics of the case. He knew, however, that random violence was highly unlikely, unless there was a mad carpenter on the loose. Whoever killed Denise White had planned to do so and had planned very carefully. He also—assuming it *was* a male—was likely to have known her. Why else would she be at that place at that time? Denise was intelligent and perceptive. She was highly organized. She was good with people. She was conscious of the potential danger that surrounded her and constantly aware of the need for security. What and who could possibly have brought her to MacArthur Park at that time?

Before he could ask Clemmer another question, his cell phone rang.

He looked at the caller i.d. screen. "Excuse me," Dearing said, "I have to take this."

Clemmer nodded his understanding and approval. He heard only half of Dearing's conversation: "OK," he said, "I understand; I'll get right back to you."

19

Wilshire and Coronado

Charles was making his way west from the park, checking side streets and alleyways, looking for Dempster Dumpsters and other trash receptacles. He had zipped his poplin jacket at the waist and placed a fresh plastic bag with carrying handles and a set of plastic gloves inside of it.

He carried a Starbucks cup in his right hand—the ubiquitous symbol of membership in the middle class. He was dressed too simply to attract panhandlers but too nicely to attract the attentions of the police or private security guards engaged by the hotels and other businesses along the boulevard.

When he came upon a dumpster he sought the side that was least visible to other pedestrians and made a quick visual inspection. The principal collection company—Reeder's--had emptied a number of the receptacles that morning, but some were managed by other businesses and had not yet been serviced. The trick was to vault into the dumpster, search its contents, and get back out without staining his clothes in too obvious a way or making so much noise that his search attracted the attention of security personnel.

If he had had the available time he would have fabricated a uniform of some sort and passed himself off as someone working in an official capacity, but with the clock ticking and the trail cooling he could not afford that luxury. That was a pity, since the lack of a plausible uniform increased his possible exposure. Except for mugging and pickpocketing, there was no activity considered less desirable in a neighborhood aspiring to commercial respectability than dumpster-diving.

He was working on the assumption that any object capable of effectively hammering a 16-penny finishing nail would be too cumbersome to carry in a pocket and that the workman's outfit that the murderer had been wearing would be unlikely garb for an individual walking along Wilshire Boulevard in the late evening. He assumed that the overalls would be quickly discarded, once they had served their purpose of concealing more commonplace clothing and absorbing any blood splatter that had resulted from the assault. So far, however, he had been unable to locate either the clothing or a likely instrument for driving in the nails.

The principal contents of the dumpsters were either small mountains of intact paper, bagged shreds, or discarded foodstuffs, with occasional fast food wrappers, cardboard and Styrofoam cups, Kleenex, and other materials contributed by passers-by. He also found a discarded, heavily stained baseball cap, an umbrella that had long since ceased to be functional, a large number of used, disposable diapers, and a significant number of soda cans and beer bottles, the most popular brands being Diet Coke and Bud Light.

In the third dumpster he inspected he found a piece of lead pipe, approximately 18" in length, the surface of which was scratched and pitted. It was an unlikely tool, but he picked it up by the ends and slipped it into the plastic bag. He continued to walk west, toward the Clinic and Vince Dearing. Unaware of each other's presence, they were working the same neighborhood, but for different evidence and in different ways.

At Wilshire and Commonwealth he was passed on the street by an Asian couple whose eyes were focused on the sidewalk in front of them and a tourist couple whose eyes were moving between the map in the man's hand and points east. All four were doubtless unaware of the fact that they were walking through an extended crime scene.

In a side street on the west side of Commonwealth he found a dumpster that had been freshly painted in dark tones of forest green, with white lettering indicating the company that serviced it. As he approached it, he tried to catch the smells of spoilage and decay that were so close to the scent of death, but, mercifully, there were none. The access lid on the left was raised above the container; black plastic garbage bags were visible in the separation between it and the base. He raised the lid on the right and saw that some of the bags had fallen from the other side into the available space there, though that side of the dumpster was largely empty.

Looking again, he noticed a rear door on the north side of the building fronting on Commonwealth. Whoever emptied the company's trash had probably taken the path of least resistance and thrown it into the side of the dumpster nearest to the door. Beneath the pile of scattered bags on the right side of the dumpster Charles thought he saw the base of a handle. After climbing in, he carefully moved the bags, exposing a hammer that was too new and too good to be simply thrown away. He slipped on his plastic gloves, opened his plastic bag, picked up the face and claw of the hammer by the tips of his index fingers, and lowered it into the plastic bag.

Progress.

20

Vermont above Wilshire

Dearing had clicked off and told Clemmer he'd catch up with him later. When he got to his car in the Clinic parking lot he punched in the numbers for Cloke's cell.

"Charlie, whatever you have, I can't come to you; I've got to stick around here and meet the officers and cadets coming in to help me with the Clinic files. How about getting together someplace nearby?"

"Sure, no problem; give me a sec here."

Cloke googled and then browsed some sites.

"There's a Starbucks on Wilshire, a block and a half from the Clinic."

Dearing smiled. Isn't there always, he thought. "I need a line of sight, Charlie, so I don't miss the support people when they arrive. There's a takeout place across the street. It looks like there's a table or two there that'll work."

Cloke pulled up outside fourteen minutes later. He was carrying a wrinkled manila folder. Dearing had held the lone table in the carryout by ordering some coffee and sandwiches. "Hope you like ham and cheese," he said.

"That's fine," Cloke said, "as long as they were made this month."

"What have you got, Charlie?" Dearing asked.

"Results on the GSR tests. Both positive and both conclusive."

"You did both the absorption analysis and the electron microscope scan."

"Right. *I* didn't do it, but the labs did and I talked to both technicians to verify the results. There weren't any doubts."

"Impossible to make any assumptions about the weapon, I guess," Dearing said. "A tiny .22 revolver can throw off more GSR than a .44 magnum."

"Right," Cloke responded. "It all depends on the quality of the piece, the amount of wear and tear it's sustained, the brand of ammunition… all I can tell you is that her purse contained a weapon that had been fired recently enough to have a detectable amount of GSR transfer to the fabric lining the bag."

"Anything registered in her name?"

"Nothing."

"I didn't think so."

"Why not?"

"I don't know; somehow it would have made everything too easy. Did you tell Lieutenant White?"

"No, I thought you'd want to do that."

"Right, thanks. Was there any GSR on her clothing?"

"If there was, the quantity was insufficient for measurement. There may have been a little bit on two fingertips. Again, it's hard to tell."

"That would make sense," Dearing said. "When she reached in her purse for something she would pick up a little of it."

"Right," Cloke said.

They sat there staring at one another as Dearing took a sip of his coffee.

"The sandwich tastes pretty good," Cloke said, taking a second bite.

After Cloke finished and left, Dearing called Frank White. "Lieutenant… Vince Dearing."

"What have you got, Vince?"

"Two things, lieutenant. We're about to start searching the client files in your niece's clinic. Lieutenant Carlow has detailed some people to help me. There are over 10,000 files and we want to work through them as quickly as possible."

"It has to be done by hand?"

"Yes, sir, they're not computerized in any way."

"OK." The disappointment was apparent in his voice. "What else do you have?"

"The GSR tests are both in on your niece's purse. They were both positive. We ran both the AA test and the SEM test, just to make sure. Charlie Cloke talked to each of the technicians and they verified the results. There isn't any doubt on either of them."

"How about on her clothes or skin?"

"There may have been a little on her fingertips. There wasn't enough residue for a reliable measurement. I assume she was right-handed…"

"Yes, she was."

"If there *was* any, it was on the tips of her index and middle fingers. She could have had some transfer when she reached for something else in her purse."

There was silence for nearly thirty seconds.

"Lieutenant…?" Dearing said.

"I was just thinking, Vince. If she *did* have a weapon with her she wasn't able to get to it in time to do her any good."

"Right, lieutenant," Dearing said, "I'm sorry …"

21

San Pasqual at Wilson, Pasadena

Charles parked his car on San Pasqual, locked it, entered the western terminus of the Caltech campus, and walked southeast toward the Church Lab. He had not been followed, either on foot or in a vehicle. His wife Mary was waiting for him in her departmental office and when he walked through her door she stood and embraced him.

"It's so sad, Charles," she said.

"I know, Mary," he answered, "I know."

She gathered up her things and he walked her to their car. Charles turned onto Wilson, drove north and then east, around the campus, to Hill, and headed north to their home in Altadena.

Twenty-five minutes later, having checked the neighborhood and their house, Charles was sitting on the back porch overlooking their small garden. Mary approached him, carrying two glasses of iced tea. "Well, Charles White," she said, "are you going to tell me what you've been doing or do I have to read about it in the newspaper?"

"You won't have to do that," he answered. "I've been downtown, trying to be of service."

"Service? From the smell of your clothes, Charles, I would have thought you'd been riding on a garbage truck."

"That's very observant," he said. "There's some truth to it. I've been looking for evidence."

"And did you find any?"

"I may have."

"And are you going to tell your nephew?"

"As a matter of fact, I have already left a message."

"And what was this evidence?"

"I'm not sure that it *is* evidence, but I found a hammer."

"A hammer?"

"Yes. Whoever killed Denise drove nails into the port-o-let so that she would not be able to escape from it."

Mary didn't respond, but Charles could see the tears forming at the base of her eyes.

"I think she was already gone," he said. "I don't think she struggled or suffered further."

Mary continued to stare at him, waiting for him to continue.

"It's a new hammer and a good one. It's not the sort of thing that anyone would throw away. It was in a dumpster a few blocks from the park. Frank can take it to the lab and they can check it for prints and other possible evidence."

"Like DNA."

"Yes."

"And where is it now?"

"In the garage, in a plastic bag, locked in the car trunk."

"And how did you know where to look?"

"I talked with a homeless man in the park who told me that he saw the person who nailed up the port-o-let walk west on Wilshire away from the park. I just walked down the street and checked alleyways and side streets until I found a dumpster that had something in it that looked suspicious."

"And did the homeless man describe the other man to you?"

"Yes, but it wasn't very detailed. He was a person of average height and weight with hair showing underneath his hat. He was wearing overalls."

"Is that all?"

"That's all."

"It's something."

"Yes, it is."

"And if there are prints on the hammer it could be everything."

"Yes."

"And when the police put the prints in their computer and check with the FBI and find out whose prints they are, you're going to let them do their job and pick the man up and lock him away."

"That sounds more like a directive than a question," Charles said.

"It *is* a directive," Mary said. "I don't want you to go out and kill the man, because if any mistakes are made we could have a second tragedy for this family."

"I understand," Charles said. "I knew you'd feel that way. That's why I called Frank."

"And have you told me everything?"

"Of course I have," he answered.

"Would you like some more iced tea?"

"No, thank you. I think I'll go upstairs and get out of these clothes and take a hot shower."

"Before or after you start sharpening the knives you have in your closet?"

"You really believe you know me, don't you, Mary?"

"It's not a matter of belief, Charles White; it's a matter of certainty."

"Well, this time you just happen to be wrong."

"Is *that* right?"

"Yes, it's right."

"And how can that be?"

"Because I sharpened them before I left," he said, sliding one out of each pocket, removing them from their sheaths, and exposing the blades to the sunlight, which gleamed along the edges and created bright, intermittent reflections against the exterior wall of the house.

22

Hill Avenue, Altadena

"So what do I tell my captain, Charles—that an anonymous source left a major piece of evidence on my doorstep?" He and Frank were sitting on Charles's back porch, drinking coffee after a full dinner.

"The captain will understand, Frank. He trusts me; we've done business before."

"I noticed something else, Charles. It came through from the Pasadena PD. There was an incident today near the main library. A short, black man broke the nose and wrist of a local citizen."

"Really?" Charles said. "Was there a report on the citizen? Was he a banker...a cardiologist or...?"

"Actually it was a young man suspected of being a member of the WB 40's."

"Hmmm," Charles said, "curious name. Would that refer to Washington Boulevard and a youth gang that frequents the western end of that thoroughfare?"

"As a matter of fact it would," Frank said. "His friends report that he was minding his own business after visiting the library to do some serious research. He was accosted by an abusive young man, when the black man entered the picture and further assaulted him."

"And was the other young man a person of color?"

"Apparently not," Frank said.

"So it was unlikely that he and the short black man were related."

"Yes. That would be unlikely."

"So the black man accused of assault simply wanted to join the fight, even though he and the abusive individual were unrelated and outnumbered."

"That would seem to be the case."

"And this black gentleman...was there any report on his likely age?"

"The report described him as being *aged*."

"So he was elderly?"

"Yes."

"That will be a very difficult case to solve," Charles said. "It's hard for me to imagine an elderly black man entering a fight involving younger people with a preponderance of numbers who had no relationship with that man."

"Yes, it will be difficult," Frank said. "If there *is* such a man, however, it would probably be a very good idea for him to cease and desist for a period of time while the wheels of justice turn."

"I fully agree, Frank. I think that would be very good advice," Charles said.

"Now about that hammer..."

"I'm sorry I don't have more evidence," Charles said. "I also wish I had a better description of the perpetrator, but I hope that what little I've added will be of use."

"I'll talk to the captain," Frank said. "If you hadn't found it, it would be in a landfill in the desert by now."

"Very hard for the police to talk to the homeless in the park," Charles said. "I thought it would be easier for me."

"And you remember the informant's name and you could provide a physical description," Frank said.

"Absolutely," Charles said. "I'd be grateful if you'd distance me from the process though."

"What do you mean?"

"Talk to several people in the park; don't let the informant know that he was being singled out."

"So that you could return and continue your investigation."

"I didn't say that, Frank."

"I don't want you on Washington Boulevard either."

"Speaking speculatively," Charles said, "purely speculatively, you understand, I would doubt that the gang member in question would be out on the street before too long. It sounds to me as if the elderly black gentleman in question might have decided to pursue his actions in order to convey a message of some sort."

"Right," Frank said. "The advice still stands."

"I appreciate it," Charles answered. "You always have my best interests at heart; that's why you're my favorite nephew."

"Denise was your favorite niece, Charles. I mentioned this earlier, but I'd like to reconfirm it…"

"Yes?"

"You did *not* loan Denise a weapon of any kind."

"I told you I didn't, Frank. I had no idea that Denise was in any danger."

"Understood," Frank said. "Neither did I. If we had, we might have saved her from all of this…"

"All we can do is seek justice for her now," Charles said.

"Yes," Frank said, but I have a nagging suspicion that you would like to do that in some very swift and violent way."

"You know that I have *always* been a friend of justice," Charles answered.

"Yes, especially that of the swift variety."

"Swift justice is guaranteed in our Constitution, Frank."

"A swift *trial*, Charles."

"Oh yes," Charles answered, "a swift trial. That would be very nice…*very* nice…unless, of course, events are such that it turns out to be impossible…"

23

Vermont above Wilshire

"Detective, I'm proud to announce that as of this moment we have combed through 65 files."

"Thank you, Officer Frehley," Dearing said. "And what have you found?"

"If you exclude all of the elderly women and all of the people who have never had a brush with the law, there are only 12 individuals we would want to follow up on."

Dearing realized that everyone had already done the mental math. At a 12-out-of-65 rate, they would have between two and three thousand names to study in depth when they completed their run through the full wall of files.

"Of the twelve," Frehley continued, "nine have been arrested and four convicted of felonies. Eleven of the twelve have no visible means of support, but six of the eleven have cars. It's not a full rogues' gallery, but all twelve look rough around the edges and capable of doing something that would land them in the front pages of the *Times*."

"So what are you telling me?" Dearing asked.

"Nothing, Detective; I just wanted to give you an update and a sense of our progress."

"What you're telling me is that we're looking for something smaller than a needle in a larger-than-usual haystack."

"Well…yes, sir. Free medical care in a neighborhood like this…it brings out a large cross section of criminals along with a lot of poor people. And if you believe that poverty and crime are related..."

"I understand," Dearing said. "I can do the math. Unfortunately we don't have anything else at this point, so keep looking."

"Of course," Frehley said. "And as soon as we turn anything that looks promising we'll let you know."

"Remember," Dearing answered, "it's not just a predisposition to crime or violence. There's probably something personal going on here. Look for incidents that could have led to a face-to face-murder with a hand-held weapon. Maybe she denied treatment to someone or, more likely, medication. Maybe somebody came onto her and she declined the offer. This wasn't a utilitarian crime, with somebody getting hit over the head and then robbed. It was weird...and it was planned. Like we've been saying...unless there's a homicidal carpenter out there, acting on impulse, this was a highly organized event."

"Understood, Detective, but one of those twelve in our first pile worked construction, so we included him, even though there was nothing suspicious in his file."

"That's fine," Dearing said. "He *should* be in the pile. You know what I'm saying..."

"Sure," Frehley answered.

After making a cursory run through the twelve files, Dearing decided to go across the street to the takeout to get his men some coffee. He caught the charred-caramel scent of burned coffee dregs the moment he opened the Clinic door and smelled the acrid air on the street. The city seemed to be full of it. He walked across to the takeout anyway. "Not worry," the owner said. "Make fresh coffee. Not use same carafe."

He was obviously perturbed. A young man wearing a stained apron was skulking behind him—doubtless the person whose inattentiveness had created the situation. The owner said something to him in Korean and the young man sent off body signals that suggested he would like to disappear into the plastic-laminate wallboard.

Dearing ordered six black coffees and picked up a box of glazed Krispy Kremes. When he put them down on the counter beside the cash register his cell phone rang. It was Cloke.

"Got a development," he said.

"What's that, Charlie?"

"Lieutenant White's uncle found a hammer in a dumpster."

"Where?"

"On Commonwealth, right near you."

"Any prints?"

"No, it's completely clean."

"Damn," Dearing said.

"It looks like a likely bit of evidence, though. It's practically new—not the sort of thing that anyone would throw away."

"Brand?"

"A Stanley. Probably no more than a few million in Southern California."

"Right. What do they run?"

"That model? Around thirty bucks list, usually discounted to the low twenties."

"Could have been shoplifted," Dearing said. "We shouldn't assume we've got a middle-class perp."

"That's right," Cloke said. "There's a little more too…"

"I'm listening, Charlie."

"Charles White talked to a homeless guy in the park. Says he saw the man hammering in the nails. Average height and weight, wearing overalls and a hat. Maybe like an old fedora or something. It wasn't a baseball cap. The guy said a *hat* hat."

"Interesting."

"The homeless guy said he was dressed like a farmer. Says he saw him finish hammering in the nails, then leave the park, walking west on Wilshire."

"No sign of the overalls yet?"

"Nope, sorry. The lieutenant has some people on the way to check the dumpsters and any other likely place that they could have been discarded. Also, some people at the landfills."

"Needles in haystacks, Charlie," Dearing said. "Maybe it makes sense that the guy was dressed like a farmer."

"Yeah, I know," Cloke said. "I figure he wore the playsuit like an apron, to keep any blood off."

"Right. Also to keep the nails and hammer down in the deep pockets. You don't see too many people dressed that way at night, but anything's possible in L.A. I saw a guy in a convertible on the 405 the other day, wearing a rubber Nixon mask."

"That's strange," Cloke said. "He should have been closer to Tricky Dick's home--out around Whittier on the 605."

24

San Pasqual at Wilson, Pasadena

Charles parked on the west side of the Caltech campus, opened Mary's door and began walking her to her office.

"So where do you plan to go now, Charles White?" she asked.

"What do you mean?" he answered.

"You're walking very slowly. That means you want to give me the impression that you've got all the time in the world. You're going to walk me to my office, stroll nonchalantly away until you're out of sight, and then jump in the car and race right back downtown, aren't you?"

"I don't know where you get those kind of ideas, Mary," he said.

"Because I know you and because I heard something heavy bounce in the trunk when you hit that speedbump on the side street."

"That could be a tool. I may be going to Frank's condo and help him fix the trap in his kitchen sink."

"That's a possibility," she said, watching the koi in the reflecting pool that paralleled the sidewalk, "but I wouldn't bet any serious money on it. Besides, if you *were* going to Frank's you wouldn't say that you *may be going* there. You never lie, Charles; you just conceal things."

"You know what?" he asked.

"What?"

"It's hell being married to a woman who knows me that well."

"And you think it's hell that I'm worried about you ending up in jail?"

"I'm grateful that you're not worried that I could be hurt by the person who killed our niece."

"Like I said, I *know* you, Charles White. I'm not worried that you'd lose; I'm worried that you'd be caught and found guilty."

"I appreciate that vote of confidence," he said.

"My question still stands. Are you going back downtown?"

"If I do, you can be assured that I will take all due precautions and be back in time to pick you up this afternoon."

"See that you do," she said, turning and entering her building.

He walked back to the car at an easy pace and put his key in the trunk lock. Standing in the gutter so far below the level of the sidewalk, he thought about the fact that on those few occasions in which it actually did rain in southern California it was capable of raining profusely. It hadn't done so in awhile. The tangle of ivy on the devil strip between the sidewalk and gutter was parched and covered with dust.

He opened the trunk and saw that the tire tool had bounced out of the plastic well in the corner below the rear taillight. Mary had heard it when he drove over the speedbump a few minutes before he parked on San Pasqual. He returned it to its position in the well and slid the plastic strap around it, securing it in its place.

Then he peeled back the tufted lining covering the base of the trunk, exposing the top of the recessed case beneath it. Moving the rings of numbers adjoining the lock and then releasing the catch, he opened the case. He first removed his Glock, slipping it inside his jacket, and then removed a piece of fresh flannel from the case and wrapped it around the handle of an unregistered Kel-Tec P-3AT, an eight-ounce pocket pistol that was easily concealed if he needed a backup and easily employed as a throw-down if the situation required one. Keeping the flannel in place, he slid the P-3AT into his jacket pocket. Extending his hand to the small of his back, he verified the presence of his makeshift weapon for silent kills—a set of oak handles with a length of piano wire strung between them.

He then closed and locked the case, returned the trunk lining to its normal position, closed the trunk, got into the car, and drove west to Lake, south to California Boulevard, and west to the parkway and the freeway beyond.

II

BACK STORY

25

Great Falls, Virginia

G reat Falls Park, since 1966 a unit of the National Park Service, sits 14 miles upriver from Washington, D.C. The centerpiece of the 800-acre park is the system of 20-foot falls and cascading rapids that result from the Potomac's dropping 76 feet in less than a single mile. Above the falls the river is 1000 feet wide. As the water plunges through Mather Gorge—just below the falls—the river narrows to a width of 60-100 feet. The rapids here are the most spectacular of any river in the eastern United States.

Gwen Harrison had spent her final college years focusing on geography rather than geology, but she knew the falls' geologic history. After the last ice age and the change in the levels of the oceans, the river was forced to carve a deeper path as it plunged toward the sea. The site in which this natural drama played out is situated between the Piedmont Plateau and the Atlantic Coastal Plain, in an area since termed the *fall zone.*

A scene of intense natural beauty and power, it is also a setting anchored in deep history. George Washington helped develop a plan to construct a series of canals which would provide a route from the eastern seaboard to the then-new settlements in the Ohio valley. Of these the Patowmack Canal of Great Falls was the largest and, ultimately, the most difficult to design and construct. Completed in 1802, it operated for 26 years, lifting and lowering boats filled with corn, wheat, rye, flour, tobacco, pork, beef, pig iron, and more. The most significant engineering feat of eighteenth-century America, the ruins of the Patowmack Canal may still be seen at Great Falls Park.

After the death of the canal but before the creation of the National Park Service's facilities, two early-1900's entrepreneurs—John McLean and Steven Elkins--built an amusement park on the site. Tourists caught a trolley in Georgetown and traveled along the river, enjoying the overlook decks, observation tower, dance pavilion, evening light show, carousel, and lovers' lane along the canal's ruins. They stayed at Dickey's Inn and were able to purchase five trolley tickets for the princely sum of 25 cents. Floods and the automobile ended all that and the amusement park dissolved into history.

Gwen was standing at Overlook 2, mulling over these things and others as she watched the falls and sipped home-brewed coffee from an insulated, plastic cup. Past experience (she held a season ticket to the park) taught her to distrust the coffee at the snack bar in the Visitor Center courtyard. The picnic tables had not yet been claimed by the day's visitors and the human sounds that would soon follow had not yet begun to compete with those of the river. The clouds above the gorge were thick and gray, but there was no expectation of rain, despite the fact that the air was heavy with moisture and the wind from the southwest was brisk.

She came here often. It was a place for her to think through the course of her life and that life's options. If they could not all be sorted out, the beauty of the place offered ample compensation for the winding drive along Georgetown Pike and the increasing period of time that that drive required. There were many things to think through today. She knew their likely consequences. She had considered them again and again and each time she did she saw the degree of their inevitability and knew how far they diverged from her personal aspirations and dreams.

Assigned to the Washington Bureau at the personal insistence of the Director, she sensed the plans that he had in mind. After some early wins she had been posted to Washington and run through a gauntlet of special training and special assignments. The FBI conducts operations in everything from counterterrorism to major thefts of jewelry and gems. So far it seemed as if she had cycled through every office, bureau, and division, but that dealing with 'Indian Country' crime. The Director had told her, explicitly, that it was 'ridiculous' to assume that her native blood somehow provided her an awareness of the provisions of the Indian Country Crimes Act, the Indian Country Major Crimes Act, the Assimilative Crimes Act, or the Indian Gaming Regulatory Act. Nevertheless, it was the single area investigated by the Bureau that remained for her to explore.

Proud of her family and her people (a direct-line ancestor had fought with Crazy [or, more properly, 'Enchanted'] Horse), she systematically avoided seeing that heritage as a possible source of professional leverage. From the time that she led her class at Quantico to that in which she was successful in resolving a series of counterterrorism cases, the Bureau had other plans, plans which she adamantly resisted. She told the Director that 'with all due respect, she had no intention of becoming a poster child' for Bureau diversity. She supported that diversity but rigorously strove to dissociate her family history from her performance evaluations, lest the latter be inflated or in any way be called into question.

The Director had pulled back, but he had not given up, and he continued to attempt to impress upon her the importance of her 'life story' for aspiring agents who might see her as a 'powerful role model'. Her newest fear was that the rapid change in assignments which she was experiencing was part of a prelude to a posting that could be perceived as beyond her age and Bureau experience. She would not—in the fullness of time—resist such an assignment, but she did not aspire to it now, preferring authentic *field*work to any form of repetitive deskwork.

The call from the Director's office had come last evening. The message was terse: "Special Agent Harrison, this is Louise Bennett, the Director's assistant. He needs to see you immediately. I've scheduled you for 11:00 a.m. tomorrow. Please call and confirm receipt of this message."

The Director was returning to Washington from a trip to Miami, arriving (she said) at approximately 9:45 a.m. If that was correct, Gwen knew that 11:00 would be his first available appointment. That was good news. If he was priming her for an assignment she was likely to resist, there would be less urgency in the scheduling. He knew she was too smart to succumb to any artificial schmooze or strokes and would not, in any event, have scheduled a private luncheon or other blandishment, but there might have been coffee and a chance to slide back in their chairs and go through the motions of a *bona fide* career talk. Scheduling her before he had a chance to attend to any other Bureau business suggested that there was a real problem at hand and that he wanted her to be involved in some way in its solution.

Hedging the bet, she had checked the flight schedules. Unless his assistant was deceiving her, and he was arriving earlier, there was an American flight due in at Reagan National at 9:47. It was a 737-800 with a first class section; that would be his choice over an Embraer low-ceiling 50-seater.

She checked every online news service and every Bureau log to which she had access. There were no particular issues or events that jumped off the screen. The state of the nation had not changed appreciably over the last several days; it was the normal slow motion riot of calculated political maneuvering, aided and abetted by edicts from sympathetic cable- and mainstream media sources, dark prophecies from the blogosphere, and a fetid stew of unsubstantiated rumors. A terrorist plot to blow up the Barcelona airport (middle-east, not Basque-separatist-inspired) had actually been discovered and prevented, but the constituent events had transpired months earlier and the announcement of the successful operation was time-delayed to both quell fears and leverage political advantage. An aerosol can containing what had been suspected to be ricin was discovered in a dormitory at Penn State, but the gastrointestinal results initially attributed to ingestion of the toxin were later found to be caused by conventional food poisoning. The usual hate-and-threat chatter picked up through routine internet sweeps had not been considered exceptional and no alerts—of any kind—had been issued.

She would learn what was actually occurring in a little less than two and a half hours. In the meantime she took a sip of her coffee and thought through the alternative scenarios she had not yet considered. Perhaps she had offended a rating officer and her career was about to be sidetracked. Perhaps a report she had filed had failed to address important questions. Perhaps someone close to her had been hurt or compromised. There were few *good* things that would generate a first-appointment meeting with the Director of the Federal Bureau of Investigation.

26

Pennsylvania Avenue, The Hoover Building

Director Gradison's office mirrored his personality. The furniture was Spartan, the decorations few. It reflected his time in the military, where each commander knows that his tour will be brief and his office will have an endless succession of later occupants. The carpet was two grades higher than that in the hallway and the room featured a dark hardwood chair rail with matching crown molding, but there were no photographs, prints, or other images on the walls beyond the Bureau seal behind the Director's desk.

Gradison answered to "General" as well as "Director"; his military career had spanned three decades and included assignments to the Joint Chiefs, a set of security agencies, and NATO. As a three-star he had served as the Superintendent at West Point and was still referred to as the most 'intellectual' supe since Andy Goodpaster. There was no question that he was politically savvy and capable of serving multiple administrations without leaving a trace of personal partisanship in the public record.

His plans for a revitalized Bureau were anchored by his support for its diversification, the point on which Gwen's concerns turned. The success of his directorship would ultimately hinge on his ability to address issues concerning organized crime and, preeminently, his ability to prevent terrorist incidents, but his investment of personal capital in the notion of a fully-diversified workforce of special agents was never far from his thoughts. For him it was a high altar, one on which she had no interest in being sacrificed.

Gwen arrived at his office a few minutes early. The Director's assistant, Louise Bennett, asked her to have a seat on the couch in their waiting room. The mahogany table in front of it contained that morning's editions of the New York Times, Washington Post, Boston Globe, Los Angeles Times, Chicago Tribune and Wall Street Journal. When asked if she would like coffee, Gwen answered, "Not just now, thanks."

"If you change your mind, let me know," Mrs. Bennett replied.

The Director arrived at 11:08. He was carrying a garment bag. "Good morning, Gwen," he said. "I'm sorry I'm late; come right in."

He put the bag in the small closet in the corner of his office and asked her if Mrs. Bennett had offered her coffee.

"Yes, sir, thanks."

"I'm going to have some," he answered. "Want to reconsider?"

"Thank you, sir; I *will* have some," she said.

He pressed the intercom button and politely requested two cups. "Black for you?" he said to Gwen. She nodded yes and he added "Both black, Louise. Many thanks."

"Sorry to do all this on short notice," he said. "You can relax on one count, however. I didn't call the meeting to ask you to appear on the covers of any magazines."

"I appreciate that, sir," Gwen said.

"Not that I haven't given up completely," he added, "but this is something more pressing."

"What can I do, sir?"

"You remember a woman in your class at Quantico, a woman named Denise Willett?"

"Yes, sir, I do."

"Her name was not Willett. Her name was actually Denise White."

Gwen tried not to register any surprise as she waited for him to continue.

"Denise was operating undercover. She was a certified nurse practitioner. Her family believed that she had relocated to northern Virginia to work at Fairfax Hospital; they were not aware that she was here to receive Bureau training. You actually knew her reasonably well, didn't you?"

"Yes, sir, I did. We worked together on a number of occasions."

"I'm sorry to have to tell you this so abruptly, particularly after dropping the information about her identity on you, but Denise was found dead in Los Angeles less than two days ago."

"Foul play, sir?"

"Yes, Gwen. She was stabbed to death. Her body was found in a port-o-let in MacArthur Park."

Gwen blinked, trying not to show any emotion. "Are there any leads, sir?" she asked.

"No, nothing significant yet. The LAPD is working on it."

"And are they aware that she was a Bureau agent, sir?"

"No, they are not. We've held that back for a reason."

"Can you tell me why, sir?"

"Yes, of course."

He didn't elaborate, so she continued. "And you want me to help with the investigation?"

"Yes, Gwen, I do."

"Tell me what I need to know, sir, and I'll be on an afternoon plane."

"I will," he said. "It goes without saying that her assignment was of the utmost secrecy."

"Yes, sir," Gwen said, holding her expression and keeping her thoughts to herself. The assignment must not have been too secret, she thought, not if Denise ended up in a pool of blood in a portable toilet in a public park.

27

Pennsylvania Avenue,
The Hoover Building

The Director removed a key from his pocket, unlocked his lower left desk drawer, and took out a thin manila folder. "Denise was involved in a top secret activity called *Operation Dogtag*," he said. "It is top secret because of the technology involved and that technology's ramifications for future counterterrorism activities. It is essential that the technology not be compromised."

"And you believe that it *hasn't* yet been compromised, sir?"

"We doubt that it has, but we can't be sure. The one thing that we do know is that our agent has been murdered. That's not a good sign."

Gwen nodded without speaking as the Director continued.

"The concept is very simple. Denise was a nurse practitioner. She was able to utilize the technology without raising any suspicions. Her identity as an agent had been carefully concealed and—as far as we know—her cover had not been penetrated."

Gwen thought about that metaphor and the stab wounds to Denise's body. "And the technology, sir?"

"Extremely simple in concept, but difficult to engineer. Let me back up for a moment." He paused before continuing. He was playing with a paperclip, gathering his thoughts. "There is an irony in the activities of terrorists. They seek to destroy our culture and our society, but they have no hesitation in taking advantage—selectively—of the fruits of that culture. Terrorists in sleeper cells, for example, routinely utilize the services that our society provides. One of those services is free medical care.

"Denise was working as a nurse at something called the Community Health Clinic, an entity of the University of Southern California which emerged from an earlier program in USC's School of Social Work. The Clinic provides health services of various kinds in a transitional neighborhood west of downtown Los Angeles. There are multiple terrorist cells in the Los Angeles basin, one of which contains a prominent member who resides in that neighborhood.

"As I said, our concept was very simple. When one or more individuals from that cell came in for free flu- or other vaccines, Denise would provide it, using what appeared to be a common, Biojector needle-free injector system. Actually, she had two Biojector devices—one for the general public and one for the terrorists.

"The Biojector is a common instrument. It has three components: the injection system proper, a disposable needle-free syringe, and a carbon dioxide cartridge. It's rugged; it's ergonomically designed for right or left-handed users; and it will deliver over 100,000 injections. Basically it forces liquid medication through a tiny orifice that is held against the body. It creates a very fine, high-pressure stream of medication that penetrates the skin and deposits the medication in the tissue beneath.

"They are particularly common in clinics such as the one at which Denise worked, since they provide an exceptional level of protection against accidental needlestick injuries. Public clinics are high-risk operations, with a significant number of patients infected with HIV and Hepatitis. Hence the Biojector. And because of that high-risk situation, the use of the Biojector does not raise any suspicions. In fact, it raises everyone's collective comfort level.

"The Biojector used for the terrorists, however, was not an off-the-shelf model. Along with the stream of liquid medication—which was real—it was designed to inject a nanochip capable of functioning as a homing device. With the chip in place we would be able to track the movements of the individual in question in virtually any location, around the clock. Because it enabled us to keep a safe distance we could move in or out, as needed, and identify the locations which the individual frequented and the individuals with whom he came in contact."

"So the Los Angeles field office conducted the surveillance?"

"No. There were four individuals involved, with a lead agent. Three reported to that agent, who, in turn, reported directly to me. When the right time came and appropriate intelligence was developed, we would make the decision to let the regional office know selected details that had surfaced as a result of the operation, but they would not be notified concerning the program or the technology. The plan was to move Denise—and individuals similarly trained—to sites across the country, widening the net of the terrorists who had been tagged and deepening the quality and extent of the intelligence that the tagging yielded."

"How far along was the program, if I might ask, sir?"

"One key individual had been tagged; the surveillance of that individual had been ongoing for three months."

"So it was something of a pilot program."

"Yes."

"Is there any reason to believe that the subject who had been tagged might have become aware of his situation and taken steps to eliminate Denise?"

"No, not as yet, but that's where I want you to begin. You will meet with the lead agent and work with her. She's expecting to see you tomorrow morning."

28

LAX

The Bureau characteristically scheduled meetings within LAX, since the facility was vast, with countless nooks, crannies, and dark corners and anyone following a local agent there would first require a boarding pass and then need to clear security before entering the gate areas. Airline club meeting rooms—again, requiring membership and proper identification for entrance--were frequently used, with their frosted glass providing additional security and privacy. Today, however, Gwen had been instructed to meet her contact elsewhere, the precise location as yet unidentified.

She was told to secure a rental car—no Bureau sedan this time—and proceed north on the 405. She expected to be directed to the Getty—another convenient site for meetings, since entrance required time-sensitive tickets, the facility included multiple meeting sites, and the height above the Sepulveda Pass combined with the noise from the freeway, limited any opportunity to eavesdrop with parabolic microphones. From the heights above the 405, words quickly disappeared into the wind.

She checked in with the Director's office as soon as she turned onto the freeway and crawled into the northbound traffic but she was directed to go east on the 10, rather than continue north on the 405, then connect with the 110 north, and promptly exit at west 6th and drive into the downtown area. Twenty minutes later, she did, and was directed through the high rises, past the library and the cathedral, where she picked up a

Bureau tail car and was instructed to drive back to the 110. There were now at least four eyes and probably six watching for any cars that could be following her to her destination.

This was high security indeed, but in the event that anyone on the other side was sophisticated enough to be able to penetrate the Bureau process, there would be a team ready to intercept them and draw intelligence or, potentially, arrests, from the experience.

Gwen's ultimate destination turned out to be the Westin in Pasadena, the former Doubletree, which was the centerpiece of a complex that included freestanding restaurants amid a system of fountains, terraces and courtyards. When she parked in the underground lot no one followed her but the Bureau tail car, which parked nearby, with clear lines of sight to her vehicle. One agent would doubtless provide security within the building, while a second would keep an eye on her vehicle, insuring that no one attached homing devices, bombs, or both, to it. She got on the parking lot elevator, took it to the hotel lobby, walked to the Westin's elevator, rode two levels, and walked to the numbered room given her by the Director. She lifted her right arm to knock and the door opened before she could do so.

"You won't need your weapon," a friendly female voice said, as Gwen slipped her hand from her jacket pocket.

"My name is Elizabeth," the woman said. "I'm glad to meet you." She extended her hand to Gwen, who grasped it, shook it gently, and then walked to a couch and chair arrangement in the anteroom of the mini-suite.

"You weren't followed," Elizabeth said. Her voice was quiet and calming; it could even be described as vaguely therapeutic. The woman was small, no more than 5'2" in height and no more than 100 lbs. in weight. She was dressed like a school teacher or librarian—a simple blouse and prim suit, with tiny pearl earrings and a simple gold necklace with pearl pendant. She had short hair and little makeup. Softly feminine, but without any notable physical features, she could fade into a crowd like the gray agents that Hoover had always sought. Gwen wondered if her glasses were necessary or part of an attempt to temporarily alter her appearance.

"Could I see your left shoulder, please?" she asked.

Gwen slipped off her jacket and pulled back the sleeve of her blouse, exposing the now-healed results of two gunshot wounds and a shower of glass fragments from a shattered windshield.

"Sorry," Elizabeth said, "but you know it's the best form of identification, particularly if the wounds are complex. You've healed very nicely, especially from the 9mm."

"No problem," Gwen said, reassured by the woman's professionalism. Since each wound had been received at a different time it would be extremely difficult to re-create their effects on an impersonator, particularly if the plastic surgery was done within so recent a period of time.

"I'm glad you're here," Elizabeth said. "I didn't know Special Agent White well, because our operation had been so highly compartmentalized, but I knew her well enough to respect her skill and her courage. We are at a loss to explain how her cover could have been blown, if, indeed, it *was* blown. We took every precaution and every pain. The level of secrecy that we have maintained has been nearly absolute. Contacts have been kept to the barest minimum. And, of course, until we learn something to the contrary we are assuming that her cover was not penetrated and that there is some other explanation for her death."

"I understand," Gwen said. "It would be very helpful if you would tell me everything that you're at liberty to divulge."

"I'll be happy to," Elizabeth said. "There isn't much…"

29

North Los Robles, Pasadena

"Agent White was staying in an apartment in Silver Lake, but actually operating out of a building in Los Olivos…"

"That's a *long* drive," Gwen said, "what…150 miles?"

"A little less than that, from Silver Lake. Remember: Angelenos drive 50 miles for a special hamburger or pizza. The facility is completely secure, completely nondescript and purposely remote. Following her there without exposing yourself would be very difficult. Workplaces are public; apartments are visited routinely by building supers and landlords. A subsidiary office in the city would immediately raise suspicions. The image projected was that she was a workaholic who broke away from time to time for trips up the coast. The unlikeliness of the facility was its principal feature."

"And the computer setup there could be accessed from a distance in the case of an emergency…"

"Yes, by her and by us."

"I'd like to visit it, if only to try to get a feel for the nature of her assignment and work habits."

"Certainly. We've gone over it, of course, but you're welcome to have a look for yourself. The computer was highly encrypted and the hard drive stripped the moment the Director learned of her death." She handed Gwen a key. "The address is on the tag."

"Thanks," Gwen said. "Tell me about the principal suspect."

"His name is Mahadi. He's Syrian. His cell is not, formally, a part of Al-Qaeda, but they share Al-Qaeda's vision and goals. As you know, in Arabic the term means *the base* and suggests more a loose federation than an airtight network. He himself has collaborated with them directly, however, so he's close enough to them to be of significant interest to us in a number of ways. He purports to be a student at Cal State-Los Angeles and he *does* take classes there and maintains the enrollment status required for visa purposes. He's dotted all the i's and crossed the t's, but he's left plenty of time in his schedule for extracurricular activities of the kind that interest us much more than them. I understand that the Director explained to you the nature of our operation..."

"Yes."

"He was tagged three months ago. Prior to that he was under surveillance, but not the kind of surveillance of which we're now capable. We've identified at least six members of his organization. As you know, it's not like a Moose lodge with regular meetings. Nearly everything is done electronically and every aspect of their operation is heavily circumscribed. The other individuals are mostly based in Los Angeles, but there's one individual in Orange County and one in the Bay area. They have not yet conducted any formal operations, but we've picked up chatter suggesting that they're getting closer to the capability of mounting something small but nasty."

"Where was he at the time of her death?"

"That's the problem. He was at Lake Tahoe."

"*Lake Tahoe?*"

"Yes. Technically he's studying for a master's degree in accounting--cost accounting, actually. The cost accountants were meeting in Lake Tahoe and he was there with one of his professors."

"How about the other members of his organization?"

"All accounted for at the time of Agent White's death and none in the immediate vicinity."

"They could have hired someone, but they generally don't like to do that."

"No. Too dangerous."

"What's your best guess on what happened?"

"We really don't know. Like I said, we're checking everything we can, but holding open the possibility that the murder was not directly connected with her work in the Bureau."

"And that's where I come in, since you don't want me sniffing around the members of your principal's cell and raising any suspicions in the process."

"Right. Our operation continues and, as far as we're concerned, it's been quite successful. We don't want to see that success jeopardized in any way, particularly if the death of Agent White is, indeed, unrelated."

"If I was Mahadi or a member of his organization I would want to do everything in my power to encourage the perception that it *was* unrelated."

"Of course…and then buy time to determine how the tagging operation—assuming they've figured it out—could be turned to their advantage."

"So I should stay in close touch with you."

"As necessary, but through the Director."

"Understood."

"I'm told that you know the area already."

"I lived here awhile when I was in high school."

"The Director said you lived in the San Gabriel Valley."

"South Pasadena and Arcadia."

"Nice places. Good schools."

"Yes, that was very important to my parents. Neither is probably affordable now."

"Right."

Gwen expected a follow-up observation or some other formulaic pleasantry, but Elizabeth volunteered nothing—no phone number, no address, no personal statement of any kind from which one might draw a useful conclusion. The Director would have appreciated that. Good fences make good neighbors in a top secret operation. Gwen might be working with her tomorrow or might never see her again. Expert counterterrorism work required a highly-integrated team, but within certain areas of the process you might never encounter or even be aware of the identities of your teammates. Ultimately you were alone, you and a disembodied voice at the end of a cell phone line, your only constant companions your wits, your weapons, and your senses—all hopefully in a state of high alert.

30

Carpinteria, the 101

Gwen left the Westin, circled through the back streets of Pasadena, and eventually took a lanai room at the Langham Huntington. The rate was above the government per diem but that could help divert attention, since an agent's staying there would generally not be expected or anticipated. The principal reason, however, was the hotel's multiple freestanding facilities and multiple points of ingress and egress. The three-floor lanai building was physically separate from the main building, which could be accessed at the lower level from the pool area or at the ground floor level from the hotel's historic picture bridge.

Now surrounded by freestanding million-dollar homes on the hotel's property and insulated from the main building by multiple parking areas, the Japanese garden, birds-of-paradise-encircled Horseshoe garden, and spa building, the site was a maze of entry and exit points, providing elaborate cover and concealment that would prove useful if the hotel grounds suddenly turned into a combat zone.

She also liked the site since it was familiar to her. Her parents had taken her there for Sunday dinners at the Tap Room when the hotel was still a Ritz-Carlton. Originally the Wentworth, it remained the site of choice for old-money Pasadena weddings. Her parents commented on the fact to her. They still had hopes for a collection of grandchildren but were less insistent on the point now.

Gwen's memories of the hotel were all positive. Her memories of the Santa Ynez Valley, however, were far less pleasant. As she drove into Carpinteria she remembered a weekend, years ago, when she and several of her high school classmates had driven to the Valley for the weekend, taken a set of rooms in an inexpensive motel, and settled in for an extended party. When things got out of hand Gwen attempted, unsuccessfully, to persuade her classmates that they would come to regret their actions and should slow things down. When the boy she was with tried to take advantage of a situation that was fast deteriorating, she separated from the group and returned to the city on a Greyhound bus. It was neither an easy nor a pleasant experience, but she had too much pride to ask for help from a member of the group and did not want to worry her parents unnecessarily or ask them to drive that distance in order to pick her up. She also thought of what her father might do in the face of the situation and considered it better, on balance, to walk away rather than resolve that situation in an atmosphere of anger and potential violence.

Today she had taken the back road to the 101 and the coast, first driving out of Pasadena and taking the 210 to the north end of the San Fernando Valley. Traffic spaced out the farther you got from the city; if anyone was following her they would have fewer places to hide than on the 134, a catch-as-catch-can demolition-derby tour of Glendale, Burbank, and North Hollywood. Driving through the Simi Valley, a conservative stronghold and bedroom community for many members of the LAPD, she had anticipated the farm country north of Camarillo and Oxnard, a stretch of land and sky that still offered a sense of what the land was like before the onslaught of postwar GI's who flocked to the Los Angeles basin and the valleys beyond.

Carpinteria was the haven of blue collar workers who couldn't afford Santa Barbara and couldn't even think of living in the intervening Montecito, where seven-figure teardown cottages were now the norm. At Santa Barbara she faced a decision—continue north on the 101 or split off at the 154, driving past the Rancho del Cielo, Ronald Reagan's 688 acre ranch in the sky, and—farther north and west--the shrinking but still bold outlines of the 3,000+ acre Lake Cachuma. The former was easier, but more exposed, the latter more scenic, but also more dangerous and more confining, with locals who were aware of every twist and turn through the mountains, driving at high speeds and taking high risks.

As she drove along the 101, with the Pacific coming in and out of view, she pushed the thoughts of her high school experience from her mind and thought about the Valley in a more detached way, her geographic training easing out her personal memories.

The Santa Ynez mountains are nearly unique, aligned as they are, east to west rather than north to south. They are young, only about five million years old, rising along the Santa Ynez Fault, with steep slopes and rugged topography. The transverse range results in unique weather, with warm, nearly rainless summers but occasional monsoonal showers. The chaparral survives these conditions, but depending on the season and the moment the mountains can either be lush and green or soft, angular patterns within a stark moonscape. Live oaks are common and, with the area's vineyards, add to the sense of life amid death and plenty amid austerity.

Whether you were driving in through the Gaviota Pass to the south or from Lake Cachuma and the east, as Gwen had chosen that day, what awaited you within the Valley could never be anticipated. Checking her map and checking the tag attached to the key which Elizabeth had given her, she drove on, clearing her head for the task at hand.

31

Los Olivos

Denise's makeshift office was little more than a toolshed behind a Phillips 66 station a block and a half from the village's principal intersection. A now arty watering hole with a little over a thousand residents, described by the local Chamber of Commerce as *charming*, Los Olivos was originally a stop on the stage line and, later, the Pacific Coast Railway line. The Victorian overlay of its prominent buildings and the continuing existence of Felix Mattei's early hotel—now a popular site for weddings with a restaurant featuring generous helpings of comfort food—pointed up its nineteenth-century past. The service station looked like a relic of the 1940's, its detached outbuilding functional but architecturally nondescript.

The building was accessible from a side street and could be entered or exited without drawing any attention from curious eyes. Gwen unlocked the door, entered, and was struck by the room's stark emptiness. The stained and cigarette-burned oak table on which the computer sat was chipped at the edges, the computer itself an aging Dell relic, with switches and buttons from another era. The guts were new—standard Bureau mystification—but the hard drive *had* been stripped, as Elizabeth said, and nothing remained but a browser and a standard suite of office software. The plastic case and keyboard were smudged with oily fingerprints and on the table, next to them, was an unsharpened No. 2

pencil and a yellow legal pad with a line of fragmentary bits along the top edge, from which earlier sheets had been indiscriminately torn.

The scanner and printer were of a newer vintage, but the paper had been removed from each of the printer's trays, as had—for some reason or other—the printer's toner cartridge. On the floor next to the desk was an office refrigerator, large enough to contain two mini- ice cube trays, a few bottles of water or soda and a sandwich or salad. The shelves and compartments were empty now. Gwen thought about Denise and about her need to do periodic, uninterrupted work in a secure environment, but there was a profound sense of loneliness pervading this space, a loneliness that further contributed to the sense of isolation that Denise must have experienced daily in her undercover role.

The only item on the otherwise-blank and windowless walls was an aged Union 76 calendar that was smudged but otherwise unmarked. No personal items of any kind were in evidence. The corners of the room, like the ceiling rafters, were heavily cobwebbed. Gwen checked the lock, strike plate and door jamb, looking for signs of illicit entry, but found none. The space was secure, but completely devoid of any evidence or interest.

After insuring that she was not being followed, Gwen drove south into Solvang and west into Buellton, picked up a cup of coffee, and headed south on the 101. She stopped in Santa Barbara, got a sandwich and a second jolt of caffeine, and drove down the coast to L.A.

She was determined to find something, perhaps something personal, anything that might somehow refresh her memory of Denise and help her to find her killer. She had accessed the address of her Silver Lake apartment through public databases and decided to drive there directly rather than return to her hotel.

Two hours later she was working her way around the gates, cameras, and locks of Denise's building. The easiest lock proved to be the one on Denise's own apartment door. Using a generic tool and applying the right amount of pressure, she was able to turn the knob and enter the darkened space. She closed the drapes, removed a small flashlight from her purse, and began to inspect the apartment.

It was sparsely furnished, but it at least contained personal items. Gwen thought that one of the jackets and one of the caps in the living room closet looked familiar and she recognized a piece of costume jewelry in a tray in the top of Denise's chest of drawers. Unaware earlier that Denise was actually a trained nurse practitioner, the white tennis shoes and blue scrubs hanging in the bedroom closet struck her as odd and unfamiliar. The Denise that she knew carried a 9 mm sidearm, not a stethoscope or set of tongue depressors.

There was nothing in the apartment that indicated any connection with the Bureau, and very little of a directly personal nature, except for a set of family photographs on top of her chest of drawers. Gwen did not recognize any of the individuals in the pictures, since none had visited Denise during her time at the academy and none had attended their graduation ceremony. She looked further, checking the backs and the undersides of individual drawers, and ran her hand around the inside base of that and other pieces of furniture. She looked in each corner of each cupboard and closet, hoping to find a wall safe or hidey hole. She looked for loose molding, for fresh paint or freshly-dried spackle. She checked sink and shower drains and the linings of drapes and bases of electrical fixtures, linoleum-tile joints, the undersides and seams of area rugs, the toilet tank, and each of the apartment's two throw pillows.

The only things she had not checked were the works and panels of the electric range and refrigerator. She reached in her purse, took out an adjustable screw driver with multiple blades in a small plastic case and suddenly heard a voice. It was a deep voice, a male voice. Its message was short and to the point: "Freeze. Raise your hands slowly or I will be forced to shoot you, and I will shoot you in the head."

32

Silver Lake Boulevard at Earl

Gwen raised her hands and turned slowly toward the sound of the man's voice. "Please don't shoot," she said. "I don't mean any harm."

"What are you doing here?" the man asked.

"Denise is my friend. I came to visit her. The super let me in."

"Your name?"

"Jane. Jane Scott."

"The super wouldn't let you in. Security is too important here."

"Well, he did. Where is Denise and who are you?"

"Denise is dead," the man said. "She was murdered. The super knows that. He wouldn't open the door without first checking with the investigating officer."

"Murdered?" Gwen said, her expression falling and eyes narrowing.

"Yes, murdered," the man said, looking at her closely.

"Can I lower my hands?" Gwen asked. "I'm not going to attack you."

"Yes, but keep them in front of you where I can see them."

His gun was now aimed at her heart. He continued to stare at her. Eventually he spoke. "How did you come to know Denise?"

"We worked together at Fairfax Hospital…in northern Virginia. Denise and I are both nurse practitioners. You still haven't answered my question. Who are you?"

"I'm Denise's uncle. Empty your purse on the kitchen counter. Don't reach inside. Turn it upside down."

She emptied it slowly, holding the extra clip against the side of her purse with her fingertips. The contents tumbled out onto the kitchen counter—a lipstick, compact, comb, packet of tissues, wallet, and keys.

"Now drop the purse on the counter."

Gwen did so as gently as possible but the sound of the clip hitting the counter was still audible.

"Deceit is very dangerous," Charles said. "Let's try that again. This time keep your fingers away from the side of the purse."

She tried to position the clip behind the packet of tissues and wallet.

"That appears to be a clip for a 9 mm automatic," Charles said. "Turn slightly to your left and very slowly lift the back of your jacket with your left hand."

She did so, revealing the handle of her weapon and the flap of the leather folder containing her Bureau credentials.

"You *have* been deceitful," Charles said, "but I have to compliment you on your duty weapon. The Sig Sauer P320 compact is an excellent choice. I have to admit to a preference for the full-sized model. The military has just concluded a major contract with the manufacturer. Those will mostly be camo rather than black, of course. By the way, you needn't bother showing me your Bureau credentials, Agent Harrison. I thought you looked familiar when you identified yourself as Jane Scott. You simply don't look like a Jane and your reputation *does* precede you."

She studied his face as the realization sank in. "As does yours, Sgt. White. Can I put my hands at my sides now?"

"Of course, but you still haven't answered my question."

"Which question was that?"

"What are you doing here?"

"I'm investigating your niece's death."

"The LAPD is already doing that; why is the Bureau involved?"

"I might ask you the same thing. I doubt that the LAPD would be comfortable with a person of your skills and reputation on the case."

"I'm just doing what I can to help; that's all. Now, my question…"

"Let me ask you something else first."

"What would that be?"

"Why don't you think I look like a Jane?"

33

Silver Lake Boulevard at Earl

"I can understand your interest in wanting to change the subject, but I need to know why the Bureau is involved."

"I'll answer in a second; this is important to me. Don't you think I've downplayed any notable features? I've never liked the expression 'Plain Jane' because it pigeonholes all the Janes. Besides, I have a friend from college named Jane who has a Ph.D. in Electrical Engineering and looks like a Swedish model, but maybe it's a subconscious thing; I don't like the stereotyping of Janes, but the Bureau doesn't want us to attract attention to ourselves. They want us to fade into the background because it makes us more effective when we're following people or working undercover. 'Jane' sounds, I don't know, more...*generic*; I thought it worked."

"Hard to stay anonymous or inconspicuous when your face keeps turning up in all the papers and across the internet," Charles answered.

"That's what I told the Director," Gwen said, "but he wanted the publicity, at least at the time. He always wants it both ways—fame *and* anonymity. He'd be *very* unhappy to learn that I was made so quickly this many miles from home."

"Can't *have it* both ways. Can't have a good *tracker* and also want the press to notice the fact and cover it."

"I appreciate your understanding that, Sgt. White. Not everyone does."

"Charles. And I'm still waiting…"

"Gwen. And I'm afraid I can't tell you everything."

"Let me start and make it easier for you," Charles said. "For one thing I know that Denise never worked at Fairfax Hospital."

Gwen was silent, letting him continue.

"I made a call. Acted as if I owned an apartment building and needed a reference on Denise's past employment and personal reliability. I got a golden-tongued answer and lots of details, but it didn't sound quite right. Nurses move around a lot. Happens all the time and it's not a big deal. It was almost as if she was ready for my question and reading from a long and carefully-written script. I called an old Army buddy, a man named Woody Green, one of my corporals in the Central Highlands. Woody works as an orderly at Fairfax Hospital. As old as he is, he still has an eye for the ladies. I know if Denise had ever worked there *he* would have noticed her. Told me he never saw her. If *Woodrow Green* didn't see her, she wasn't there."

"Have you said anything about this to the LAPD, Charles?"

"Not just yet."

"I'd appreciate it if you didn't."

"She was in Washington to work for the government, not a local hospital, wasn't she?"

"She was there to receive training."

"Then I would conclude several things. With all of this snoopy-poop cloak-and-dagger she was on a top secret assignment."

"Go on…"

"She was either a Bureau agent or some sort of operative for the Bureau, since the federal agencies are still protective of their own turf, even in the days of Homeland Security, and they wouldn't send one of their own top agents to investigate the death of an individual from another organization."

"Yes, and…"

"She was definitely on *our* side. The Bureau would investigate criminals and suspected criminals, but Denise wasn't one of those."

"No, she was not."

"And you know what she was working on, but you can't tell me the details."

"I don't really know the details; the Bureau compartmentalizes those things."

"They would have to tell you something, however, if only to provide a local contact and a rough outline of her activities. They didn't send someone from the regional office, so they didn't want them involved. Thus, she must have been engaged in something very secret. She was working at the Clinic for the Bureau, not simply to better the lot of humanity in the neighborhood…"

Gwen nodded and let him continue.

"So there was some connection between the people who came through the Clinic—or worked there—and the operation in which she was involved. Have I been wrong in anything I've said so far?"

"I knew that you were a great field soldier, Charles. I didn't know how astute you were as a student of our work."

"Well, when you're retired as I am, you have time to think about such things. I have another thought…"

"Yes?"

"It wouldn't aid you in your efforts if I shared what I've learned with the LAPD, even though my nephew Frank is a lieutenant there and would appreciate the help."

"That's true."

"And even though you have to maintain confidentiality it's clear that I've already figured out most of the things that you're not at liberty to discuss."

"Go on…"

"And I don't have to know the most secret details, at least not at this point."

"Right."

"So I believe that we should work together. We have the same goal—to bring a murderer to justice—and we have the same motivation to maintain secrecy in the process. You *did* know Denise, didn't you?"

"Yes, I did."

"And were you close?"

"Yes, we were, but I didn't know her real identity at the time and somehow feel bad about that, though there's no reason in the world that she should break the confidence she was asked to keep."

"I didn't see her as often as I would have liked to, but we were always close," Charles said. "She didn't tell any of us that she was doing this kind of work but we all still loved her."

"I understand your feelings and I know that you understand her situation. She couldn't tell you. The mission demanded it."

"I've always been thought of as someone who was what we called 'mission-oriented'," Charles said. "I think we'd make a good team."

She reached out to take his hand, but he sensed a certain reluctance or concern.

"What's wrong?" he asked. "Are you still worried because I recognized you?"

"I should have worn some glasses," she said.

"Wouldn't have helped," Charles said. "I've been hunkered down here for six and a half hours, turning over possibilities in my head. I had hoped that the perp would show up, looking for something that might incriminate him. This time of night...it wouldn't be a workman; it could only be somebody bad or somebody good. And I know the good ones already. They're at the Clinic or back at the PAB.

"The killer was male, so I had to figure that you were good, but not local. Who crosses state lines to help solve crimes?"

"So the dye job and new 'do didn't help at all?"

"Not under the circumstances," Charles answered, "but most don't have the time that I do to check on such things. I think if you put on those glasses you'll be fine. I *knew* the Fairfax Hospital story was phony; no one else does. They won't be suspicious the way I was."

"I hope you're right," she said.

34

The 110, just South of the 10

D ave Carlow's phone rang over to the duty sergeant's desk. "This is Vince Dearing," the voice said. "Is Lieutenant Carlow available?"

"Bill Hennessey, Vince. He's meeting with the Captain. He should be back in 15 or 20 minutes."

"If he comes out early tell him I'm on my way, Bill. I should be there in about 5 or 10 minutes; I need to talk to him immediately."

"Will do," Hennessey said.

Vince knew that he would have to log some time on one of Carlow's oak client chairs while the new lead on the White case was swirling in his head. Carlow's desktop would be covered with file folders, his walls blanketed with commendations and award-ceremony photographs, while the smells from his old three-pack-a-day habit still permeated the folds of his fabric-covered desk chair. The screensaver on his aging Dell would be, as always, a Dragnet-inspired photograph of City Hall, the tower slightly distorted because of the pixel density of the original picture.

When Dearing sat down in the lieutenant's chair, the top of the nearest stack of folders would be level with his chin. Carlow liked to see everything that was in progress spread out before him. The folders also formed a barrier between him and his subordinates, a fact that constituted a subject for office jokes and amateur psychologizing.

While he waited, Dearing would think through the evidence and information that he had turned, so he could speak quickly and directly to Carlow without any hesitation or rethinking. He wanted to watch the reactions in his eyes. With the scant resources at the division's disposal every report was a kind of pitch. The lieutenant would be world-weary, a stained, half-filled coffee cup in his hand, collection of ballpoints in his breast pocket, and seldom-used service 9 mm automatic in a short holster on his hip. Later Vince could put everything down in his notepad, but time was of the essence now and he wanted to get the information to his lieutenant as quickly as possible. Perhaps others could be assigned to help work with him on the lead. The lieutenant's call.

Carlow would pause for a moment before he could begin and offer him coffee; Vince would pass, anxious to get to the subject at hand. He would then spring the news about the lead, which would pique Carlow's interest. After hitting the wall with the Clinic records they needed a new development, even if it was something of a long shot. A similar crime. A USC connection. Carlow would scoot forward in his chair, hit Vince with a series of insistent questions, coming more and more to life with each answer and each follow-up.

Stumbling upon the lead had mostly been a matter of luck, though the old adage was probably true: luck *does* come most often to those who are prepared for it. After constant combing of the endless shelves of Clinic files it had fallen into his hands like a gift from the heavens. The right query. The right data base. The answer that lit up his laptop screen. Maybe even a case-breaker...

The freeway traffic slowed as he drove, start-and-stop, through downtown. The Angelenos were at least merciful in their willingness to permit lane-changers to move toward exits or to roll the dice and try other lanes when traffic appeared to be moving at a better pace in one than in the other. Driving was less of a competition here and more of a shared burden.

There were even some clouds and a touch of blue sky above the

San Gabriels; the yellow haze that characteristically clung to the towers above the four-stack had moved east, toward the desert. For a second Dearing was dazed as a lane opened briefly and the driver of the dark sedan behind him gave him a short honk to signal the opportunity. Vince raised his right hand in a gesture of thanks and took the sudden opening, accelerating toward the interchange and the ultimate exit onto Broadway that would take him to the Police Administration Building.

The surface streets were as clogged as the freeway. As he sat waiting for the traffic to move he noticed that the driver of the dark sedan had followed him from the freeway. He had probably been polite because he suspected they were going in the same direction. What was good for Vince was also good for him.

When the cars ahead did not move for the next 35 seconds, Vince saw the driver behind him drive out of the line of traffic and approach the side of his car, a dangerous move in light of the possibility of sudden oncoming traffic. If Vince were a traffic cop he'd be reaching for his ticket book.

As the driver pulled up, parallel to Vince's unmarked cruiser, the man lowered his window and lifted his arm. The sound of the gun, the shattering of the driver's side window on Vince's car, and the blood splatter on the far window, windshield, seat, and headliner came simultaneously. A mercy shot. That was the good news; it did its work instantly and definitively. Vince slumped gently against the wheel, his body listing to the right, his heartbeat stilled forever. His cell phone rang and vibrated in his breast pocket—eight full rings before the eventual silence.

35

100 West 1st Street—The Police Administration Building

"Run all the film," Carlow said. "There's a camera at each interchange. I want to know what cars were behind him and who was driving them. Talk to the witnesses again. Jog their memories. Anything could be of use. I will *not* tolerate the murder of one of my detectives within sight of our headquarters. Go over Dearing's car. If somebody was following him they might have gotten close to the vehicle earlier. Dust every inch of it. Crawl around underneath and check for tracking devices. Did the shell casing fall into the street? Check with the people processing the scene. Look in the gutters, the sewers...everywhere."

As the members of his team scattered, the phone on his desk rang.

"Carlow," he said.

"Dave, Frank White. What have you got?"

"Good afternoon, Frank...such as it is. Vince Dearing was coming to see me. Somebody shot him just outside of our building. No real leads yet. The witnesses say that it appeared to be a middle-aged man. He was wearing sunglasses and an unmarked baseball cap. Driving a late model sedan. One thought it was a Mercury, another thought a Ford. Dark green, nearly black. Heavy traffic...the guy was right behind Dearing... he pulled out of the line of traffic, came up along side and shot him. Dearing died instantly. The last call on his cell phone was from his daughter in Chicago. That's it."

"You said he was coming to see you, Dave…"

"Yes. He had talked to the desk sergeant. It sounded urgent."

"What about his notepad?"

"No entries since last night. Nothing recent worth talking about."

"How about his men at the Clinic?"

"There was only one there at the time when Vince left. The others were at lunch. He told us that Vince was working on his laptop and then suddenly said that he had to leave. This was about an hour and twenty minutes before he was shot."

"So he made one or more stops on his way to your office."

"Right. It looks as if something caught his attention and he went out to check on it, or on something related to it, before he came here to meet with me."

"Was he working any other cases?"

"Yes, but nothing this big."

"So wherever he was heading, he probably had at least a half hour to get there and a half hour to get back. Unless, of course, it was someplace nearby, in which case he could get there quickly and spend a longer period of time on the scene."

"Right," Carlow said.

"From Wilshire and Vermont you can go pretty far in thirty minutes, especially if the traffic isn't too heavy. You're basically looking at an area the size of the entire Los Angeles basin."

"Unfortunately."

A uniformed policewoman came into Carlow's office. "Just a second, Frank," he said. Covering the phone with the heel of his hand, Carlow spoke to the policewoman.

"What is it?"

"We've got an owner i.d. on the dark sedan, lieutenant," she said.

"Name?"

"Yes, sir. Clemmer, William. Age 52. Culver City address."

"Thanks. Get a team ready."

Carlow got back on the phone. "Frank, we just got an i.d. on the owner of the sedan."

"Anybody we know?"

"Denise White's supervisor at the Clinic."

36

Vermont above Wilshire

The two vans arrived simultaneously at the Clinic parking lot. Carlow, a detective, and six uniforms emerged, the latter all wearing protective jackets and helmets, and all carrying automatic weapons. After pausing momentarily at the door, they stormed into the building, converging on Clemmer's office. With a cup of coffee in one hand and a sheaf of papers in the other he was standing in the outer office, between work stations, staring at the armed team like a man suddenly encountering a large wild animal in his living room. A drop or two of coffee spilled over the side of his cup.

Carlow and the detective, Art Herbert, turned Clemmer around, frisked him, and escorted him into his office.

"Did you find my car?" Clemmer asked. "I've been expecting a phone call, not an assault team."

"Did you report it missing?" Carlow asked.

"Yes, of course," Clemmer responded.

Herbert took out his cell phone and stepped outside the office.

"Your car was used in the commission of a homicide," Carlow said, as the two of them sat down. "We have the car and its license plate on tape. The murder occurred less than an hour ago, on West 1st Street."

"When, precisely?"

"Approximately 40 minutes ago."

"I haven't left the office since I came in this morning," Clemmer said. "I tried to go out for lunch, but discovered that my car had been stolen and came right back in. I wasn't gone for more than 2 or 3 minutes. I've got a whole office full of witnesses who can testify to that."

Herbert came back in. "The theft of the vehicle was reported an hour and 35 minutes ago, lieutenant."

"Who was killed?" Clemmer asked.

"The victim's identity hasn't been released yet," Carlow said.

"Was it Detective Dearing?"

"Why do you say that?"

"Because he left in a hurry and he hasn't come back since then."

Carlow didn't respond.

"I don't like this at all," Clemmer said. "If somebody was watching him and stole my car to continue following him, the person has been at the Clinic or just outside of it. If he actually saw Detective Dearing close his laptop and get up and hurry out, and figured that he had discovered something (as *we* all did) the killer was actually waiting inside our Clinic. This morning. Armed. Unrecognized."

Carlow looked out through the glass partition marking Clemmer's office and surveyed the individuals waiting to see the nurses. Five women. Six men. Four children and two infants. Soiled clothes. Unwashed hair. Desperate expressions. Storm trooper-like policemen stood in their midst, armed to the teeth, and they paid little or no attention to them, the weight of their own lives pressing upon them and their familiarity with the threat of violence so deep and of such long standing that the policemen's presence was little more than a brief episode in an otherwise unremarkable Tuesday afternoon.

Not all of them could be criminals—certainly not of the stature of someone who could blow out the eye and skull and brains of a detective within sight of police headquarters—but they could all fade into any backdrop, deceive any observer, and wear their hardscrabble lives and experiences like a disguise that could defy the best efforts of the most attentive observer. They had seen, heard, and felt it all and were not about to be ruffled by the simple matter of a room filled with armed officers. Where was Vince Dearing's murderer now, Carlow wondered. Sitting in that room? Standing just outside the door? Standing above a sink filled with bleach, washing his hands of GSR, preparing himself for his next move?

37

The Pasadena Library, Central Branch

"This is interesting," Gwen said, twisting the screen of the library desktop computer so that Charles could read it.

"Parallel case, in some ways," she added. "The only problem is the time frame."

"2002," Charles said. "Long time ago."

"The victim was found in a men's room stall. Bludgeoned, not stabbed, but you've still got the public rest room, violent homicide, and USC association."

"Behind the iMAX theatre?" Charles said, focusing on the small print and the black and white photograph. "California Science Center, Exposition Park. Right next door to campus."

"And the victim was a USC professor."

"Couldn't be a connection with the Clinic," Charles said. "It didn't exist then. Maybe something purely random. Professors hang out around the Park, but people come to the iMAX theatre from all over southern California."

"Right," Gwen said. "It could be two separate, totally-unconnected events."

"Anything there about the door being nailed shut?"

"No, but the door to the facility and the door to the cubicle were probably made of steel. At least there's nothing in the story about either or both of the doors being nailed. That would be an interesting detail, worth reporting if it actually happened. Plays to a common fear—being trapped in a small space. Papers would seize on it instantly."

"When was the body found?"

"The next morning," Gwen answered. "They lock up the toilets right after the last screening, so unless the perp had a way of getting into the facility later that night, he did the killing in the time between the last showing and the lockup. Tricky for planning."

"If he'd done it earlier somebody would have seen the blood, or maybe heard the last groans."

"Right. Whenever I've been there they cleared out the theatre and the park very quickly. Security reasons. Not a good place to walk around in after dark. The victim could have been one of the last people out…the concession stand was closed…the lights were dimmed…and he decided to make one last trip to the men's room before getting on the freeway. Fatal decision. The perp could have followed him in, killed him, and then turned off the light, so that whoever was responsible for locking up simply looked in, saw the darkness, locked the door, and took off."

"Maybe a last-minute decision," Charles said. "Kill him there rather than risk anybody seeing him do it outside or hear the blows being struck."

"The investigating officer figured that the victim was struck outside of the cubicle and then shoved inside, since there was a heavy blow to the back of the head in addition to several blows to the face. Hard to hit somebody in the back of the head in that enclosed space…"

"Unless the victim slumped forward or was pulled forward."

"Right."

"The most lethal blow would be to the temple, not to the face or back of the head."

"Right," Gwen said, "but most amateurs wouldn't know that."

"Yes, and most professionals wouldn't bludgeon somebody to death. They're into efficiency, not anger. If they want to get your attention they shoot or stab the victim in the eye."

"I agree."

"Did they find the weapon?" Charles asked.

"Yes. It was right in the waste paper bin. A ball peen hammer. Covered with blood, hair…a few other things…everything but fingerprints."

"That's another point of connection," Charles said. "Carrying a hammer to a crime scene. And the case was never closed…"

"Not yet," Gwen said.

"What was the movie that night?"

"The Rolling Stones at the Max."

"Doesn't sound like something that would bring out a college professor," Charles said. "Usually they'd go for something about giant turtles or Chinese dams."

"There's another possibility. He may not have been in the area to see a movie. The Trojans played Notre Dame that evening at the Coliseum. They even won."

"Whatever he saw, I hope he enjoyed it," Charles said. "I know he didn't enjoy what happened afterwards, in that toilet stall."

38

Vermont above Wilshire

Carlow had taken over the case. Everyone who had visited the Clinic that day was identified, located, detained and interrogated. Pictures were taken of each and shown to the witnesses who were present at the scene where Vince Dearing was shot. The driving record and DMV status of each were checked. Some had their own cars and had driven to the Clinic. Some were sufficiently incapacitated to prevent their operating a vehicle. Some of the women could not have successfully impersonated a male driver and a number of the Clinic's clients were unlikely to have been able to hotwire Clemmer's Taurus.

The only physically-plausible suspect was an individual named Hernandez, who had three witnesses prepared to testify that he was in their company for large segments of the period in question. He also had his own car—an aged Nissan rattletrap with a leprous body but still-functioning drive train. One of the witnesses, a woman named Gomez, testified that she had ridden in it, with Hernandez, eight miles from the murder site, at approximately the same time that the crime was being committed.

Carlow also investigated the staff who were on site that day. All were familiar faces with alibis and character witnesses. Gerry Burke, the IT support person, commented that he had seen a person near the receptionist's desk who looked more like a mechanic or electrician than a Clinic patient. The receptionist was away for a moment and the man was thumbing through various pamphlets and handouts. No one else had seen the individual and Burke's description was too generic to be of any significant value. He had only seen the man in profile and was unable to describe any salient facial features. "Who would know that something was going to happen and that we'd be asked about it later?" he said. "It was just a guy looking at some pieces of paper. Probably on a break. Clearing his head for a minute or two before he went back to work."

"Was he wearing a jacket or anything in which he could have concealed a weapon?" Carlow asked.

"Not that I remember," Burke said. "I think he was wearing a colored tee shirt, but I couldn't swear to it."

"Facial hair?"

"I don't think so, but I was looking from the side. He might have had one of those 'soul patch' things or something. I couldn't really tell. And honestly, lieutenant, I wasn't paying that much attention. He didn't look dangerous or anything."

"Hair color?"

"I don't know. It's hard to tell. Working guys...they're sweaty. Sometimes they have dirt in their hair...drywall dust...paint...cobwebs. They crawl around in dirty places. Stuff gets attached. They look all salt-and-peppery and then they take a shower and look completely different."

"He *looked* salt-and-peppery?"

"Maybe. I *know* he didn't look all dressed up for a date or anything."

"And you say he was around 5'10" to 6'."

"Yes, something like that."

"Average build."

"Yes. He didn't make any big impression. I would have noticed if he was really fat or really skinny."

"Age?"

"Hard to tell with guys like that. They drink a lot, smoke a lot. Somewhere between 40 and 60 is as close as I could get."

"Was he holding a baseball cap?"

"Not that I remember."

"How about his shoes?"

"Couldn't see them. I was behind a computer screen. I couldn't see anything below his waist."

"If you *do* remember anything else, give me a call," Carlow said, handing him one of his cards.

"I'll do that, lieutenant. I promise I will."

As Carlow finished questioning him his cell phone twitched. He removed it from his pocket and checked the screen. Incoming from Frank White. His third attempt in the last twenty minutes. Carlow hit the answer button. There was nothing to report but he figured he owed him the courtesy of at least telling him that and reassuring him that they were increasing all of their efforts, even if there were no positive leads yet. They were simply running faster on the same treadmill, but what else could they do?

39

Exposition Park

"The doors are steel now," Charles said, "and they don't look as if they've been replaced in the recent past."

"Prison-like, isn't it?" Gwen answered. "Cinder block. Drab colors. Minimal fixtures. Purely functional."

"High crime area," Charles said. "They call it a park, but open space surrounded by a neighborhood like this is a place to hunt, not to picnic--especially with all the rich targets from the suburbs who walk through it."

"I was here once on a date," Gwen said. "We got some dinner and then drove in for the evening show. There was a car in the lot. Old, but not broken down. Black guy sitting behind the wheel when we arrived. We saw the classic iMax movie—the one from the Air and Space Museum: "To Fly". Real short; less than half an hour long. There was also a movie about penguins and the trailer for a movie about some islands--the Canaries I think. They had a break between the two short features--to change the filmstock. I guess the iMax reels are huge. Anyway, when we came out we noticed that the black guy was still in the car. I was curious. I wanted to check him out, see who he was, find out why he was there… but my date probably would have gotten nervous, and anyway, the guy didn't budge from his seat. We were the last ones out of the lot. As soon as we left, he left, and all the lights were turned off. Then I realized who he was and what he was doing there. Undercover cop. Protecting the moviegoers, watching their cars; keeping an eye on the grounds and the dark corners."

"Little guy, barely visible behind the wheel."

"Yes," Gwen said.

"Calvin Hopper," Charles said. "Retired GI. Combat engineer. Close friends call him Sap; short for *Sapper*. His specialty was clearing minefields. Much easier duty watching a parking lot…"

"You know them all, don't you Charles?" Gwen asked.

"Never know when you might need them," Charles answered. "Got to stay in touch."

Gwen paused and then continued. "So a man walks into a rest room, gets hit on the back of the head with a ball peen hammer, shoved into a toilet, and then has his face turned into bloody mush with another 8 or 9 blows. There's a lot of splatter, but the perp doesn't have time to stop and clean up. He drops the hammer in the waste paper bin and walks away. He's smart enough to either wear gloves or wipe his fingerprints from the handle of the hammer. No other evidence left behind, at least nothing reported to the press. If they *did* have anything, it didn't lead to any convictions."

"High risk, don't you think?" Charles asked.

"Yes," Gwen answered. "Just like MacArthur Park, if the two *are* connected. Lots of chances to be caught and even more chances to be seen. Not the way I'd do it…"

"Go on," Charles said.

"If I had to kill somebody I'd do it in private, not in public. Disguise myself somehow…gain the victim's confidence. Show up at his front door with a uniform on…something official…something that could get him to open the door. Maybe a postal outfit and a nice package in my hand. A present…all he has to do is sign for it, tear off the brown paper and look for the ribbon and fancy wrapping…when he opens the door I'd slip in, do the job, slip back out and disappear. Low risk."

"I agree," Charles said. "So why do it this way?"

"Time constraint? The person had to be killed quickly; not enough time to take the safe route; too much at stake. Maybe the person knew something, something big."

"Possible," Charles said. "At first I was thinking that the act was done on impulse. Sudden rage, maybe."

"Me too," Gwen said, "what with all the blood and overkill…but it all seems too planned for that."

Charles reached inside his jacket. "Cell phone," he said.

Gwen nodded.

"Yes, Frank?" Charles said. "When?…Where?…OK, thanks…don't worry, I won't…"

He clicked off and put the phone back in his inside jacket pocket.

"Vince Dearing. Shot downtown, just outside the Police Administration Building. Little over an hour ago. Male perp. Generic description. Ball cap. Dark glasses. Stolen car—owned by Denise's supervisor."

"Who no doubt has an alibi…"

"Yes. They figure the killer was stalking Dearing. Dearing left the Clinic suddenly and the killer followed, stealing the first available car."

"Dearing knew something. That's why he was killed in the worst possible place. Good God, right outside of LAPD headquarters. It was the perp's only chance for a clear shot. The need had to outweigh the risk."

"Maybe we've got a pattern," Charles said.

Gwen nodded in agreement.

"Dave Carlow's taken over the case."

"Dearing's lieutenant?"

"Yes," Charles said.

"Is that a good thing or a bad thing?"

"Probably a good thing," Charles said. "At least it raises the profile of the case. The lieutenant has the juice to add more officers to the investigation. He also puts his own reputation on the line."

"If the killer followed Dearing from the Clinic he was hanging pretty close. He must have seen something, seen some sort of reaction from Dearing. Otherwise Dearing could just be leaving for lunch. No reason to steal a car to follow him unless there was something out of the ordinary going on. The chance of being caught was high. That time of day…the owner himself could just be getting ready to go out to lunch… he discovers his car missing…files a report…suddenly the thief is caught following the principal investigator on a homicide case. He's got some serious 'splaining to do. Why take that kind of risk? He was *desperate*, Charles."

40

Exposition Park

"I agree, but I still don't understand the violence level with the other two killings, assuming, of course, that they're related."

"A serial killer would strike more often," Gwen said. "The monkey would be clawing at his back, urging him on. I've never heard of a dormancy period that long, unless, of course, he was in prison and unable to do anything. Anyway, I don't see a serial killer here. Murdering an undercover FBI agent suggests that we're dealing with something other than a thrill killer. Let's assume that the Dearing murder was committed in order to silence him. We have to assume that it was related to Denise's death, since the car was stolen from the Clinic. This wasn't some old adversary of Dearing's, seeking some overdue revenge; it was somebody concerned about his current case. So let's go with our hunch. The perp saw some reaction in Dearing, feared that he would take the investigation to the next level and get too close for comfort. So he shot him. No opportunity for anything up close and personal, except inside or right outside the Clinic. Too close, for any number of reasons..."

"Right. So he follows him for...I don't know...an hour or so. Maybe Dearing saw something in one of the data bases and went to check for himself. Then he drove to the admin building. The perp figured that Dearing had made the connection between what he knew earlier and what he suddenly learned. His next stop was Carlow's office and his next step would be a ratcheting up of the investigation. As soon as the perp saw that Dearing was heading for LAPD headquarters he knew that he had to take him out."

"Maybe he stopped off at Exposition Park," Gwen said.

Charles let that sink in. "Could be…but what about the violence? If he's a guy who kills people when they learn things he doesn't want them to learn, why all the blood?"

"Possibilities…let's see," Gwen said. "He's an *amateur*. He doesn't know how much blood you have to lose in order to die, so he wants to make sure. He's *desperate*. He's afraid his victim might cry out and draw help. He wants to silence the person at all costs. He can't risk doing something more surgical. He's *up tight, repressed*. When his blood is up and he let's go he has trouble stopping. He's a *borderline psycho* and the victim presses one of his buttons…says something to him…something that sets off the lightning in his brain. Maybe…maybe he's just carrying more *anger* than he can bear."

"I'll tell you one thing," Charles said. "I don't care very much about whatever it is that's gnawing at *him*…I just want to find him and take him down."

"That's a must," Gwen said. "First, we've got to find out more about the college professor. We know Denise and we know who she was working for and what she was doing…"

Charles gave her a look, but didn't speak.

"*I* know what she was doing. And it's not really material, Charles. The object of her work was hundreds of miles away during the commission of the crime and he wasn't in the U.S. at the time of the earlier murder."

"Are you sure?"

"Reasonably sure. There's nothing in the Bureau data bases to suggest otherwise, but I'll check again. Knowing the person with whom she was concerned suggests to me a very different approach to the problem."

"The other person would have used a bomb."

"I didn't say that, Charles."

"The other person would have tried to take out a few more in the process, maybe a couple thousand."

"Again, Charles, I didn't say that."

"But I'm not too far off."

Gwen stared without changing her expression.

"That's what I thought," he said.

"Like I said," she responded, "we know about Denise; we don't know about this other victim. Let's assume the two events are connected. We should begin by finding out who he was, what he did, and why someone might have wanted to kill him."

"I can tell you two things right off," Charles said. "His name was Appleman and he made a lot of people very angry."

III

RED CITY

41

Exposition Park

"Geoffrey Appleman," Charles said. "With a G, not a J."

"Sounds British," Gwen said.

"I think he was from Minnesota, actually, but I don't remember all the details. I just read the obituary that ran at the time of the murder."

"What made everybody so angry?"

"A book he wrote."

"Any details?"

"Not in the obit. They just said that the book had been very controversial and sparked a negative reaction in the university community."

"We need to know more," Gwen said. "What department was he in?"

"History," Charles said.

"Let's check him out."

The current department chair was a man named Stuart Stern. When he learned that Gwen and Charles wanted to discuss Geoffrey Appleman he suggested that they meet in the library, in a soundproof study room.

"I'd rather meet here than in SOS [the shorthand abbreviation for the Social Sciences Building]," Stern said. "Geoffrey's name still raises the faculty's collective blood pressure."

Short and thin, Stern was wearing dark trousers, a plaid shirt and threadbare maroon sweater, which circled his throat, pinching the sides of his shirt collar. His salt and pepper beard clung tightly against his face, with scattered blank spaces exposing acne-scarred cheeks.

"You said you were doing research on Geoffrey's death?" he said.

"Actually we're working on a project that deals with violence on university campuses," Gwen said.

"And you are...where?"

"We're freelancers, not academics," Gwen said.

"I see."

"What can you tell us about the professor's death?" Charles asked.

"Not a great deal, I'm afraid. I was here, of course, but I didn't have any personal knowledge of the murder, apart from what appeared in the paper."

"What about the man himself?" Charles asked. "I understand that he was not particularly popular on campus."

"Geoffrey was a gadfly," Stern said. "Such men are useful, but it all comes down—in the end--to whose horse is being stung. He managed to upset nearly everyone. I don't believe that there were many tears shed at his funeral."

"You attended his funeral?" Charles asked.

"No. I believe it was a private service," Stern responded, as he shifted uncomfortably on the cushionless, oak library chair.

"Was he an unpleasant person?" Gwen asked.

"I wouldn't say so; generally he avoided personal confrontation."

"He irritated people by his writings," Gwen offered.

"Yes, sometimes."

"And was there one thing in particular..."

"Yes," Stern said. "His last book."

They all stared at each other as Stern sat silently. Before Gwen or Charles could prompt him he began to speak again.

"It was titled *Red City*. I don't remember the exact subtitle. It was something like 'a study of the structure of the contemporary university'."

"It didn't just deal with USC, then?" Gwen asked.

"No, though this university offered a number of examples of the things which troubled Geoffrey."

"Have you read it?" Charles asked.

"Of course," Stern answered, impatiently. "I read all of my colleagues' books."

"That must keep you busy," Gwen said.

"Not that busy," Stern said.

"Could you summarize the book for us?" Charles asked.

"Yes, I suppose so," Stern said, pausing again and shifting in his seat. "The core notion is that the modern university aspires to be a socialist *polis*."

"A *polis*?" Charles said.

"Yes, like a Greek city-state. The community is small, by world standards, but it cherishes its independence. While it can be ruled by a tyrant it is generally ruled by an oligarchy. Many of these oligarchies are also timocracies, since the few who rule are also rich, or at least well-compensated. The community tolerates them because the *polis* is putatively democratic and explicitly socialist. Socialist *ideology* mutes concerns over potential tyranny—at least most of the time—and socialist *policy* is systematically sustained."

"Forgive me, Dr. Stern," Gwen said, "but that sounds *very* academic."

"It *was* very academic, but some of Geoffrey's statements were more explicit."

"For example?" Charles asked.

"Geoffrey said that academic socialists have been able to create a society on campus that the American people would routinely reject at the ballot box."

42

Doheny Library, USC

"How is it socialist?" Gwen asked. "I thought that private schools like USC were generally criticized for being elitist."

"The key point for Geoffrey," Stern said, "was a survey of university budgets that was done at the time. It concluded that while the growth in the number of students and the number of faculty was modest, the growth in the number of non-professorial academic staff was astronomical. Essentially, the universities had taken on a vast array of roles that Geoffrey considered alien to their central function--education."

"For example?" Charles asked.

"For example, support centers for gay and lesbian students and students of color. These, by the way, are now being expanded to include trans- students and students who are questioning their orientations and have not yet settled on one. There is growing pressure at USC, for example, to provide such services for asexual students."

Gwen was about to express surprise that such individuals would possess the impulse and energy for political mobilization, but thought better of it and let Stern continue.

"These kinds of services, Geoffrey argued, are basically available on demand. When added to all of the other offices that deal with ethnicity, gender, and various aspects of identity politics, they constitute a bureaucracy beyond that contemplated by the leftist fringe of either the red states or the blue. The staffing of such offices is made possible by general revenue funds. In other words, a significant share of each student tuition dollar is being used to provide services for a segment of the community that is proportionally small. *Their* tuition dollars go there as well, of course, but the majority are paying most of the costs for the minority. Geoffrey's point was that the university's mission should be to provide education, not psychological or medical services. If individuals sought such services they should pay for them themselves, separately. The university's role is to develop and disseminate knowledge, not provide therapy."

"He was more conservative," Charles said.

"Paleolibertarian, actually. That's how he would identify himself," Stern said. "The point was one of principle. Geoffrey himself was actually gay. That's not widely known, but it's a fact. His objection was to the reallocation of resources, not to the orientation of some individuals. His conception of the university's role would now be considered narrow. When he was in college, of course, there were virtually no services such as those which he questioned."

"And far lower costs," Gwen said.

"Yes, that would be Geoffrey's point," Stern said. "When he was a student, room and board charges were approximately the same as tuition; now the latter is 5-to-6 times higher. Student housing is much improved, as is the food served therein, so they have not been standing still, but the cost of tuition has literally skyrocketed. The reason is—according to Geoffrey—that the university has become a vast welfare state, providing endless services, some academic, many not. Most are very expensive and from both an educational and utilitarian point of view, often questionable. From a political point of view, however, they are inestimably important. The inefficiencies simply mirror the cognate inefficiencies of centrally-planned socialist economies. We would not support a system such as that in our everyday political lives, but it is forced upon us in the modern university. If Harvard adds a new office to their list of politicized support services or a new program of scholarship set-asides, we all must do the same, whether we can afford it or not, since the ideological integrity of the institution trumps its educational effectiveness. The university has become a polity unto itself, a polity that socialist theorists would recognize at once."

"And this made people very angry," Charles said.

"Yes. Geoffrey retorted that their anger at something so self-apparent indicated the degree to which the dominant ideology had pervaded the *polis*."

"As you said earlier, Dr. Stern," Charles responded, "it all depends on whose horse is being stung. If *you* were one of the people whose position depended upon that ideology you would perceive his comments as a threat."

"Yes," Stern replied. "For a time there were suspicions that some member of the university staff might have actually killed Geoffrey. We all thought that quite preposterous."

"Why do you say that?" Gwen asked.

"Because Geoffrey was obviously *right*. The dominant ideology *was* so pervasive that no one could possibly imagine the university administration responding favorably to his book and taking action on it. There were some pieties to the effect that '*Professor Appleman has reminded us of the importance of efficiently utilizing our resources for the advancement of our intellectual community*' but never a moment's thought that anyone would be closing down the Black Cultural Center or Office of Disability Services. It is interesting though…"

"What's that, Dr. Stern?" Gwen asked.

"Someone just killed a nurse at the School of Social Work's Clinic over on Vermont. The Clinic didn't exist at the time of Geoffrey's book, but it was precisely the sort of thing that he had in mind—in this case the university providing free medical care. In some ways this was worse, since the clients weren't even members of the university community. Part of *outreach*, presumably. The universities are expected to do such things now. It's possible that he might have argued that such entities are better than PILOTs. At least we control the dispensing of the services."

"PILOTs?" Charles asked.

"PILOTs: payments in lieu of taxes. Universities are tax-exempt organizations. Some are pressed to make such payments to compensate for the loss of tax revenue to their surrounding communities. I studied at Yale, for example. The city of New Haven has received such payments from Yale for years. *Outreach*, on the other hand, can be cited whenever the threat of a PILOT is raised. The university can quickly list all of the services it is currently providing the community without cost. That keeps the politicians at bay, at least for the moment. This is precisely the sort of thing that keeps Geoffrey spinning in his grave."

"But there's one thing he could say," Gwen responded.

"What's that?" Stern asked.

"At least he's not bleeding anymore."

43

Doheny Library, USC

"What are your *own* thoughts on Professor Appleman's theory, Dr. Stern?" Charles asked.

"Like most theories it covers some of the data, but not all. You should, for example, also talk to Daniel Stein. He takes a very different view."

"Is he in your department?" Gwen asked.

"No, he's at UCLA. He's their education historian."

Stein was not in his office when they called, but the departmental secretary told them that he didn't mind taking calls at home and gave them his number. He agreed to meet them at his apartment on Venice Boulevard. The space was filled with brick-and-board bookshelves. What wouldn't fit on the shelves was stacked on the floor. The kitchen table had been moved to the living room and contained a computer, a tray of note cards, a stack of books with paper slips protruding from the pages, a large ash tray, and a seldom-washed glass covered with visible fingerprints. The furniture was early-graduate student, with stains, scuff marks and noticeable fabric tears.

Charles and Gwen introduced themselves, using aliases, told him again that they were working on a study of violence on college campuses, and reminded him that they had spoken to Stuart Stern, who had suggested they meet with him.

"Over at the University of Spoiled Children."

"Sorry?" Charles said.

"It's a tired joke," Stein said. "UCLA's explication of the USC acronym. I hope you don't mind if I smoke." He had already taken out a cigarette.

"It's your home," Gwen said, politely. "We're grateful that you're willing to speak with us."

"Professor Stern told us about a book by Professor Appleman—the man who was murdered some years ago in Exposition Park," Charles said.

"Nice man, for a crypto-fascist. His gayness may have softened the edges a little."

"Professor Stern described him as a paleolibertarian," Charles said.

Stein smiled. "A trimmer like Stuart would say something like that."

Gwen let that pass. "Have you read Professor Appleman's book, Professor Stein?"

"It's more of a screed than a book," Stein said, "but, yes, I've slogged through it."

"And what do you think?" Gwen asked.

"It's preposterous, of course. On the economics alone he's clearly delusional. *Red City* is the sort of trade book that keeps the right-wing publishers in business."

"I believe it was published by a university press," Gwen responded.

"Yes, as I said…"

"Tell us more about the economics, Professor Stein," Charles said.

"Sure," Stein said, taking a drag from his cigarette and picking at one of the toes protruding from his sandal. "Geoffrey is troubled that the universities have set up some support centers for their students. For starters, the students and their parents are paying, so if they're not unhappy, why should he be? But leave that aside for a moment. His argument assumes that students are creatures of pure intellect. They have no bodies, no drives, no emotions. They are racially and sexually homogeneous. They are fully formed at the age of 18 and are not undergoing any developmental changes. They're like detached brains in a science fiction film. They do not interact with other beings. Their personalities—if that is an appropriate term--have no social or political dimensions. Ultimately they have no souls, if you're more comfortable speaking that way.

"Any *economic* account of a phenomenon must take into consideration all of the dimensions of its discrete elements. Geoffrey clearly got an F in Econ 101 (or stopped attending when he got a headache from the *complexity* of the subject).

"Apart from all that, the book is absurd on its face. Just because one area of an organization has grown, it does not follow that its relative size is disproportionate to its level of importance. It is possible, for example, that certain areas have been *neglected* in the past. When that problem is addressed, people such as Geoffrey Appleman see it as part of a leftist plot rather than as a long-overdue attempt to right a long-tolerated wrong. Have either of you ever been in Heritage Hall?"

"I haven't," Gwen said.

"No, I haven't," Charles added. "What is it?"

"It's a shrine," Stein answered, "a shrine to USC athletics. It's like a chapel. Soft lighting. Jerseys, statuary of the saints…O. J. Simpson…John Wayne…I don't know what it cost, but it wasn't cheap and it tells you where the university's values really lie. You take the entire budget of all of the support services that troubled Geoffrey Appleman and set them beside the budget for USC football and then tell me that USC is a socialist city-state. I'll tell you what that university is; it's a shill for corporate southern California and a major player in the entertainment industry. And so is UCLA," he added. "There. I can be fair."

Charles and Gwen sat silently, waiting for him to continue.

"Check the budget for information technology at any major

university. It'll be bigger than the budget for the library. Yes, some of that money goes to research, but where does most of it go—to bandwidth that enables students to download popular music, to wi-fi in dorms and student centers where they can play video games or sit in the corner and watch porno movies. There's nothing very secret here. Geoffrey Appleman did not uncover any great plots or underground societies in the modern university. I hate to disappoint you, but there's no Priory of Sion there. He identified what are little more than a series of sops to the progressive faculty and the handful of minority students who are allowed to squeeze through the door. Have you ever seen any place whiter than USC? And in *that* neighborhood? The real budgets speak volumes. The modern university is a summer camp for rich people. Despite what you read, it *is* run *like a business*. A huge business, with billion dollar budgets commonplace and multi-billion dollar endowments increasingly commonplace. Have you ever heard of 'enrollment management'?"

"Yes," Gwen said. Charles nodded in agreement.

"The fiction is that it's designed to add diversity to the student body. If you believe that I may also be able to interest you in buying a freeway or two. The levels of minority enrollment more or less stay the same though there are pieties offered up to the effect that the university is *committed* to expanding their numbers. There has to be that occasional bow to legislative black caucuses…but what does the enrollment manager really do? He or she tries to achieve the best level of SAT scores—a sop to USNews rankings for the university's p. r. department—at the same time that he tries to attract the largest possible number of rich students, people who pay the full tuition and don't draw on any of the scholarship moneys. That's why they include international students in the diversity numbers. Sure, the grad students may come from China and India, but grad students don't pay tuition anyway. Where do the *undergrads* come from? The Middle East oil states? The mansions on vast Latin American plantations?

"It's a business. And everybody contributes, including the federal government. We're talking hundreds of millions of dollars in research support for places like USC and UCLA and half of that or more going to so-called 'indirect costs', so tax dollars underwrite the infrastructure of these businesses."

"But the grants support research," Gwen said, "and much of it deals with human health."

"And who does *that* make rich?" Stein asked. "Ever heard of university-industry partnerships? The industry we're usually talking about is pharmaceutical or military. Ever taken a look at the Department of Defense's budget and the amount that it spends—in universities—for R&D? They're not very interested in human health."

"So your take on all this," Charles said, "is that Professor Appleman was dead wrong, that the university is not a socialist state, but a capitalist state."

"I'd say it was a bulwark of capitalism, a bulwark of the *status quo*, with an occasional crumb thrown at the natives to keep them from growing too restless. The crumbs and scraps quiet the consciences of the faculty, the money reassures the trustees, and the athletics and so-called 'information technology' departments distract the students by keeping them endlessly entertained."

"And the rest is mostly a sham?" Gwen asked.

"Follow the money," Stein said. "See how little of it is going into the classroom. Thirty percent? Maybe thirty-five in a small liberal arts college? You know what the real surprise is…"

"What's that?" Charles asked.

"That they continue to get angry at people like Appleman. You don't blame what's wrong in a *polis* on the village idiot."

44

The Santa Monica Freeway

"I didn't finish college," Charles said. "I took courses through the University of Maryland sites around the world, whenever I could. I'm not saying that Stein or Stern or Appleman is wrong, only that they're worried about a university that I never experienced. For me it was all very practical. GI's wanted an education; they went to simple classrooms in simple buildings; they took courses; they got credits. I'm sure the global programs made some money for the University of Maryland, but they also served a purpose and met a need."

"Right," Gwen responded. "My experience was a little different. I went to a private liberal arts college in Ohio where there were a lot of small classes and a lot of nice new buildings. Basically, we were paying for the size of the school. No matter how many students you have you need a laundry and a registrar, a financial aid director and a math department. The smaller you are the less benefit you get from economies of scale. The good side is that the students feel as if they're getting more personal treatment. Facilities were a big issue also—especially to a group of eighteen year-olds. Stein's right about computer support. My college also bragged about its exercise facilities; in that regard the school *was* a kind of summer camp. I don't think my tuition dollars were going so much to the handholders as they were toward infrastructure and debt service for capital projects. The buzzwords were *high tech* and *high touch*. Any way you slice it though, one thing is pretty clear."

"What's that?" Charles asked.

"The university that Appleman and Stein describe is a world with a lot of money and a lot of anger, anger bordering on rage. At least *they* seem angry."

"They've always said that academic politics is a full-contact sport," Charles said. "Maybe the city is red with *blood* rather than with socialism."

"This one certainly is," Gwen added. "The problem is Denise. I can imagine why somebody might want to hit Appleman with a hammer. Or Stein, for that matter. I can't see why that same person would want to kill *her*, unless, of course, the two cases are unrelated."

"That's going to be the trick," Charles said, "...finding a connection between the two (assuming that there is one). All we've got at this point is a set of similar locations—areas with a potential for violence, each near USC--and bodies found in rest room facilities."

"Right," Gwen said. "I very much doubt that we'll learn that Appleman was an undercover Bureau agent and I can't see how Denise would have angered anyone the way Appleman did."

"I agree," Charles said, "but they're both dead and whoever killed them is still at large, despite the gap in time between the events. I know what I'd like to see…"

"How about the case file on Geoffrey Appleman?" Gwen asked.

"You took the words right out of my mouth," Charles said. "I also know who can get it for us."

They met with Frank at his office at the PAB. Charles introduced Gwen (complete with thick, non-prescription glasses) as "a friend of Denise's from D.C.," noting that they had met at Denise's apartment and that she had volunteered to tag along and help in any way that she could.

"She's great with a computer," Charles said. "She found another case, one from the early two thousands—a professor was killed in the rest room at the iMax theatre in Exposition Park, next to the USC campus. We asked a few questions and we found out that the professor had written a book that made a lot of people angry."

"We've checked Dearing's laptop to see what he might have turned," Frank said, "but he erased the history of the sites he had visited. They've got somebody with more IT skills looking at it now. Tell me about this professor and his book."

"It was a book about universities," Charles responded. "He said that they were spending too much money on support services rather than education…said that this was distorting the universities' budgets and playing hell with their traditional functions. Somebody must have disagreed because they found him beaten to death with a ball peen hammer. The case was never closed, as far as we could determine."

"So you've got a major time lapse between the events but both murders took place in rest rooms, both involved the use of hammers, both had a USC connection and the earlier victim was complaining about the kind of services that Denise's clinic later provided."

"That's right," Charles said, "exactly."

"What was the first victim's name?" Frank asked.

"Geoffrey Appleman," Charles answered. Gwen sat silently with her hands on her knees, the dutiful assistant.

"Sit tight," Frank said. "I'll be back."

He returned ten minutes later, carrying a thick manila folder that was worn and wrinkled.

"Who handled the case?" Charles asked.

"Lou Davis," Frank asked. "Cashed in in early 2010 and moved to Idaho; died a few years later. Natural causes. Cancer, as I remember. Lou wasn't the shiniest bulb in the chandelier but he was very thorough. Plodding sometimes, but tenacious. His close rate was high. Wasn't able to close this one though."

Frank flipped through the documents in the file, pausing to study several of them. "It appears that he did have a prime suspect however."

45

The Police Administration Building

"William Dennison," Frank said. "Close personal associate of the victim's."

"Gay lover?" Charles asked.

"How did you know that?" Frank asked.

"We talked to the chairman of the victim's department at USC--History; he remembered him well...told us that he was gay."

"Interesting wrinkle," Frank said. "What was it to him—a simple rest room or a tea room? Violence against a gay man there wouldn't be surprising...it could all have been sudden and, in effect, random...some kind of misunderstanding...he hits on the wrong guy and pays a heavy price...but maybe the lover was in the area...maybe found him with somebody else...? The only problem is the hammer. And it's a big problem. Speaks to premeditation...loudly and clearly...unless the lover suspected him of something and brought a hammer along just in case."

Frank flipped through more pages. "Dennison was Appleman's research assistant--a graduate student--not a carpenter or plumber. Grad students don't generally carry hammers, at least not in History. More likely to use a field expedient, pick up whatever was handy." He flipped some more. "Alibi was shaky...Dennison claimed to be in his apartment all night. Two people confirmed it, but each differed on the time frame. No positive evidence to link him with the crime. Lou interrogated him;

said in his notes that there were a lot of tears. He believed the guy's story. No real evidence to swing things the other way.

"Rolling Stones movie that night at the iMax. Multiple people testified that they could not imagine that Appleman would have had any interest in seeing it. Lou figured that he was keeping an appointment there, probably hadn't seen the movie at all. That would speak to the premeditation issue and further reinforce Dennison's alibi. No reason to meet with Dennison there unless the two of them actually wanted to see the movie and no reason to want Dennison there if he was meeting with somebody else, especially if it involved something romantic."

"It may not have been romantic," Charles said. "Could have been some other motivation for killing him. Robbery, for example, if it was random. Maybe he resisted and the killer overreacted."

Frank nodded, paused, and read several pages closely. "Multiple affidavits concerning their relationship," he said. "All agreed that everything was copacetic. No rifts between the two…fidelity all around. Appleman was conservative in his attitudes and in his personal behavior. Not a cruiser. Ditto Dennison. They had been together for some time."

Frank paused again and got on his computer, clicked on his browser's icon and searched for Dennison's name. Then he sifted through the hits, stopped, downloaded and printed a single page. "Dennison, William," he said. "Associate professor at the State University of New York in Albany. There since 2005. Over 50 years old now. Check out the picture. He looks sad."

"Same guy?" Charles asked. Gwen leaned forward, studying the blue eyes, with heavy bags and wrinkles, and the neatly-trimmed beard and moustache beneath them. No tattoos or features suggesting a violent personality.

"Lists a USC Ph.D., received a couple years after Appleman's death. Teaches American history," Frank answered.

"He *does* look sad," Gwen said. It was the first time she had broken her silence. "Any information on his height or weight?"

Frank checked Davis' notes in the file folder. "Small…5'6", 130 pounds…at least at the time that Lou questioned him."

"He wouldn't get any taller than that," Charles said. "I talked to that homeless guy at MacArthur Park. He said the guy walking away from the port-o-let was average in height and weight. Didn't say anything about a beard either, though the killer could have shaved."

"Always worth checking," Frank said, "but on the face of it it looks as if Lou's assumptions were right. Let's see what else is here…

"Appleman had a sister. Lou's notes say that she confirmed Dennison's version of things."

"Still around?" Charles asked.

"Let's see…" Frank answered, turning back to his computer. After a set of quick keystrokes he leaned forward to read the screen. "Yes," he said, "here she is—Jane Appleman, Department of Classics, Pomona College."

"I think Denise's friend and I should pay her a visit," Charles said.

"Under what pretense?" Frank asked.

"I don't know just yet, Frank, but don't be concerned; we'll think of something that won't jeopardize your relationship with the LAPD," Charles answered.

Frank was still shaking his head as they left his office.

As they drove east toward the desert the sky darkened into grayish-yellow streaks as the trapped valley air formed a layered fabric of thick smog. Charles could feel the pollution settling against his skin and taste and smell the acrid particles that constituted it. He commented on the fact and Gwen nodded in agreement.

She had called first to insure that Appleman's sister was available to meet with them. When the departmental secretary told her that she was scheduled to hold office hours for most of the afternoon they left promptly, allowing ample time for potential traffic snarls and slowdowns. As the cost of housing drove middle-class Angelenos farther north and east the principal freeways clogged in new and unexpected ways. Appointment times had become little more than optimistic guesstimates.

Pomona College is part of the Claremont schools, an Oxbridge-like alliance of freestanding undergraduate institutions sharing a common graduate school. Pomona is the gem in the consortium and enjoys a deep endowment with a strikingly high endowment dollar-per-student ratio. Everything is on a small scale compared with USC or UCLA but the presence of institutional money is palpable. Charles commented that Geoffrey Appleman would have worried about the manner in which it was being spent.

His sister Jane's department was in Pearsons Hall. When Charles and Gwen arrived she was meeting with a student. The door was cracked but her voice was crisp and clear. It was also deep and carried an aura of authority. Gwen imagined a stiff wool suit with a scarf and antique pin. Her hair would be short and tight against her head. There would be an actual cup and saucer and a favorite pen resting on a desk blotter with a burgundy leather frame.

When the meeting was finished and the student rose and opened the door Gwen was startled by the image before her. Jane Appleman was dressed in a brown granny gown with a carved, ebony necklace. Her shock of straight white hair framed her face and her wrists were covered with copper bracelets, her fingers with large-stoned rings. If the Pomona campus was a functional architectural mix of east coast and west, Jane Appleman was an earth mother with discordant overtones of Wellesley and Bryn Mawr.

Her office was Hollywood-academic, with a butler's tray table, wing chairs, dark-hardwood bookcases and the kinds of silver, crystal, and walnut accessories that are seldom seen in real offices at real colleges.

The dominant color of her books was Oxford blue, with standard editions of Greek and Roman writers on one wall and the works of modern commentators on another. Charles had asked Gwen to lead the questioning and she began by complimenting the professor on the beauty of her office and its appointments. Her response was a formulaic nod and smile and a clip, "How can I be of help to you?"

"We'd like to talk to you about your late brother," Gwen said.

"Geoffrey died years ago," she answered. "Why now? And why you?"

"There's been a recent case with some similarities. The victim was a friend of mine and a relative of Mr. White's. We're making unofficial inquiries; if we learn anything of potential significance we'll share it with the authorities."

Charles wondered why Gwen revealed that, but said nothing.

"That seems rather irregular," Jane Appleman said.

"You can verify that with Lieutenant Frank White of the LAPD; Lieutenant White is also a relative of the victim. Technically he is not the lead detective on the case, because of that relationship, but the LAPD sees the possibilities of a relationship between the recent crime and the murder of your brother as extremely remote. They are concentrating their efforts elsewhere."

"And so you were told to waste your time if you wished."

"Precisely," Gwen said.

"Tell me about the similarities between the two crimes."

"A nurse in her early 30's was found stabbed to death in a public port-o-let in MacArthur Park. She had been working at a USC clinic, a service provider of the sort criticized by your brother in his book *Red City*."

"Geoffrey did not criticize service providers. He criticized the source of their funding."

"I understand," Gwen said. "The two events are very distant in time and both scenes are high crime areas. Hence the remote possibility that they could be related. Still, the death of Mr. White's niece is a tragic event for those who knew and loved her. Hence we are pursuing every possible link."

"I should think there would be an equally violent event if Mr. White locates the individual who killed his niece before the authorities do."

46

Pearsons Hall, Pomona College

"I live near Pasadena," she said. "I am quite familiar with Mr. White's, or should I say, Sergeant Major White's career."

"The details have often been exaggerated," Charles said.

"Or suppressed?" she suggested.

Charles held a Mona Lisa smile as Gwen interposed, "Regarding your question, Professor Appleman…"

"Yes?" she responded.

"You could be of *significant help to us* if you would tell us about your brother."

"What would you like to know?"

"You told Detective Davis that you believed Dr. Dennison had no involvement in your brother's death…"

"Absolutely. Bill loved Geoffrey and the feeling was reciprocated. I haven't spoken with him in awhile, but I know that it took years for him to come to terms with the loss."

"Do you believe that the act was one of random violence?"

"I simply don't know," she answered. "I think it very unlikely that someone would take a hammer with them to the movies and I doubt that anyone seeking anonymous sex would either. At the same time, I am unaware of anyone who would be motivated to murder Geoffrey, particularly in so violent a manner."

"His book angered people."

"In a sense," she answered.

"I beg your pardon," Charles interjected. "We've been told that your brother's book made people *very* angry."

"There was anger, of course," she answered, "but the debate was largely an academic one. Some anger was expressed through overheated rhetoric in reviews and conference presentations, but that was really an example of intellectual posturing rather than something approaching actual physical violence. It was a foregone conclusion that Geoffrey's arguments would not prompt the universities to change their practices in any significant way. Academics build arguments and erect theoretical structures in the hopes that the end result will be a small, incremental gain, not a root-and-branch abandonment of existing practices. Besides, the arguments were largely a stalking horse…"

"For…?" Gwen asked.

"For a defense of the traditional curriculum. The arguments for more traditional structures and infrastructures were a not-very-subtle argument for more traditional values and the curriculum that embodied those values. The new array of support services grows out of the contemporary curriculum and it reinforces its particular directions. It all focuses on the student's self-concept and so-called 'wellness'; it is geared in part to the new student demographics and the degree of preparation which contemporary students bring to their academic work. Put bluntly, the academy has become more democratized. The percentage of students who attend college has risen dramatically, often in inverse proportion to their level of preparation. They require such services for both their academic success and their personal comfort levels. The university requires that they succeed because it is dependent on their tuition. A 1% increase in a university's retention rate translates into millions of dollars in tuition revenue. Universities are businesses. They may sometimes look like Esalen encounter centers, but that's just the flip side of their efforts to influence student persistence and hence protect the bottom line."

"That's very interesting," Gwen said. "Your brother was much more of a traditionalist, even as a gay man."

"*Indeed.* Geoffrey was a Straussian. Weren't you aware of that?"

"I'm not sure what that means," Charles said.

"Leo Strauss?" Gwen asked.

"Yes, of course. In some ways the father of the neocons, though I doubt that Strauss would have thought of himself in that specific way. He sought to bring about a rebirth of classical political philosophy, absent the scholastic hermeneutic."

"At the University of Chicago," Gwen said, letting the prior statement pass.

"Yes, of course, for the majority of his career at least. Geoffrey studied with him."

"But your brother was a historian," Charles said, "not a political philosopher."

"Yes, but they mixed and matched a lot there," she answered.

"What you're saying," Gwen added, "is that this would all be part of a complex debate of which the average person would have little awareness."

"Of course. The people who operate support services would not have been troubled, so long as the individuals to whom they reported were unmoved, and they would be unmoved because they would never have taken note of it. There was a dust-up for about two or three days in the USC student press—probably instigated by one of Geoffrey's colleagues—and then the matter was quickly forgotten."

"Could such a colleague have been willing to continue the fight in a different forum?" Charles asked.

"Yes, of course," she responded, "but in a scholarly journal--certainly not in a public rest room. Besides, the movie that evening concerned some rock band or other. It would be bad enough to risk being seen at a popular film; this would be beyond the beyond."

"So what would they actually have fought over?" Gwen asked.

"Heidegger and Nietzsche, of course. Strauss had his own strong views, but with the rise of postmodernism the two of them were in the ascendant while Strauss's star was on the wane. This was all ultimately about *relativism* and *tentativeness* within the modern university."

"Whoever killed your brother…" Charles said.

"Yes…?" she interjected.

"…seems to have been *very certain* about what he was trying to accomplish."

"Yes, indeed," she said. "That's why I doubt very much that the person was an academic. And certainly not a postmodern multicultural relativist."

"So what does that leave us with?" Charles asked.

"Not very much, I'm afraid," she answered.

47

Pearsons Hall, Pomona College

As they walked back to the car Gwen said, "I think that was helpful."
"How so?" Charles asked.

"If she's correct, that eliminates several categories of possible suspects."

"Yes, but it doesn't offer us any alternative."

"I'm not so sure," Gwen said. "It suggests that Geoffrey Appleman was killed for a completely different reason."

"As yet unknown…"

"Right," she said. "As yet."

The next morning Gwen called the Director from her hotel in Pasadena. She asked him if there were any new developments with the terrorist cell that Denise had helped the Bureau track.

"None," he responded. "I'll let you know immediately if Elizabeth develops anything new and relevant."

She told him about her meeting Charles; the Director seemed aware of some of the facts, including the details of Charles's background. "Be careful," he said. "He's highly skilled, of course, but the political fallout from a collaboration with a private citizen could be extremely negative."

"I understand, sir," she said. "Right now he's very controlled and very focused."

"The advice stands, Gwen."

"Understood." She then briefed him in detail on the Appleman case.

"I'll see what we have here. You've run the normal files, of course."

"Yes, sir. I was hoping for something additional."

"A miracle?"

"I don't expect miracles, sir."

"Sometimes we need them," he answered. "This seems like a long shot, particularly with the time lapse between the events. I'd be more hopeful if the community were smaller and the chances of random violence were more remote. A hammer is one of the most common household tools. Sooner or later one of them has to turn up at a crime scene. If the events were closer in time a *pattern* might be established. I suspect that a garden-variety search engine would turn up a succession of violent crimes involving hammers...in nearly all cities and states."

"It would, sir; I've checked already."

"The case is more interesting in what it doesn't say than in what it does. The similarities are there but so are the dissimilarities. The two victims are both USC employees (putatively, at least, in Denise's case); both are killed in comparable locations; both events involve hammers, etc. etc. But consider the differences—youth/age, black/white, female/male, straight/gay...these are diametric opposites. The professor could have been considered wealthier and a better target for street crime, but neither case appears to involve robbery. There's no evidence to suggest that Denise ever knew Appleman. She was in grammar school in Detroit when he died. We'll check, but most black school kids in Detroit don't spend much time—if any--in California and most college professors don't spend much time—if any--in Detroit."

"We're missing something," Gwen said, "but I'm still encouraged by the fact that we're able to eliminate some possibilities and extend the search in other directions."

"I suppose so," the Director responded. "In the meantime I'll check everything available at this end and let you know if we turn anything, anything at all."

"Thank you, sir," she said.

She clicked off and called Frank's office. It took a few minutes to locate him, but when the desk sergeant did, Frank took the call. "I'm sorry to bother you, Lieutenant," she said, "but I had a couple of questions about the Appleman case."

"Just a second," he said, rearranging the paperwork on the top of his desk. "OK, I've got the file. Shoot."

"Did Detective Davis check Appleman's email files?"

"I think I saw a note to that effect. Let me check again…yes, most of them had been trashed, so he had to go through the university server. Nothing of any great moment. All pretty routine; nothing that could be considered suspicious. As I told you, Lou could be a plodder but he didn't usually overlook things. He was a green-eyeshade type; he could chain himself to a desk and root around in piles of documents for days."

"How about telephone records?"

"Just a sec…again, nothing momentous. And Appleman didn't have a cell phone. Too early for that. Lou checked out his home. The guy lived almost like a monk. No cable television. A very basic sound system. 'Very old school' Lou says in his notes. Conservative—classical music, classic books. Old family furniture. No obvious indulgences except for some expensive wines. The guy was a relic, maybe even a fossil."

"That squares exactly with the kinds of things his sister told us. Did Charles brief you on our meeting with her?"

"Yes, he did. He didn't say much."

"There's not much to say, except for the fact that she doubted very much that any of the likely readers of his book would have reacted to what he said there with physical violence."

"Right," Frank said. "Anyway, there's nothing in the file that offers any hints of a *personal life*—other than his relationship with Dennison, of course. He didn't go out of his way to hide that relationship and according to Lou there really wasn't anything else *to* hide. This guy read books, wrote books, taught about books, sipped sherry and slept with his socks on. His travel was confined to scholarly meetings. His VISA card summarized his purchases at the end of the year. He'd occasionally buy some food from gourmet grocery stores, but he spent next to nothing on clothes. He drove a 10 year-old car that offered cheap, reliable transportation and little else. His only major expense was books and journal subscriptions. Sorry. I wish there was more…"

"I understand, Lieutenant. Thanks very much," Gwen said. She asked Frank for Appleman's and Dennison's addresses at the time of their deaths, jotted them down, thanked him again, clicked off her cell phone and walked over to the window. She stared at the yellowish glare and the haze clinging to the tops of the fan palms across the San Gabriel Valley, finished the bottle of juice sitting on the edge of the desk, and called the valet parkers to bring her car around.

48

The Langham Huntington, Pasadena

She didn't have to drive far; Appleman's former home was four minutes from her hotel. As she turned onto Lake from Oak Knoll Circle and looked at the peaks and slopes of the San Gabriels in the distance she thought about the fact that there are really six or seven Pasadenas—the pricey sections along Orange Grove, above the Rose Bowl, along the arroyo, and in enclaves like Chapman Woods; the cheap, gang-ridden and dodgy sections above the freeway, the Millennial commercial sections between Old Town and Caltech, the astronomically-pricey sections that abut San Marino, the raw commercial sections along Colorado east of Lake and along Raymond and Fair Oaks between Old Town and South Pas, and the neighborhoods of small craftsman properties between California Boulevard and San Marino on the west.

The public schools are best avoided, so those who can do so (like Gwen Harrison's parents), gravitate toward South Pas, Arcadia or—if their pockets are deep enough—San Marino. Gwen had attended high school in Arcadia. She knew the area well and realized—as she drove toward Geoffrey Appleman's neighborhood—that it was, for him, the perfect compromise.

Just beneath the Lake Street coffee bars, shops, and independent commercial mainstays such as *Pie 'N Burger*, and just above the megamansions of Arden Road and Oak Knoll sits a tiny neighborhood of quaint and attractive cottages. 'English' is not an inappropriate description, though some of the houses are Spanish revival in their essential elements. The English tone is achieved by manicured gardens and unique architectural detail. Appleman's house, for example, featured a roof in which the light green shingles were wrapped around what would normally be guttering and fascia, the result being a fairy-tale effect that suggested a remote village in Dorset or the Cotswolds rather than an island of calm two blocks from service stations, an automobile upholsterer and a mixed complex of shops and discount emporia.

A little over a block to the south was the putatively Colorado mansion used for exterior shots on *Dynasty* and across Lake, on the east side, was a well-preserved apartment complex in which William Dennison had once resided. Appleman had probably helped out with the rent; even then it would have been steeper than a graduate student could afford. The neighborhood would have appealed to Appleman's conservative impulses, met his practical needs, offered him easy access to the freeway as well as to his lover, and—in those days—been (barely) affordable for a senior academic.

Pasadena and its neighbor, San Marino, are notoriously traditional, the seats of old, Protestant money and strong, Midwestern values. Many of the restaurants and stores of Lake Street on the north, Huntington Drive on the south, and Mission and Fair Oaks to the east in South Pas date from the middle of the last century or earlier and offer the sense that one is living in a small town, a town in which the people take walks in the evening, greet their neighbors by name, and patronize established, once-upon-a-time commercial entities. There is a still-functioning soda fountain and the heavily-decorated, faded-glory, recently-shuttered *Rialto* theatre featured in *The Player* on Fair Oaks and in Appleman's time a fully-functioning tearoom in *Bullock's* on Lake, where ladies and gentlemen could pause for a civilized lunch or tea in the course of their day of shopping.

This was the tiny piece of southern California originally sought by wealthy Midwesterners who wanted to feel at home in California but enjoy much better weather than that afforded by Chicago or Cincinnati. Appleman's own home there squared with everything said of him by his sister. It was staid, traditional, and charming, a lovely image from the past. You could look at it and almost hear a warm soprano voice singing of bluebirds over Dover or nightingales singing in Berkeley Square and while it was a five minute walk from every place that he might need to go, it was worlds away, or at least fourteen miles away, from the place where—late one night--he had been beaten to death with a hammer by an as yet unidentified assailant.

Gwen sat in her car, facing north on the east side of Lake, her eyes shifting from Dennison's tidy, attractive apartment to the soft roof line and bright red rose arbor of Appleman's cottage and wondered why he would ever leave it for a dark and lonely rest room in Exposition Park.

The southbound traffic on Lake was heavy. A Lexus crossed her line of vision, then a Mercedes, a BMW, and a second Lexus. No Ferraris in Pasadena. As Gwen continued to watch, a woman walked out from behind Appleman's house. She was wearing gardening gloves and carrying what appeared to be a pruning tool. Gwen got out of her car, crossed the street, and approached her. She badged her quickly, identified herself as a law enforcement official, and asked if she would answer a question or two.

"Certainly," the woman said. "I'm happy to be of help. I'm Claire Simpson."

"Gwen Harrison," Gwen responded. "Your home is very lovely."

"Thank you," the woman answered. "We consider it very special. The flowers take a lot of my time but I believe they're worth it. They're one of the reasons why we purchased it. Bougainvillea are very common here, but somehow I prefer the roses. There are yellow roses in the backyard, if you'd care to see them."

"I'd love to," Gwen said, following her along the driveway.

"Would you like something to drink? I have fresh-squeezed juice."

"That would be very nice," Gwen said.

"It will only take a second; please sit down."

"There was a tented patio behind the house with a table and two cushioned chairs. Mrs. Simpson returned in less than five minutes, carrying a small tray with two glasses and a pitcher of orange juice. There were two ice cubes in each glass. "I don't like to water down the juice," she said, "but I just squeezed the juice and it's only been in the refrigerator for a few minutes." Gwen saw the orange tree in the southwestern corner of the backyard. There was an avocado tree to the northwest.

"This is lovely," Gwen said, as she tasted the juice. Mrs. Simpson nodded appreciatively. "I'd like to ask you a question or two about one of the previous owners, Professor Appleman."

"Certainly. Is the case being reopened?"

"Not yet. I'm just making some general enquiries at this stage."

"I'll try to help in any way that I can."

"Thanks, I appreciate that. You bought the property directly from him…there were no intermediate owners?"

"Actually we bought it from his estate. We've had it ever since. We'll never sell it; it's too special."

"Was it his sister who handled the sale?"

"Actually, his attorney. We met the sister at the closing. She was very nice. She was the principal heir, but the attorney had secured the realtor and responded to our questions after the inspections. He handled all the details and when the funds were disbursed she received a check."

"Do you happen to have the settlement statement?"

"It's in our safe deposit box. I can tell you the long and the short of it. His sister received the bulk of the money; the two real estate agents involved received their commissions and some funds were escrowed for various purposes. There was really nothing else in Professor Appleman's estate. We bought all of the furnishings with the house and gave his books to his sister. We couldn't see selling them to a secondhand bookseller when she and the attorney had been so amicable about everything else. He had an insurance policy as part of his university compensation. The attorney said that it had covered his funeral expenses. His only actual property, according to the attorney, was the house. It was a very unique case. The attorney said he'd never seen anyone with so organized a life. I'm sure there was also a bank account and checking account, probably enough to cover the attorney's executor fees. Either that or he was the beneficiary of the policy and recovered his fees that way. We didn't inquire, of course. Can I refill your glass?"

"Yes, thanks," Gwen said. "Was there any mention of a man named William Dennison?"

"The professor's *friend*."

"Yes."

"He came by and introduced himself. The professor had been gone for about three months and we had just moved into the house. Mr. Dennison lived in the apartment building across the street there. He was very distraught. I felt sorry for him. I recognized him, because the professor had had a picture of him in his library…it was one of the original bedrooms, converted for that purpose. It was a very old-fashioned picture. Black and white, with lovely lighting. Mr. Dennison looked European, like a man one might meet on a vacation in the Mediterranean. He had a white, silk shirt. It was open at the collar. He was photographed in profile. Very romantic. His sister had explained it to us and as soon as we took possession we asked her to return it to Mr. Dennison. Probably wouldn't happen now…"

"What do you mean?" Gwen asked.

"The stagers," Mrs. Simpson responded. "They advise you to remove all personal items from your house when you put it on the market."

"Oh yes," Gwen said.

"Nothing was removed when this house was put up for sale. It very much reflected the life of its owner, but then he had exquisite taste. It was almost like a small museum. That's why we purchased the furniture. Would you care to see it?"

"Yes, I would; thanks very much," Gwen said. "This is very kind of you."

"We're proud of it," Mrs. Simpson said. "You can bring your glass with you if you'd like."

"We kept our own bedroom set, of course," Mrs. Simpson said. "The professor had a lovely bed, but it wouldn't accommodate the kind of mattress we prefer. We gave it to his sister. It was antique Italian, with a lot of carving. The worm holes were authentic. It looked like something from a Tuscan villa. It may have been from one, actually."

The library adjoined the living room and dining area. It contained a long table with carved figures in the support pieces. "This is Italian also," Mrs. Simpson said. "An appraiser told us that it was probably sixteenth or early seventeenth century. Quite valuable as well as functional. The living room and dining room pieces appear to be matched with those in the library, but they're really not. They're English. Jacobean actually. They're a bit heavy for the size of the room, but they're really museum quality."

"Beautiful carpet," Gwen said.

"Yes, it's Persian, of course. Probably fifty or seventy-five years old when the professor acquired it. He was able to purchase it before the Ayatollah restricted imports of the better pieces to America. We don't use the crystal decanters there on the side table. My husband's afraid that the lead will somehow leach into the scotch or sherry and poison him. They're very decorative, however. They're not antiques, of course. That's off-the-shelf Edinburgh Crystal."

"Still very lovely," Gwen said. "Tell me about the iron pieces on the bookshelf."

"Those are English, eighteenth-century. Probably early eighteenth-century. They're actually rush light holders. They're there instead of candelabras. Candles for the poor, in a sense. Pieces of rush would be dipped in animal fat, clamped into the holder, and then lit. A poor substitute for candles because of all the soot, but better than sitting in the dark. For us they're conversation pieces more than anything else, though there is a certain amount of beauty in their functionality."

Between the bookshelves was a surrealist pencil drawing of Don Quixote tilting at an abstract windmill. Gwen couldn't approach it because it was high on the wall and recessed between the shelving. "Is that a Dali?" she asked.

"Yes, my husband's favorite. That's ours, not the professor's. We probably couldn't afford it these days. We purchased it many years ago and it comes with us wherever we move. I think that's a good place for it. Somehow it works with the old furniture."

"Old subject," Gwen said.

"Yes, it is," Mrs. Simpson said. "Can I be of any further help? I'd like to get back to the roses before the midday sun."

"I very much appreciate your help," Gwen said. "Just one more question; do you happen to remember the professor's attorney's name?"

"Of course. He's very well-known. His name is Donald Fell."

49

South Lake Street, Pasadena

M rs. Simpson checked the local yellow pages and wrote down the attorney's address and phone number on a yellow post-it note. "Here he is," she said, handing the note to Gwen.

Gwen thanked her again, returned to her car, and phoned the attorney's office. Once past the receptionist Gwen spoke with the attorney's assistant—Dorothy Caldwell--who asked a series of questions.

"Could you tell me the purpose of the meeting?"

"Yes, of course," Gwen answered. "I would like to speak with Mr. Fell concerning one of his late clients. The client was murdered; Mr. Fell handled his estate. There is a possibility that the investigation will be reopened."

"Are you an officer with the LAPD?" the assistant asked.

"I'm a federal agent, Ms. Caldwell, but I'm cooperating with local officials," Gwen said.

"Donald is in court now, but I expect him to return at 10:45. Could you come at 11:00? You may have to wait a few minutes if he's running late."

"That would be fine, Ms. Caldwell. I appreciate your help."

"Of course. We'll see you then. You have the address…"

"Yes, I do," Gwen said, and clicked off. Interesting, she thought. All the signals pointed to a one-man office with both a receptionist and private assistant. Perry and Della, together again.

With 40 minutes to kill Gwen walked up to California Boulevard, bought a coffee at *Peet's* and sat in the window, absorbing the warmth of the morning sun. It was too early to call the Director for a simple check-in, so she called Charles. His cell phone rolled over and she left a brief message, telling him that the owner of Professor Appleman's house had discussed his personality and behavior—to the extent that she could—and confirmed Gwen's previous impressions. Gwen also told him that she was going to meet with the attorney who had handled the professor's estate.

She put her cell phone down on the table next to her cup and waited for it to ring, but it didn't. When she finished her coffee she bought a bottle of water and returned to her car. She drove up to California, turned left and headed west.

Donald Fell's office was in a classic craftsman on Marengo, just east of the Parkway. As a private home it would sell in the low seven figures. The complete architectural deal: a low-slung roof, wide eaves with exposed roof rafters, a large porch with square columns, wide brackets at the roof cornices, and a prominent chimney of heavy, raw stone. The interior would include dark wood paneling with matching furniture, built-ins, and stained glass. The porch contained an actual shingle that read **Donald Fell, Attorney-at-Law**. From the size of the parking area behind the building it appeared that Fell had purchased the property behind him, torn it down, and created convenient parking space for his clients. From the street Gwen could see a dark wooden fence, draped in bright red bougainvillea.

She rang the bell, identified herself, and listened for the buzz of the electric lock. Entering the reception area she was greeted by a woman whose desk plate read *Ellen Ross*. Gwen introduced herself and told the receptionist that she had an 11:00 appointment with Mr. Fell. "I'm a few minutes early," she said.

"Dorothy is expecting you," she said, extending her hand to the right. "Go right in."

The former living room was now a large office with a fireplace, leather furniture and walnut paneling. The tile work around the fireplace was original, as was the carved mantle. The room was dominated by prairie-style vertical lines, with Frank Lloyd Wright-inspired lamps and rugs with matching geometricals. Dorothy Caldwell was seated on a corner couch. The pocket door to what was probably once the dining room and was probably now her own office was open. There was a china coffee cup and saucer on the table in front of her. She rose, introduced herself, and asked to see Gwen's credentials. Gwen showed her her Bureau badge and Fell's assistant asked if she'd like some coffee or tea. There was no change in her expression from the initial greeting to her looking at the badge to her asking if she'd like something to drink. Gwen thanked her. She left and returned with a matching cup and saucer. Wisps of steam floated off the top; the coffee inside smelled fresh.

"Donald called a few minutes ago. He should be here in a few minutes. If you could tell me the name of the client in question I'll get the file and save us some time."

Us. It *did* seem like a Perry/Della relationship.

"Geoffrey Appleman," Gwen said.

"Yes, I thought it might be him," she said. "I'll just be a moment."

She returned in less than a minute. "Very sad case," she said. "Such a nice man and such a violent death."

"Then you knew him," Gwen said.

"Not well. I met him on a few occasions when he came by the office and I did some of the estate work."

"His death must have been a shock."

"A terrible shock, particularly the violent circumstances. There was a great deal of publicity at the time and then it all seemed to evaporate. No evidence beyond the murder weapon. No real leads. Unlikely that it was simple street crime . . . people in that part of the city carry guns and knives, but who carries a hammer with them and who goes to a movie theatre in search of a victim? It also seemed quite clear at the time that the motive could not have been theft, since Professor Appleman had an expensive watch and a wallet full of cash. If, on the other hand, it was an act of passion, why the premeditation with the hammer? And why in such a public place? The press suspected revenge, but revenge for what? Not for his book, though that had been the subject of some initial speculation. It had appeared a full two years earlier and any notoriety it had attracted had long since run its course. Very odd…and very sad. Oh, here's Donald…"

She must have seen him on the porch, because the office was virtually soundproof and Gwen could not hear the outside door open or close. A few seconds later the main door to the office opened and Donald Fell entered. His presence was imposing, but without the pretense that might have accompanied it. Tall and well-groomed, he was wearing at least five thousand dollars worth of clothing, not counting jewelry and accessories. The plaid, soft wool suit, tailored Jermyn Street tattersall shirt, and soft red tie gave off a Buckingham Palace vibe that was completed by the brown Church wingtips.

"Special Agent Harrison…Don Fell," he said. Either the assistant or the receptionist had made a cell phone call and given him a headsup.

"How do you do," Gwen responded.

"I hope I haven't kept you waiting," he said, as he slipped off his suit jacket and hung it neatly on a hanger and hardwood hall tree. There were no red suspenders; he didn't indulge in that sort of affectation. "I had to file some papers and talk to some bailiffs and judges. I trust that Dorothy's been looking after you."

"Yes, she's been very helpful," Gwen said.

"The Appleman case," Dorothy Caldwell said. "It may be reopened."

"That would be nice," Fell said. "It's appalling that a person such as Geoffrey could be killed in so violent a fashion and the murderer escape untouched. It's a famous town for violent murder cases, but every now and then we close one. I'm sure you already know that, Ms. Harrison. How can I be of help?"

"There's one thing you could tell me," Gwen said. "I hope you won't be offended…your reputation is as a courtroom attorney…and it's a prodigious reputation…"

"Thanks," he said. "You're wondering what in the world I was doing taking on estate work."

"Yes," she answered.

"Good question; simple answer. Geoffrey was a personal friend. I did all sorts of things for him. I think I may have even notarized the sale agreement on an old car of his. We met many years ago at a function at the Huntington."

"The hotel?" Gwen asked.

"There too from time to time, but the first meeting was at the Huntington Library. I've represented them from time to time and Geoffrey had been a Fellow there. They'd trot him out from time to time to talk to trustees or donors. We met at a dinner. We were seated at the same table; I introduced myself and Geoffrey told me an interesting story about my name. Here…let me show you this…"

He gestured to Gwen to follow him to a corner table. There was a thin booklet inside a glass case on the top of it. "It's bolted and wired for security purposes…it's very valuable," he said. "This is the third page. The Huntington had a second copy and they've loaned it to me. The eighth line is the one that Geoffrey called to my attention:

And here the fell Attorney prowls for Prey;

It's a poem by Dr. Johnson, imitating a classic Latin poem about the evils of ancient Rome. He's updated it and is criticizing contemporary London. One of the greatest of horrors there—as Geoffrey noted—was the prevalence of lawyers." He laughed politely and turned the table slightly so that Gwen could read the text more easily.

"*Fell* would refer to a pelt or hide," Gwen said. "The meaning would be something like the *savage attorney*."

"Precisely," Fell said. "Very good."

"Doesn't Hannibal Lecter use the name *Dr. Fell* when he's escaped from America and is hiding in Florence?" Gwen asked.

"He does indeed," Fell said. "A++. Geoffrey was teasing me about my courtroom reputation. I told him it was quite deserved and we struck up an immediate friendship. Actually, my people came from eastern Europe. The family name started out with F-e-l and then ended in a long succession of unpronounceable consonants. The officials at Ellis Island urged them to shorten it and add an extra *l.* It's been that way ever since."

"How long were you friends?" Gwen asked.

"From the late 80's," he answered. "We'd have dinner every month or so. Usually at the Jonathan Club or some other conservative venue I knew he'd enjoy."

"I've heard nice things said about Professor Appleman," Gwen said, leading him.

"Yes. He had a great deal of personal warmth combined with a wry sense of humor. He had excellent taste—in books, in food, wine…and in people, I think. Present company probably excepted. He was a very old-fashioned man. He liked to dress for dinner, for example. He wasn't fussy, however, and there wasn't an arrogant bone in his body. He was what the academics would probably call *civilized.* That's what makes his death so incomprehensible.

"He and his friend William were very close. The relationship was academic as well as romantic. As *you* probably know, the Greeks considered male/youth relationships to be part of an idealized system of education that also entailed mentorship. I'm sure Geoffrey saw it that way, though we never discussed it directly. That's simply the kind of person he was."

"So you agree that it would have been highly unlikely that his murder could have been the result of some sexual misunderstanding."

"Absolutely. One can imagine a gay basher brutalizing a gay man, but Geoffrey was very conservative in his behavior and demeanor. He would neither have attracted nor encouraged any advances that could have been misunderstood. At the same time, if the assailant had actually been seeking anonymous sex, why would he have been carrying a hammer? I've always believed that that explanation was a non-starter. And it certainly wasn't about theft. Geoffrey had an antique Rolex that was untouched, along with a considerable sum of cash. He always had money with him because he didn't like credit cards.

"Some thought at the time that his book *Red City* might have prompted someone to kill him, but his book criticized the university's provision of services that are better done by local government or the private sector. There was no animus directed at the services or service providers *per se*. All thinking people realized that and the sorts of people who might have taken umbrage were not likely to be among those who would bludgeon a person to death with a hammer. They would have filed grievances and tried to force him to take sensitivity training or some such thing."

Dorothy Caldwell was smiling politely as Fell reinforced her reading of the situation. "So what does that leave us?" Gwen asked, first looking at her and then at him.

"I wish I knew," Fell responded. "I've spent over thirty years working in the criminal justice system. I've seen a great many disturbed people and I've been exposed to grisly forms of violence, but this makes no sense. It's like the recent case in MacArthur Park…"

50

South Marengo Avenue, Pasadena

"The nurse…" Gwen said.

"Yes. Another USC employee killed in a public, nearby location for no apparent reason. Who would want to kill a nurse? And why there? And why so late at night?"

Fell's assistant scooted forward in her seat and spoke. "Nurses know things—the results of AIDS and STD tests, for example, but even if she knew something that the murderer wanted to be kept secret, the HIPAA regulations should have afforded him sufficient protection. Besides, killing the messenger or health professional would not remove the files or lab records anyway. Perhaps there's something the LAPD or the press are withholding, but on its face it makes no sense."

Fell nodded in agreement and looked back at Gwen.

"Unless there was a personal relationship between the victim and the murderer," Gwen said, "something unrelated to the fact that she was a nurse or that she worked for USC."

"Always possible," Fell said. "If Geoffrey was still alive he'd probably be criticizing the fact that the University was providing the sorts of services offered by the clinic where the nurse worked, but he's long gone and any possible relationship between the two events is remote in the extreme. The issue is still there, but it never got much traction when Geoffrey raised it and it's as old as last year's ice water now. Besides, the assumed motives of the murderers would be in conflict. People thought

Geoffrey might have been killed for saying what he did. In this case, however, a *provider* of service has been killed rather than a *critic* of such a service. When you really think about it, the connections are almost completely circumstantial. Two USC employees are killed near campus, which is to say, near downtown. That doesn't narrow things very much. How many employees are there at USC—twenty thousand? Twenty five? How big is the area we're talking about—five square miles? Ten? And how much of that area is safe at night? Any of it?"

"And she was stabbed," Dorothy added, "not bludgeoned to death."

"Apparently the port-o-let where the body was found was nailed shut," Fell said.

Gwen held her expression. That information had not been released by the LAPD. Fell had his own sources. Someone angling for a kickback fee if and when Fell was retained by a suspect?

"But," he added, "as Dorothy said, the victim was actually *killed* by an edged weapon of some sort, so that parallel breaks down. Nevertheless, it's a very interesting detail. This is not some serial killer who only uses hammers and only surfaces every decade or two; that's clear, but either he *had* a hammer and nails with him or he found some nails there and used a rock or something to drive them in. If he had a knife and was prepared to use it, why would he bring a hammer too? Is he a psychopathic carpenter who works at night? That doesn't seem terribly plausible. What do *you* think, Agent Harrison? You're the pro here."

"I don't really know," Gwen answered. "I think you're posing all the right questions, though. I suppose it's a possibility that the person who killed her wanted to make certain that she died before she had a chance to get help. He might not have been clear on whether or not he had hit a vital organ, but he knew that she was bleeding and that if she was unable to extricate herself from the port-o-let she would eventually bleed out."

"That certainly makes sense," Dorothy said.

"An over-the-top killer," Fell said. "I gather that there were multiple stab wounds as well as some slashes…"

That information hadn't been released by the LAPD either.

"She was probably dead long before he finished driving in the first nail," Fell said. "This person wanted to *make sure*. If that's the case, there would be at least a circumstantial connection between the nurse's death and Geoffrey's. A single blow to the temple would have killed him, but the murderer struck him until his face was unrecognizable. Normally one would associate that kind of behavior with rage. Maybe this person… or these people…are into overkill. Maybe they don't know what death looks like when it occurs…or maybe they lack faith in their own ability to inflict it and reassure themselves by going too far. We *can* say that the methods were certainly unprofessional…"

"And ugly," Gwen said.

"Very ugly," Dorothy added.

"And almost surely premeditated," Gwen said.

"Yes, I agree," Fell said. "I was too flip with my comment about the homicidal carpenter. Geoffrey's killer left the weapon behind him, so it is far more likely that he brought the hammer with him to serve a specific purpose than that he carried it routinely. If he *was* dressed like a carpenter or wearing a tool belt of some sort that would certainly attract unwanted attention and immediately identify him as a potential suspect once the hammer was found. They didn't have the surveillance systems then that they do now, or at least not so many of them, but still…it would not have been to his advantage to so identify himself. Better to wear a sport jacket or something more upscale to divert attention from any possible connection between himself and a blue-collar weapon."

"I agree," Gwen said, even as she wondered why Denise's killer would have worn workman's overalls. They could be used to block blood spray and hide things, but, as Charles learned, they were the one salient thing that stuck in the memory of the homeless man in the park who had observed him.

"A carpenter usually wears a nail apron," Gwen continued, "sometimes with a metal hook on the side for a hammer. That would be a very odd thing to see at an iMax theatre. I could imagine a person dressing up like an electrician, with a belt containing all manner of things—screwdrivers, a hammer, a roll of tape, etcetera—things that could be used as weapons. An electrician can turn up at any time in any place, responding, presumably, to some outage or emergency. That could be a useful disguise, particularly for a white-collar killer, but then he would probably want to discard all of the equipment before leaving the crime scene. The equipment could divert attention from his facial features and people might see the *role* rather than the *man*, but Professor Appleman's killer only left the hammer behind."

"Right," Fell said. "Well…this has been very interesting—and I mean that--but I'm not sure we've helped you very much, Agent Harrison. What else can we tell you?"

"I'm certain you've thought of this again and again, but was there anything in Professor Appleman's estate that could provide us any help at all?"

"It was the very model of simplicity," Fell said. "Virtually all of Geoffrey's money was in his house and its furnishings. He was an interesting man. In some ways, he was not interested in material things at all. In other ways he was obsessed with them. His obsessions however, were very selective. He had a few clothes, all of high quality, but he was no clothes horse. He drove cars until they died and survived two or three temporary resuscitations. At the same time he thought nothing of spending $300 on a bottle of wine or $35,000 on a piece of antique furniture.

"At the end there was nothing really left except for the house and furniture. The food and wine had largely been consumed. He had a checking account which he drained every month and then replenished and a small savings account, which he appears to have used primarily for the emergency needs of Mr. Dennison. There were his books, of course, but they eventually went to his sister. I suspect he had given many to Dennison while he was still alive.

"He was very conservative, but comfortable in his dependency on his university for health care, long-term disability insurance, and his pension. He didn't put money away; he simply invested it—as available—in a few beautiful things."

"Did you prepare his will?" Gwen asked.

"No, he had a simple, generic will drawn up decades before. The blue backing paper had nearly faded to whitish yellow when we dug it out of his file cabinet. We have the estate papers here in our files if you'd like to see them. I think there may have been a thousand dollars or so in his checking account and perhaps fifteen or twenty thousand in his savings, nothing much beyond that. The house was worth about five hundred thousand at the time of his death and the furnishings probably two hundred and fifty. The money in his retirement account was substantial for an academic, probably around eight or nine hundred thousand; the sister was his beneficiary."

"So she profited considerably."

"Yes. Certainly by normal standards, but she was already quite comfortable. Her husband is very successful, a patent attorney I think. She teaches at one of the Claremont colleges, but she and her husband have a home near mine, by Lacy Park. On St. Albans, actually."

"In San Marino," Gwen said.

"Yes," Fell answered.

"That's the street with the huge evergreens that are lit at Christmas time."

"Exactly," he said, "so you know the area."

"We lived in Arcadia when I was in high school. Those homes are now worth millions."

"Oh yes. The inheritance from Geoffrey would have been very nice for her, but little more than a year or two's salary for her husband."

"She uses her own name rather than her husband's," Gwen said.

"Yes. They weren't married until she was already established as an

academic and had published under her maiden name. She just kept it…
saw it as part of her academic identity, I suppose."

"Well," Gwen said, "you've certainly been helpful and generous with
your time. I must be going. Thanks very much to both of you."

"You're very kind," Fell said. "I doubt that we've done all that much,
but if I can be of any additional help, feel free to call. I mean that. If I
can be of *any* help at all."

As soon as she got to her rental car Gwen removed her cell phone from
her purse. She wanted to call Charles, brief him on what she had learned
and see if he had turned anything. She removed the phone from its slip
case and saw the *1 missed call* notation on the screen. She accessed her
voice mail. The call was from the Director.

"I haven't been able to reach you," he said. "There's been an explosion
at the Clinic. Check on it at once and report back to me."

The message ended with the robotic voice-mail announcement of
the day and time at which the message had been received. The Director
had called seven minutes prior to her checking for missed calls. She
dropped the phone in her open purse and drove directly to the parkway,
speeding toward the Pasadena freeway.

51

The Pasadena Freeway at Orange Grove

Gwen had moved Charles's cell phone number to the top of her speed dial list. She hit the number 1 and then the call button but his phone continued to roll over to the leave-a-message prompt. She put her cell beside her purse on the passenger seat and merged into the left lane of the southbound traffic. Eight minutes later in Highland Park the freeway was crowded and as she approached Chavez Ravine it slowed to a crawl. The downtown exits were nearly impossible. By the time she got to MacArthur Park the traffic had come to a virtual halt. It took her an hour on the freeway and forty minutes on Wilshire to make the usual twenty-five minute drive. The boulevard was covered with uniformed officers; they allowed traffic to inch through the corridor but the first turn they permitted was at Catalina. She parked in the first available space on the north side of Wilshire and ran back toward the Clinic.

Police tape was stretched across the sidewalk a block from the building. She badged the uniforms holding back the crowd and hurried to the site. Or more precisely--what was left of it. The southern wall of the building was gone and the roof had shattered and collapsed. The windows were all blown and the damage to adjoining buildings and cars was enormous. It looked as if a directional bomb had been detonated, since the east and west ends of the structure were marginally intact. Bodies and body parts were covered by tarps and towels, the latter sodden with water as the firefighters directed their hoses at piles of debris that continued to smolder. In some cases she could see the edges of the blackened bodies amid the rubble. As she got closer two uniformed officers approached her with outstretched palms. She badged them and asked to talk to the officer in charge.

"That would be Captain Loram. He's the one standing next to the black-and-white blocking the parking area." As she approached him she saw Lieutenant White standing nearby and approached him instead. He was clearly surprised to see her.

"Gwen," he said, "how did you get past the barriers?"

"I talked my way through based on my relationship with you and your uncle," she said.

He looked at her skeptically but didn't question her further. "It's devastating," he said. "Charles should be OK, but he was unconscious when they took him out."

"I didn't know he was here," she said. "I've been trying to phone him."

"He was outside, on the other side of the building. He was hit by debris and thrown about fifteen yards. A lot of blood and surface wounds, but the vital organs appear to be intact. He almost surely has multiple broken ribs. Possibly also a fractured collar bone and broken arm and leg."

"Good God," Gwen said. "Where did they take him?"

"His vital signs were strong, so I had them take him to the Huntington Hospital in Pasadena. An extra twelve minutes or so in the ambulance, but easier check-in and probably better care. Also easier for my aunt that way."

"I'll go check on him," she said.

"He'll be sedated for hours," Frank said. "He was actually very lucky."

"It looks like the building was torn apart."

"Everybody inside was lost except for a receptionist. She had gone out behind the building to smoke; it saved her life. Lieutenant Carlow was killed, along with two uniformed officers, two Academy cadets, and all of the staff of the Clinic—Hinden, Clemmer, Billups…"

"And the client records were all destroyed."

"Yes. From the evidence available it appears that the bomb was in a vehicle, parked at the side of the building, on the wall closest to the shelving holding the Clinic records. Either that was the target and the people inside were collateral damage or the entire Clinic was the target, with the records as primary target and the personnel as secondary."

"Any read yet on the nature of the device?"

"The preliminary indication is fuel oil and fertilizer. Oklahoma City all over again."

"Probably in a van or car trunk?"

"Yes. There's not much left of any of the cars that were parked in the lot. The only thing that's clear is the primary impact point. It'll take the bomb squad and forensic team awhile to determine the likely vehicle that was used. There's one thing that's clear…"

"What's that?" Gwen asked.

"The perp's still out there and he's worried that we're getting close."

"Probably figures that this will set you back," Gwen said.

"And he's right, unfortunately," Frank said.

"I'm sure it's important to know that you're on the right track though," Gwen said. "It's like that old James Bond movie—the one where Bond is approaching the compound that's guarded by totem heads with dart guns and signs that say Stay Out. Bond says he's on the right track; all he has to do is keep going past the warning signs."

"Right," Frank answered.

"The problem is that James Bond's not like ordinary people. They can be hurt and they can die," Gwen said.

Frank nodded in approval.

Gwen hurried to her car and took surface streets toward Silver Lake and Glendale; she was planning to come into Pasadena from the west rather than the south with all of the congestion between the Clinic and the freeway. She called the Director and brought him up to speed on the bombing and her meeting with Fell and his assistant.

"So what are you thinking, Gwen?" he asked.

"I could be wrong, sir, but I don't want to be distracted by the bombing."

"What do you mean?"

"Obviously the bombing is significant. It's a big risk to drive around with a bomb in a vehicle. You can be picked up for a traffic infraction and suddenly you're compromised big time, especially if you're driving a stolen vehicle in a neighborhood with high levels of drug trafficking, with the police automatically checking nooks and crannies whenever they have the opportunity. You also run the risk of blowing yourself up, particularly if the materials used are unstable. This is also the sort of thing that attracts law enforcement from every direction and every jurisdiction—city, state, and federal. Blowing up a building is not something that's done lightly…"

"Go on," he said.

"My fear is that the locals will automatically feel that the purpose of the blast was to destroy the records, the logical implication being that the bomber, who killed Denise, was a client at the Clinic. That's possible, of course, but I keep coming back to a different question: why did the perp first kill Detective Dearing? If the reason was that he feared that Dearing might discover his name in the files, why not just blow up the files first?"

"You think he was worried that Dearing discovered something else."

"Yes. Assuming, of course, that the perp is rational and that's always a potential stretch when you're talking about a murderer. He is, however, efficient and he's been smart enough to get away so far."

"You like the possibility of a connection between Denise's death and the professor's."

"Appleman, yes. Dearing left the Clinic and went somewhere before driving to the Police Administration Building. The time gap is sufficient to take him from the Clinic to Exposition Park and then to downtown."

"He could have gone to a lot of places during that interval, Gwen."

"I understand, sir, and I agree. And there's no obvious connection between the two USC murders except for some circumstantial details. Also, the time gap between the two events is huge, but I have to believe that there's a connection between Denise's death and some other event, if not this one. The perp was following Dearing from the time he left the Clinic, because he had stolen Clemmer's car, which was parked there. He followed him to the site of Dearing's side trip; otherwise he wouldn't have still been on him when he returned to the PAB. The perp concluded that Dearing had seen the connection between Denise's death and some other event. Hence Dearing had to be killed. And he had to be killed instantly—in the shadow of police headquarters, despite the risks that that entailed. The moment that Dearing connected the dots he had to die. Whatever Dearing saw…it made the perp realize that his guilt was about to be exposed. I think that's the key and that the bombing may just be an attempt to sidetrack the investigation."

"Interesting…it sounds plausible."

"I don't have anything else, sir, not with the Center files blown to pieces all over the mid-Wilshire corridor."

"Where are you off to now?"

"To the hospital. I want to be there when Charles White wakes up. He may have seen something right before the detonation."

"Good luck," the Director said. "Keep me posted and—above all else—be careful. If he *did* see something, he could be the next target. A person who will blow up a health clinic wouldn't hesitate to blow up a hospital."

52

Huntington Hospital, West California Boulevard

Gwen took back streets to the hospital, leaving her rental in the East Parking facility. She walked up to the Hale East Tower and the emergency facilities on the first floor.

She badged the receptionist, who told her that Charles was still being treated and that she could wait in an adjoining room. When she entered the room there was a neatly-dressed, elderly black woman sitting in the room with her back against the far wall. She was wearing a black skirt, pressed cotton blouse, and low heels. She was sitting very straight; her purse was on her lap and she was reading a tattered issue of the *Reader's Digest*.

"Mrs. White?" Gwen said, approaching her.

"Yes?" she responded.

"I'm Gwen Harrison. I've been working with your husband, trying to determine the identity of the individual responsible for the death of your niece. I'm very sorry that we have to meet under these circumstances."

"Thank you for coming," Mary White answered. "It's very thoughtful of you. And you needn't worry; Charles will be fine. The number of things that *that man* has survived makes for a very long list."

"I saw your nephew at the site of the bombing. He said that your husband has some broken bones but that his vital organs all appear to be intact and his vital signs are all strong."

"Yes," she answered, smiling warmly. "Frank called me about his Uncle Charles. Charles is wiry. Even at his age he's very strong and very resilient."

"Did he have a chance to tell you why he was going to the Clinic?"

"As a matter of fact he did," Mary answered. "He said that there were two crimes, that you were investigating the one and that he was going to continue to investigate the other. He said that the two of you were a tag team."

Gwen smiled and then continued. "Did Lieutenant White tell you that Charles was outside the building at the time that the bomb was detonated?"

"Yes, he did, but he didn't know *why* he was there. It wasn't clear if he was about to enter the building or if he was outside waiting for someone or possibly watching someone."

"He'll tell us when he's in the recovery room," Gwen said.

Mary paused before speaking. Then she smiled and said, "Miss Harrison, you're actually a federal agent, aren't you?"

"Yes, ma'am, I am."

"Charles didn't say so, but he doesn't have to spell everything out for me in order for me to know what's really happening. When you're married as long as we have been it isn't always necessary to actually say the words."

Gwen just smiled.

"And somehow I have a feeling that Denise was doing more than just working as a nurse. Is that correct?"

"Yes, ma'am. It is."

"Federal agencies don't send people from Washington to investigate each and every local crime."

"No, ma'am, they don't."

"Denise told the family that she was working at a hospital in Virginia, but she was actually being trained by the government, wasn't she?"

"Yes, ma'am, she was."

"And she couldn't tell the family because she was going to work on a special assignment--something they needed to keep secret."

"Yes, ma'am."

"But you and Charles think that whoever did this to her may have also been involved in some other crime, so you're trying to find the connection between the two so that you can identify whoever it is who did these things."

"Yes, ma'am, that's exactly what we're doing."

"I thought so," Mary said. "Would you like to get some coffee or something to eat?"

"Coffee sounds wonderful," Gwen said.

They brought it back to the waiting room, in case there was any word from the ER physician on Charles's condition. Mary had chicken noodle soup. The steam floated above the Styrofoam cup and the collection of tiny noodles floated to the top and gathered against the edge.

"It didn't take long for you to figure all this out, did it?" Gwen asked.

Mary smiled. "I always have to stay on my toes. I work in the Chemistry department at the Institute. The faculty say that Chemistry is the queen of the sciences. I don't know about that, but I know that *they* believe it. They're very proud and very serious. They believe that they're on the verge of receiving their tenth Nobel prize for Chemistry. They're wonderful, but they can be a handful. It's my job to keep them happy and keep them working without any unnecessary distractions. I have to anticipate their needs and know what they're likely to say before they say it. Being married to Charles has been good practice for me. He's always involved in one thing or another and it's often the kind of thing that he doesn't want to talk about, at least not to me, since he's afraid I might worry. I *do* worry, of course, but then Charles is just like them; he has a very good record of success. *Very* good."

"I'd say that's an understatement," Gwen said. "I've seen him referred to as a living legend."

"He is," Mary responded, again smiling, "but not so much around the house."

Twenty minutes later the ER physician came into the waiting room. He was wearing surgical greens but he had removed the bags on his shoes, his latex gloves and his surgical mask. He looked very fit and his hands were steady but there were deep circular lines beneath his eyes. His name was James Berners.

"I'm Dr. Berners," he said. "Are you Mrs. White?"

"Yes, I am," Mary said. "This is our friend, Miss Harrison."

Berners nodded and continued. "Your husband is in recovery. He sustained serious injuries but I don't believe that they are life-threatening. His condition is *stable*. His right arm is broken and he has a hair-line fracture of his right leg. His collar bone is broken, but while there's no such thing as a good fracture this one could have been much worse. There were also some bumps and bruises and scrapes as well as a mild concussion. We've done full-body scans and are convinced that we've identified all of the injuries. He looks like he's been in an automobile accident. There's a lot of swelling and stitches, but he's been sedated and he's not in any pain.

"He'll need to stay here at least 72 hours and we'll continue to monitor his condition. Basically the shock wave of the explosion threw him against the wall of an adjoining building and he was hit with flying debris. Fortunately he has the physical condition of a man half his age."

"How soon can we see him, Doctor?" Mary asked.

"He'll be in his room in about thirty minutes. You can see him then, but I doubt that he'll be awake for awhile. And please don't worry when you see him. He's pretty banged up, but he's not as bad as he looks."

"Thank you, Doctor," Mary said. "We appreciate all of your help."

Berners just nodded and returned to the ER.

Mary turned to Gwen and said, "Thank you again for being here. It's a great comfort. I was afraid that whoever blew up that building might have seen Charles there and followed the ambulance to the hospital. He might have gotten past me, but I don't think he'd get past both of us." She opened her purse so that Gwen could see the Taurus Ultra-Lite .32 Magnum revolver resting on top of a packet of tissues. "Now, tell me," she said, "how many women can say that they've gotten an anniversary present like that on top of the roses and earrings and dinner out?"

Gwen smiled and opened her own purse so that Mary could see her Sig P320c. "It wasn't given with that kind of love," she said, "but it gets the job done when you need it."

53

Vermont above Wilshire

Frank White clicked off his phone and returned it to the case on his belt, relieved to hear that his uncle was expected to recover fully. His captain, Carl Loram, approached him at the edge of what remained of the Clinic building.

"Hell of a mess," Loram said. The firemen continued to spray the smoldering ruins, filling the air with black, caustic smoke. "All those good men and civilians lost. And so far we haven't recovered any of their notes beyond a single sheet. I recognized Carlow's handwriting. There were just a few names—all very generic: a Hernandez, a Kim, a Lopez...a Li. At least they had gotten through the L's. Maybe we'll find something else. At this point it looks like a massive no-win. We lose our guys and we lose their work. If we continue to hose it down we damage the remains. If we don't, the remains just burn up."

"I just talked to my aunt," Frank said. "Charles is going to be as good as new. They've set the broken bones, stitched up the open wounds, washed off the blood and loaded him up with sedatives."

"Charles'd be hard to take out," Loram said. "We can't issue him a purple heart for this, but that's OK; he's got enough of them already."

"Right."

"Let me ask you something, Frank," Loram said.

"Yes, sir. What's that?"

"What would you do now if you were me?"

"With regard to what?" Frank asked.

"The case. I want my best man on it but I don't want to worry about personal conflicts."

"You want *me* to do it?"

"Can you?"

"Of course," Frank said.

"No personal problems?"

"I don't think we can stand here and wring our hands," Frank said. "We don't have that luxury. We just lost a mountain of potential evidence along with the collective memories of the Clinic's staff and the collective work of our officers. We're just a few steps beyond starting from scratch."

"So what would you do?" Loram asked.

"Put together a team of obsessives and start digging. Try to find the gun that was used to kill Vince and see if it can tell us anything. Add the use of explosives to the other violent crimes on this guy's list of activities and make another run through our data bases. Start hitting every potential supplier of fertilizer and fuel oil within a fifty mile radius and jog their salesmen's memories. Cover the surrounding streets with officers and see if anyone noticed a strange vehicle in the area or anyone acting in a suspicious manner--futzing with the vehicle in some way or making a quick departure after parking it behind the building but then not entering the building. Search the streets, alleys, and vacant buildings in the area for any evidence that could be connected with the perp or the detonation device. Lean on the bomb squad and the forensic team for answers and evidence..."

"Anything else?"

"Find out if my uncle saw anything. We know where he was standing before the blast. We don't know why he was there."

"Any concern that someone else might be wondering if he saw anything?"

"Actually I took the liberty of calling the Chief of the Pasadena PD. They've dispatched a pair of officers to keep an eye out."

"I know," Loram said. "I called him too and he said that you'd already made the request."

"Hope that's not a problem," Frank said.

"Great minds moving on the same track? Why should it be? I think you better make some calls, get your team moving. You should be there when Charles opens his eyes and if I know Charles that will happen sooner than most people would expect. He lost his niece and he's going to wake up angry rather than relieved."

54

Huntington Hospital,
West California Boulevard

The resident in the ICU assured Mary and Gwen that Charles was not comatose, but to them he looked as if he was in a state of suspended animation. His body was rigid, his breathing so shallow as to be barely perceptible. The bloodied cuts, deep bruises and swollen eyes, cheeks, chin, lips and forehead were as stark and real as a Gross Anatomy cadaver on a steel table. He was, initially, barely recognizable. Gwen reminded Mary that the ER doctor had warned them about his appearance. She also reminded her that he was not in any pain.

Frank arrived twenty minutes after Charles was moved to the ICU. He hugged his aunt and put his left hand over Gwen's hand when he took it in his right.

"Don't be shocked," Mary said. "We've been assured that he's much better than he looks."

"I know," Frank said. "Thanks." He looked at his uncle and managed to hold his expression. "No ventilator; that's a good sign."

One of the nurses, a woman named Gail, brought a third chair into Charles's room. The three sat together, making small talk. After fifteen minutes Frank asked if he could get coffee or soda for either of them. Mary said she'd like some more of the chicken noodle soup and Gwen volunteered to accompany him. "You can't carry three cups," she said.

They were halfway down the hall when Frank turned to Gwen and told her he was grateful for her being there. "I also wanted to talk to you," he said.

"Sure," Gwen answered. "Any new developments at the bomb site?"

"No new evidence," Frank said, "but there's a new development. The captain has put me in charge of the investigation."

"That's good," Gwen said. "I consider that a positive step."

"Thanks. We're running in as many directions as possible, hoping to turn something. I'm afraid we're going to need a break, some luck, or both."

"I understand," she said. "If I can help in any way, just let me know."

"I appreciate that," Frank said. "I need to tell you something. Let's go in here for a second." They walked into a vacant waiting room near the elevator.

Gwen nodded, waiting for him to continue.

"You looked familiar to me," Frank said, "so I asked my med tech to do a little checking. He was back in the office and I was on the road. He's good with data bases, so I turned him loose. He didn't have to do anything too exotic to find several pages worth of hits. I should have realized it earlier, Gwen. You're a Bureau agent."

"That's right," she answered.

"On special assignment, obviously, or they would have sent someone from the L.A. office."

Gwen let him continue.

"The L.A. guys are actually very good," Frank said, "but they're a little...*proprietary*...about jurisdictions. They would probably be surprised to know that you're here."

"Yes," Gwen said. "I suspect they would."

"And the fact that you're here suggests that the issues with which you're dealing are above their pay grade."

"A need-to-know thing," Gwen said.

"The Bureau always likes to compartmentalize, but this particular Director has made it a way of life. The business with the history professor...

Appleman…came later, so you were sent here to be the Director's eyes and ears on *Denise's* case. That means that she was doing much more than giving people shots and salves."

"Yes," Gwen said.

"So either officially or unofficially Denise was working for the Bureau."

"Officially," Gwen said, "but under deep cover."

"You're the Bureau's prize tracker. You closed the Wolf Trap terrorism case."

"Yes, I did," she said. "My hair color was different then; I've altered my makeup a little; I try to change hats and hairstyles…preserve a little anonymity…"

Frank smiled. "You're also a full-blooded Lakota."

"That's true," Gwen said, "but I don't generally dress the part."

Frank smiled. "So were you really a friend of Denise's or were you sent because of your special skills?"

"I *was* a friend," Gwen said. "We went through Quantico together."

"Good," Frank said. "I think that helps."

"So do I," Gwen said.

"I'm guessing that if the Director bypassed the locals and brought you in that Denise was also working on something of which the locals were unaware."

"Yes," Gwen said.

"Is there any possibility that it could be relevant to our case?"

"We don't think so," Gwen said. "Let me be more emphatic. There's not a single bit of evidence connecting Denise's death to her Bureau activities in Los Angeles. The individuals related to those activities have rock-solid alibis for the time of the murder and have not exhibited any behaviors that suggest they were aware of her work or, for that matter, of her death. They don't wish us well, of course, but—again--there's no evidence that they were aware of Denise's role and, individually, they had no opportunity to kill her. They could have hired someone to do it, but we consider that a very remote possibility."

"Is it a fair assumption that the individuals under investigation are more likely to have been professionals, with access to plastic explosives and more sophisticated weapons than knives and hammers?"

"It is," Gwen said.

"So what began for you as a quiet investigation of a death related to a secret operation has become a more conventional investigation of something not only unrelated to the secret operation but potentially related to another murder that occurred many years ago."

"Yes, exactly," Gwen said.

"But you have to continue to lowkey it, because the Director doesn't want to stir up any suspicions with the local office. As far as they're concerned this is an LAPD case, not a federal one, and—from all appearances—they're right. However, you're here and the Director wants somebody on the ground who he trusts."

"He doesn't like to see an agent taken down without a Bureau response," Gwen said, "particularly not someone as special as Denise."

"And you would be comfortable with a *collaborative* relationship?"

"Absolutely. Everything has to be professional, but for me this case is primarily personal. And I don't want any limelight. I don't like it anyway but I don't want the investigation compromised. I want to be thought of as Denise's friend who's here to help. That's much more than just a cover story; it's the truth."

"I understand," Frank said. "Jerry—that's my med tech—was rooting around in the files and saw that you've always tried to stay out of the spotlight. For one thing, of course, the publicity can reduce your effectiveness. What is it that you were quoted as saying—that you just wanted to be an agent and not a diversity headline?"

"That's an accurate quote," Gwen said.

"I can understand that," Frank responded. "It's a little different for me. We've got a lot of black cops in the LAPD…not a lot of lieutenants and captains, but a lot of cops. When things happen…high-profile things… things related to the black community…the Department has a tendency to move me into the center of the spotlight. Provide some reassurance… take off some heat…maybe prepare for a little scapegoating…I hate it; it's a distraction."

"It certainly is," Gwen said.

"I just like to catch bad guys," Frank said. "I don't want to be on television; I just want to be there to hear the cuffs snap and the cell doors close."

"Otherwise we would have gone into acting rather than tracking," Gwen said.

"That's right. Now we better get my aunt some soup. It probably wouldn't hurt us either. We've got some serious work to do."

"I agree," Gwen said. "I'd only add one thing."

"What's that?" Frank asked.

"Those cuffs snapping…and those cell doors closing?"

"Yes?"

"I think a 9 mm round penetrating soft tissue would be an acceptable outcome also."

"Maybe 2 or 3 of them," Frank said.

55

Huntington Hospital, West California Boulevard

After two and a half hours of waiting and multiple trips to the vend-ing machines, Mary, Gwen and Frank had accumulated a growing collection of empty paper cups and cellophane wrappers. Frank collected them, walked down the hall, and deposited them in the trash receptacle next to the elevator. When he returned and sat down, Charles moved his arm slightly and winced. Mary was out of her seat immediately, placing her hand on Charles's wrist. He turned his head toward her and opened his eyes slightly. They were blood red.

His voice was little more than a whisper. "I hope I'm not in heaven yet," he said, "but you look like an angel."

"You *will* be in heaven if you keep doing what you've been doing, Charles White."

Then she smiled and squeezed his hand.

"Please don't break it," Charles said. "It looks like it may be the only thing that's still intact."

"Welcome back," Mary said.

"It is *good* to be back," Charles said. "How long have I been here?"

"Five or six hours," Mary said. "How was your nap?"

"I can't really say," Charles answered. "I heard the explosion and suddenly I'm here…in several pieces."

"You were blown against the adjoining building," Frank said. "About fifteen yards or so."

"Probably not a bad thing," Charles said. "Better outside than inside, I suspect."

"Everybody inside was killed," Frank said. "Each member of the staff, Dave Carlow, two of our officers and two of our cadets. Instantaneously."

"I guess that's one form of progress," Charles said, wistfully. "We can remove them all from any possible list of suspects." He refocused his eyes and saw Gwen standing behind Frank. "It's awfully nice of you to be here, Gwen," he said.

"Thanks," she said. "Can I ask you something?"

"Of course. You want to know if I saw anything or anybody before the building exploded."

"That's right," she said.

"I'm not sure. I may have. I went there to look over the facility; I was trying to get a sense of who worked where, of who might have seen what…that kind of thing. I didn't have anything specific in mind; I just wanted to get a better feel for the place. Whoever killed Denise probably had contact with her there, so I was trying to get inside everybody's head and scope out what they might have seen or done.

"I couldn't park in the side lot because it was full, so I drove up on Vermont and parked a block and a half away. I guess that's the good news, Mary; our car probably survived…"

"Don't worry about that, Charles," she said.

He smiled at her. "Anyway," he said, "I walked back to the Clinic and was about to enter the main door to the old theatre, on the west side of the building. Before I could get there I saw the flash and heard the blast and everything went black. I could feel movement, but it was as if the building moved rather than my body. I guess they both did."

"You said you *may have* seen something," Gwen said.

"Yes. As I was walking south on Vermont a man hurried past me. He wasn't running, but he was walking quickly, almost as if he actually wanted to run but couldn't because he didn't want to draw attention to himself."

"We think the bomb was a mixture of fertilizer and fuel oil," Frank said. "He may have activated it with a fuse. It could be that when you saw him he had just lit the fuse and then taken off."

"Yes," Charles said. "The problem is that I can't give you any kind of useful description of him. He was white; I think he was wearing jeans, gym shoes, and a cheap windbreaker. I didn't notice any facial hair or tattoos. He *was* wearing a baseball cap."

"A baseball cap is a good disguise," Gwen said. It hides the hair and shades the eyes. Vince's killer was wearing a ball cap. Any sense of his possible age?"

"Not a kid," Charles said, "but he was able to walk quickly and smoothly. He wasn't decrepit. Maybe mid to late 60's. Hard to say these days. People are better preserved than they used to be, especially in L.A. with all the exercise and facelifts and hair dye…"

"Any markings on the ball cap?" Frank asked.

"Not that I remember," Charles said.

"Was he carrying anything?" Gwen asked.

"I don't remember seeing anything," Charles said. "One thing I noticed…he wasn't swinging his arms. Lots of times you see people walking quickly…it's a form of exercise. They're carrying those heavy hands things or at least swinging their arms. He wasn't. It was like he was trying to be…what?…inconspicuous?"

"Sounds promising," Frank said.

"I agree," Gwen said. "Sometimes people try to look inconspicuous in neighborhoods like that because they don't want to attract the attention of muggers, but walking fast immediately draws attention. Certainly it would draw police attention. They'd figure that the person might have just stolen something. The businessmen there…in the sections of the boulevard that have been gentrified…would signal their status by their dress. They'd be in suits, not baseball hats, and they'd drive everywhere, not walk, unless they didn't have an upscale coffee bar on site. Even then they'd probably send a gofer. The only business people who dress that casually are in the high tech industries and their offices tend to be in the Valley, not in the mid-Wilshire corridor. The poor people in the neighborhood wouldn't walk quickly. They'd usually be carrying bags or babies. Teenagers would travel in groups and they'd probably swagger. This guy sounds more like a blue collar from the suburbs. If he *was* actually working in that neighborhood, he'd probably be wearing some kind of service industry uniform. If he was a tourist who'd been suckered into a nearby hotel by an address and a website, his family would be with him. I think it *does* sound promising. You did well, Charles, especially under the circumstances."

"I'm sorry I can't remember any more details.," Charles said. "I *can* say this—what I remember of the person walking away from me is consistent with the description of Denise's attacker that was given by the homeless man in the park."

"He may look fairly ordinary," Gwen said, "but if we assume that he's our guy we can still automatically eliminate the short, the fat, the young, the very old, the female, the non-Caucasian, the noticeably tattooed, the noticeably scarred, and probably some others we'll think of in time. It's a step forward, Charles."

Suddenly Frank reached for his phone. He had turned off the ring tone but had felt it vibrate. "Yes?" he said. Then he listened for a moment, said "Hold on for a second," put his hand over the base, and said, "We've got something."

IV

THE NEW YEAR'S GANG

56

Huntington Hospital, West California Boulevard

"A gun," Frank said. "A patrolman spotted it in a storm sewer, just a few blocks from the Police Administration Building."

"Better to dispose of it immediately than be caught with it during a routine pullover," Gwen said. "Sounds like we finally caught a break."

"The guy just phoned it in. He's on his way to headquarters. He's going to take it straight to the lab."

"Go," Charles said. "Don't sit around here; I'll be fine."

"It'd take us twenty minutes to get there, Charles. They'll have a preliminary report in ten."

"Well how about something to eat then?" Charles asked. "Maybe some jellied consommé with a side of ice chips?"

Gwen and Mary checked with the duty nurse, who said she'd get something for Charles now that he was awake. "Nothing fancy yet," she said. "Maybe some juice and tea."

Frank said he could eat a sandwich but wouldn't eat in front of Charles. "Don't give that a second thought," Charles said. "I'd rather have a handful of pain pills than solid food anyway."

Gwen and Mary got some sodas and sandwiches. "I hope you like ham and cheese, Frank White," Mary said. "The other choice was older and grayer ham and cheese."

"That's fine, thanks," he said.

Fifteen minutes later he still hadn't heard from the lab. He called his tech, Jerry Dailey.

"I know, Frank, I've been wondering too," Jerry said. "I'll check and get right back to you."

He called back in eight minutes. "It's a Glock 19, Frank. Four rounds expended. No prints. They're trying various exotic methods, but it looks as if it's been wiped clean."

"How about the unexpended rounds?"

"They're next; nothing obvious yet."

"Call me right back," Frank said.

"You got it," Jerry answered.

Frank clicked off. "It's a Glock 19. That's a compact 9 mm, Aunt Mary. It holds 15 rounds, plus 1; 11 were unexpended. Vince Dearing's car took at least 3 or 4," he added.

"That's probably an expensive weapon, isn't it?" she asked.

"Moderate," Frank said. "Close to $500 retail. The street value would be much higher, particularly if it couldn't be traced. It's not something you'd throw away carelessly."

They finished their sandwiches in silence. Frank was finishing his drink as his phone twitched.

"Yes, Jerry?"

"Serial number intact, Frank. Federal issue. We couldn't get any more information than that. There's a clear print on the back of one of the unexpended rounds. They just sent it off to IAFIS, with a RUSH request."

"Thanks, Jerry. Keep me posted."

He clicked off the phone and told them what he knew.

"They may drag their feet on the i.d.," Gwen said. "Weapon of choice for many," she said. "My bet: he killed Vince Dearing with Denise's gun."

"Denise's purse was found in her car," Frank said. "There was GSR but no weapon."

"She took it with her," Gwen said. "She wanted it handy. She didn't want to have to go into her purse."

"Then she knew the person and knew that he was dangerous," Frank said.

"Yes," Gwen said. She paused before proceeding, concerned that she not upset Mary.

"Go on," Mary said. "I want to hear your thoughts. We're way past the social pleasantries. We're talking about the piece of trash who killed my niece."

"This could explain the overkill," Gwen said. "He saw the gun and panicked, started stabbing and slashing as fast as he could. He didn't want to give her a chance to use it. He must have surprised her in some way, because if her gun was in her hand and she saw him coming at her with a knife she would have shot him. That's what she was trained to do."

"It could have been in her pocket," Frank said. "You could see the outline through the blue material, even at night. He made his move the instant he saw it."

"He wouldn't have known that she was a Bureau agent," Gwen said. "Her cover was tight; the family was close and *they* were unaware of her position. She and the perp were meeting under some pretense. He may have wondered why she wanted to see him, but he wouldn't have known that she was in law enforcement. He could have been edgy and brought along a weapon just in case. Or maybe he was always looking over his shoulder and always armed. For her it was different. It was past the investigatory stage; she was ready to make her move, and, as Frank said, she also knew that he was dangerous. She was armed and prepared to shoot to kill. They met and everything went south, probably very quickly. The big question is, why? What did he do to arouse her own suspicions? How did he enter the picture and sidetrack her from her other, presumably more-important work? There's one thing that's very doubtful…"

"What's that?" Frank asked.

"I don't think she was investigating the murder of Professor Appleman. That happened years earlier. It was a big deal locally for a short time, but it wasn't a national story. Besides, she would have been a grammar-school kid at the time. I doubt very much that she even knew about it."

They sat in silence for a moment.

"She had other, *significant* responsibilities," Gwen said, sounding as if she was anxious to convince herself, "and there are plenty of unsolved murders in Los Angeles, many far more celebrated than this one. She *wouldn't* have taken them on in her spare time. She didn't *have* any spare time. She was doing a full-time job at the Clinic as well as her job as a Bureau agent. Somehow this guy just walked into her life…"

"And then took it," Mary said.

57

Huntington Hospital,
West California Boulevard

"There's something we're missing," Gwen said. "I want to talk to the sister again. No one knew more about her brother than she did. Excuse me…"

Gwen went down the hall and checked the local white pages on her iPhone. Jane Appleman had her own number listed. She picked up on the third ring.

"Professor Appleman, Gwen Harrison. We spoke earlier about your brother."

"Yes?"

"I need to speak with you again. Would it be possible to do that today?"

"I wasn't planning on going into the office," she said. "I've got somebody here installing a counter top and I'm meeting my husband for an early dinner."

"I'm in Pasadena, Professor. You're nearby, aren't you?"

"Yes, in San Marino. On St. Albans. Do you know where that is?"

"Just above Huntington Drive?"

"The corner house at the end of the first block. On the west side of the street."

"I can be there in about ten minutes, if that works for you," Gwen said.

"Make it thirty," she answered. "I've been rooting around in the garden and I want to wash up a little."

"I'll see you then," Gwen said. She returned to Charles's room and told them that she had secured an appointment and would report back anything that she learned that could be of any possible use.

She walked to the parking lot, doing her best to survey her surroundings as inconspicuously as possible. Charles was down. Carlow was dead. Dearing was dead. And Denise was dead. Whoever had done it had done it without hesitation and under circumstances that could easily have compromised him. If he passed Charles on the street and then saw him hurtle through the air he could have had the presence of mind to find a vantage point and observe the investigatory process. Perhaps he had followed her to the hospital. Perhaps he had followed Frank. Either way, she decided to inspect the undercarriage of her car. Nothing there. She then popped the hood and checked inside the engine compartment. Again--no obvious explosive- or other devices.

She then started the car and drove slowly out of the lot, heading north to Colorado. No one followed her out of the lot, but when she entered the lines of traffic on the surface streets it was impossible to tell who was there by happenstance and who was there by design. She decided to make her way through several multi-tiered parking lots, beginning at the Target lot on Colorado and then driving to the Macy's lot on Lake, entering the latter on the east but exiting on the west. If someone *was* following her, he was very good, because the ramps were both complex and convoluted and the traffic was heavy. As she drove below California, past Appleman's former home, the traffic began to thin and by the time she drove into San Marino it had slowed to an occasional trickle. As the home prices escalated and the boulevards widened, so did her field of vision and anyone attempting to follow her would have difficulty doing so without revealing his likely intentions.

On Oxford Road she saw a house with long grass, a For Sale sign, and a driveway that looped around to a rear-load garage. She made sure that no one was visible on the street behind her, then quickly turned into the driveway and parked behind the house. No one came to the window when she did so and the property to the south was enclosed with a dense shrub fence that reduced sound and blocked lines of sight. She turned off the motor and waited for a full five minutes, thinking about the kinds of questions that she might ask Jane Appleman. Where should she start? What do you ask when you need to discover something as yet unknown?

58

St. Albans Road, San Marino

As Gwen approached Jane Appleman's street she considered the fact that the professor's sister could also be at great personal risk. If, indeed, she held the information that constituted the connection between her brother's death and Denise's (even if she was unaware of the fact), she could easily be targeted for a form of elimination as bloody as that of the growing list of victims.

Rather than increase that risk Gwen parked in the rear of a commercial lot on Huntington Drive and walked to her home. She first slipped on a jogging jacket, white athletic shoes and a baseball cap and transferred the items in her purse to a mini-backpack. San Marino chic. As she walked up St. Albans Road she swung her arms rhythmically as if she was in full heel-and-toe exercise mode.

Jane Appleman met her at the door. She seemed surprised at Gwen's appearance but didn't comment on the fact. Gwen could smell the fresh scents of expensive soap and shampoo. Her hair was still damp and she was wearing a silk dress with a flowered print. This time she looked more like a grande dame of San Marino than a Pomona professor. There were fresh flowers throughout her mini-mansion, with stargazer lilies providing the primary scent.

"Tea, coffee, juice or mineral water?" Jane Appleman asked. "I can also do something stronger."

"What are you having?" Gwen asked.

"Strong coffee. The kind you could float a horseshoe in."

"That works for me," Gwen answered.

"Good," Jane said.

Gwen could hear a rubber hammer tapping from a distant corner of the house. The counter top installer. In a butler's pantry or utility room? She could also hear Jane opening cupboard doors in the kitchen. A few minutes later she returned with a mahogany tray containing two cups and saucers, some cloth napkins with silver rings, a small china coffee pot and matching creamer and sugar bowl. She put the tray down on the glass-topped coffee table and poured. Gwen declined the cream and sugar and Jane took a sip of her noticeably hot coffee.

"I needed that," she said, putting down the cup. "Now what can I tell you?"

"I'm not sure," Gwen answered. "I'm missing something, but I don't know what it is. Perhaps if we talk I'll learn something I didn't know earlier or we'll focus on something I had somehow overlooked. As you know, there's been a recent murder, one that had some commonalities with your brother's. The separation in time is huge, but somehow I keep coming back to the fact that the two events must be connected."

"Because you don't have anything else?" Jane asked.

"Possibly," Gwen answered, "but more because no other explanations are working. At this point the number of deaths has multiplied. The initial investigator of Denise White's death has been killed, as has the lieutenant who replaced him. The building in which Denise worked has been blown up and all of the staff there perished in the blast."

"The Clinic building, down on Vermont…"

"Yes," Gwen said.

"It was on the news before. Terrible."

"Sergeant White…who accompanied me earlier…"

"Yes?"

"He was standing outside the Clinic when the bomb went off. He survived, but he's been hospitalized."

"And are you concerned that I might be next?"

"I thought it best to take precautions," Gwen answered. "I didn't want to park in your driveway and I changed my appearance slightly in an attempt to look more like one of your neighbors."

"I thought that might be the case."

"I don't want to alarm you unnecessarily," Gwen said. "Whoever is doing this may not have made the connection at all. Besides, your brother died many years ago and his killer has continued to escape notice, so it would be logical for him to assume that you don't have any evidence that could implicate him. Hence, he's left you alone. So long as we're discreet he may continue to do so."

Jane shook her head slightly, and sipped her coffee. "Let's proceed as if that's the case," she said. "I appreciate your not drawing any unnecessary attention to your visit. Now, how can I help?"

"We know that the first investigator had visited a site just prior to his death. We have a good fix on the time frame and a trip to Exposition Park prior to his arrival at the Police Administration Building would have been very doable. He would have had time to park and check the crime scene of your brother's death, even take a few notes if he had wanted to."

"But why do you think he would have gone there?"

"Because when you search the LAPD data bases and indicate the common elements shared by your brother's and Denise's murder the screen lights up with hits detailing the circumstances of your brother's death. If *I* could get that result Detective Dearing could get that result. He was killed just before he reached police headquarters—the worst possible place for a murderer to strike."

"So the killer would have had to have been very desperate."

"Exactly," Gwen said.

"And you're thinking that he either followed Detective Dearing from the Clinic or had staked out the site in Exposition Park and picked him up there."

"Yes. Almost surely the former."

"Then it would have either been someone who was completely anonymous at the Clinic or someone who was seen there regularly, such that his presence would not arouse any suspicion."

"Yes," Gwen said. "Very good."

"It's still a stretch," Jane said. "I know what a mathematician would say about the number of possible points to which Detective Dearing might have driven while he was en route to LAPD headquarters."

"It would be a very large number," Gwen said.

"Yes, but the commonalities between the events and the data base hits reduce the number considerably."

"Yes," Gwen said. "It's still a stretch, but it's all we have."

"Then where do we start?"

"Did your brother keep a diary, Professor Appleman?"

"A diary? Not that I know of."

"A journal? Perhaps a notebook of some sort?"

"Come with me," she said. "Let's have a look."

In the rear of the property was a small guest house. "Geoffrey's books are here, along with many of mine and my husband's." The space was approximately 1,000 square feet in size and nearly all of it consisted of book shelving. There was a library table and chair with a desktop computer and a leather loveseat nearby.

"This is beautiful," Gwen said.

"It's a fabulous place to work," Jane said. "I have to keep the blinds drawn though—too many distractions otherwise. Have a look here..."

She directed Gwen's attention to the lowest shelf of a corner bookcase. "These are notebooks that Geoffrey kept, but I believe that they're notes for his books, not personal materials. Feel free to take a look. I haven't checked them in a long time."

Gwen removed one of the folders and studied it. They were all in brown leatherette. She wondered if these were the originals or if Appleman's sister and brother-in-law had had them replaced with the leatherette containers so that they conveyed the sense of a matched set. Books are furniture as well as instruments and most peoples' old notes are contained in scuffed folders or stained, tattered boxes.

Appleman had a simple but elegant system for taking notes. His sources—books, articles, and primary texts—were sorted alphabetically in each ring binder. At the top of each entry was the full bibliographic reference for the source. While there were a few rough notes, most of the references were complete quotations, so that he would not have to recheck them later. He obviously erred on the side of completeness. Down the left margin were the precise page references of the quotes. If they covered more than a single page he inserted a prominent slash mark at the original page break. It was clear that he didn't want to go back and recheck his sources later—a good plan since materials disappear or are on loan, particularly when you are most in need of them.

Some entries were very brief, no more than a page. Others were long. Important books, for example, might yield twenty or thirty pages of notes and quotations. The entry pages were all numbered, *seriatim.* Then, at the front of the collection of binders that served as the grist for each book-length project, he had listed the chapters that the book would include and the themes and ideas pertinent to each chapter. Each of those themes and ideas then had a set of corresponding numbers, *viz.* 127/22-23. The number 127 was the page in the binders and the 22-23 corresponded to the note or quotation on page 127 from pp. 22-23 of the source text. He didn't identify the individual binders because he continued the page numbering from binder to binder.

Hence he read all of his materials, took his notes and recorded his quotes, and then put them—alphabetically by source—in binders. He then numbered all of the pages. At that point he had a good idea of what he wanted to say in his own book, broke his general ideas into chapters, themes and individual points and went back to read through all of his notes. Each time he found something pertinent he made a note of the individual reference on the relevant chapter/theme/idea page, so that by the time he was ready to actually compose he had both a general outline and a full set of supporting references.

Very efficient. But nothing personal. The notebooks formed a substantial portion of the basis of his professional life but they offered no insight whatsoever into his personal affairs. Gwen commented on his cleverness and efficiency but then asked if there was anything else— personal letters, for example.

"Geoffrey was really not a letter writer," his sister said. "He was a talker. He *could* do email, but most of his communications were terse and utilitarian. Simple things: 'much appreciated' or 'see you at 7:00.' Seldom any more than that. He had a university computer at home and in his office and we returned them after his death. I don't know whether or not there would be anything left on the university's servers.

"There must have been correspondence concerning his business affairs, letters from editors and publishers—that sort of thing—but we didn't find any. I think that as soon as Geoffrey completed a project he discarded everything concerning it, except, of course, for the scholarly materials which he used to compose the book. He kept those because there was always a chance that he might reuse them. A book that he had read for one project might also be relevant for a later project. Once one of his books was published, however, all of the related paper was pitched. He didn't leave any copy-edited manuscripts, galleys or page proofs. 'They've got the actual book now,' he would say, 'and the rest is just clutter.'"

"I wonder if he kept any floppies?"

"We didn't find any. And we cleaned out his campus office as well as his home. He was more trusting than I am. I back up everything. Middle child syndrome."

"How about photographs or greeting cards—something that might carry an inscription?"

"No, sorry. He had a set of framed pictures of Bill. I returned them to him after Geoffrey's death. Otherwise all of the materials that he had framed were art pieces. Would you like to see them?"

"Yes," Gwen answered. "And thanks again. This is very good of you." To herself she thought that they were just about finished anyway. How many dry wells can you stand to drill? And what would be her recourse if the professor's sister had nothing more to offer than what they had seen so far? Gwen made a mental note to herself to ask the sister for William Dennison's address and phone number. Her next step was likely to be a trip to Albany, New York. The longer they waited the greater the chance that Appleman's killer, *Denise's killer*, would be toasting his successful escape while they chased phantoms and will-of-the-wisps, with time out for the funerals and burials of the murderer's more recent victims. Her watch was battery-powered and silent but for an instant she thought that she could hear its tick, striking against the nerves in the back of her brain like a small steel hammer.

59

St. Albans Road, San Marino

As they climbed the stairs to the home's third level, Jane gave Gwen an abbreviated version of the building's history. "We purchased the home from the Henreids," she said, "no relation to the actor. Walter Henreid was the president of a large California bank. His wife's father had owned an insurance company in Hartford, Connecticut. They had four daughters—all fixtures of the local society scene. When they purchased the house the top floor was an attic storage space. They remodeled it completely for their daughters. They cut in two dormers, installed hardwood flooring, floor-to-ceiling mirrors and a ballet barre. The dance floor actually has a floating subfloor that provides both resilience and stability. You'll notice the spring in it right away. It is, to all intents and purposes, a fully professional dance floor. Must have cost them a tidy sum. Not a problem, though; they had plenty of money. When the girls grew up and made their debuts the ballet space became ballroom space. I'm told that at times they even brought in large ensembles to play for the girls, their friends and their dates."

"High society," Gwen said.

"Yes, very much so," Jane answered. "My husband and I don't have children and most of our friends would rather eat and talk than dance, so we had the mirrors removed and turned the space into a gallery for Geoffrey's art. I think you'll find it interesting. In some ways it's a bit odd…"

Gwen wondered what she might have meant by that, but she didn't have to wait long to find out. A broad staircase with intricately-carved and gilded banisters connected the second level of the house to the third. It was slightly over-the-top, created, no doubt, with the Henreids' little princesses in mind. The ballroom—now gallery—space was huge: at least 30' x 40'.

And it *was* odd, at least to anyone with a strong aesthetic sense. The north wall consisted of art prints and drawings, the south of oil paintings of birds, particularly waterfowl.

"See what I mean?" Jane asked.

"Yes," Gwen answered, as she walked into the center of the room, flexing her toes to feel the give in the floor. The art prints included Miro's *The Sun Eater*, an image of a wide-eyed boxy figure with a bright red sun within a blue torso that was covered with bars. Next to it was Dali's *The Horseman of Death*, an image of a skeletal figure, riding a spectral horse with some remaining flesh past a stand of cypress trees masking a large tower. Then there were four prints from Rouault's *Miserere* series and, finally, the prize piece of the collection, a Picasso drawing that Gwen had never seen copies of before: a minotaur/satyr-like figure sitting between two female nudes, with the remains of lunch on a small table.

"Not exactly homoerotic," Jane said, "but certainly erotic. Geoffrey said that the title was something like *Satiety*, but that it should have been called *Sex, then Lunch*, or *Lunch, then Sex*. He bought it in Barcelona. It cost him a small fortune at the time, but it would cost a large fortune now."

The paintings of the birds contrasted with the art prints and Picasso drawing in their style as well as subject matter. They were realistic representations of common species: quail, jays, blue-wing teals, Canada geese. They were very nicely done, but absolutely different in nature and subject from the works facing them on the opposite wall.

"Geoffrey was an interesting person," Jane said. "Not so much internally-riven or contradictory as he was *complex*. I'd say he was many-sided. Maybe just two-sided actually, but certainly not schizophrenic and certainly not Jekyll-and-Hyde-ish. There was a part of him that was heavily aestheticized. At the same time there was a part of him that loved the simple and popular. He liked to read Catullus, for example, and he read him in Latin. He learned Spanish in order to read Cervantes. He also loved Dorothy Sayers and P. D. James, Ngaio Marsh and Mary Roberts Rinehart. At the time of his death there was a set of Hume's history of England on his desk and a novel by Margery Allingham on his nightstand. He loved foie gras and a nice Margaux but he also loved Dodger dogs and draft beer. Sometimes his colleagues would tease him about his 'bows to populism' and he would take great offense at it. He prided himself on his own breadth of taste and actually offered historical explanations for its narrowing since the early nineteenth century."

"That's *very* interesting," Gwen said, not simply being polite. This was the first discussion of Geoffrey Appleman that had actually added new information to the mix.

"The artwork mirrored Geoffrey," Jane said. "The more highbrow things were hung among his professional books and antique furniture. The bird paintings were hung in the parts of his home that were more personal—the spaces that would generally not be visited by others. Geoffrey hastened to point out that he was not concealing them; they were simply more *personal*. 'One exhibits one's silver and crystal,' he'd say, 'but not one's shoes and socks. That doesn't mean that the latter are less important than the former.'"

Gwen approached the oil representing the blue-wing teals. "Owen Gromme," she said.

"Yes, they're all by Gromme," Jane said. "He was a very interesting man. He began his work as a taxidermist, actually. He worked at the Field Museum in Chicago and at the Milwaukee County Museum. Eventually he devoted all of his time to painting. Some of his more interesting work dealt with the birdlife in the Horicon Marsh. It's actually the largest freshwater cattail marsh in the United States—a nice day trip from

Madison or Milwaukee. The marsh is best-known for the Canada geese there, but Geoffrey told me that there were over 250 other kinds of birds that were common to the area. Geoffrey loved to go there. He'd never hunt, of course. Of the 30,000+ acres of the wetlands two-thirds are federal and a third state. You're only allowed to hunt in the state portion. And hunt they do. The cottage industries surrounding the marsh sell blind materials, decoys, camo outfits…they rent boats…you know you're getting close as you drive there because all you see are service industries and pictures of Canada geese."

"That's a long way from southern California," Gwen said. "Did he go there when he was a student at the University of Chicago?"

"No, he went there when he was at Madison."

"I didn't know he *had* been there," Gwen said.

"Oh yes, he left as a kind of protest."

"Protest? I thought your brother would be too conservative for that," Gwen said.

"Oh he *was* conservative," Jane answered. "This was during the late sixties and early seventies, the time when some conservative professors relocated because of their disappointment at the manner in which their universities' administrators handled *student* protests. Allan Bloom and Walter Berns left Cornell; they were also Straussites, of course. And Geoffrey left Madison. After they blew up Sterling Hall…"

60

St. Albans Road, San Marino

"What did you say?" Gwen asked.

"I said that Geoffrey left Madison after the radical students blew up Sterling Hall. There was actually a whole series of events at that time. First came the Dow riots and then the TAA strike and the bombing of Sterling Hall. The bombing weighed on him most heavily. The TAA strike was simply annoying, though for him its implications rose to the level of principle."

"The TAA?" Gwen asked.

"The teaching assistants' association, their union. They went out on strike over a host of issues. What most bothered Geoffrey was that they wanted unfettered control of the courses they taught. He saw that as a faculty responsibility, as, indeed, it was."

"Please tell me more about Sterling Hall," Gwen said.

"Of course. I dare say this all happened before you were born," Jane said. "Sterling Hall housed the Math Research Center, which was funded by the Army. They didn't do classified research, but they worked on problems that the military was anxious to see solved. The building also housed the physics department. The MRC was a prime target of the student radicals and a group of them simply took it upon themselves to blow it up. This was in 1970, August I think. They called first before detonating the bomb, but there was a young man inside who didn't receive the warning. He was a physics postdoc named Robert Fassnacht. He died in the blast."

"I know that it was historically significant," Gwen said. "Along with the Kent State shootings…"

"Yes, it was. Kent State happened in the spring. The two events together helped change public opinion about the war. What troubled Geoffrey was the utter irresponsibility of the Sterling Hall affair. The university hospital was just down the hill from Sterling Hall and the blast shattered windows, with shards of glass striking patients. The bomb was incredibly powerful. For all the students knew, they could have blown up half of the city. In fact, it took quite some time to discover the manner in which the bomb had been delivered, since the van which contained it was literally blown to pieces. He would not have approved of the bombing in any case, but the ignorant use of such a powerful device was very troubling to him."

"And what did the bomb consist of?" Gwen asked.

"Something very common," Jane said. "Nitrogen fertilizer and fuel oil."

Gwen was staring at her silently.

"What is it?" Jane asked.

"That's what was just used to blow up the Clinic," Gwen answered.

"Surely you don't believe that the events could be connected," Jane said. "That was over fifty years ago. And they used something similar in Oklahoma City, I think."

"I don't know if the events are connected," Gwen said, "but until today I didn't know that your brother had been in Madison in 1970. Coincidences are always interesting."

"Geoffrey was a junior faculty member at the time," Jane said, "which is to say he was largely invisible. He wasn't involved in any of the actions or any of the official decisions and he didn't get up on any soapboxes or do anything confrontational. He was conservative in his behavior as well as in his thought, after all. He simply wrote a private letter to his department chair, dean, and chancellor, explaining his feelings and his actions and then he moved on. His first book had been awarded the Bancroft prize the previous year and USC was very happy to hire him. Case closed. Or so I thought. I should have mentioned this earlier, but then it was all so long ago…"

"Don't worry about it," Gwen said. "I know now. That's what's important."

"How do you think the events could be connected?" she asked.

"I don't know. I'll have to check on some things," Gwen said. "This has been very helpful, Professor, and, again, I'm very grateful for the hospitality as well as the information."

"If there's anything else I can do, please don't hesitate to call me."

"I won't," Gwen said. "In the meantime I think you should be very careful. I don't want to frighten you, but I think you should keep in mind what's happening here. I'll ask the LAPD to work with all of the local authorities to protect you."

"Do you really think I'm in danger?"

"I think we are all in danger, until whoever's done this is brought to justice, Professor."

"Then you should be careful as well."

"I know. Thank you," Gwen said.

Gwen left by the rear door and worked her way west to Old Mill Road, returning that way to Huntington Drive. She got in her car and drove quickly through the back streets of San Marino until she was convinced that she had not been followed. Then she drove to her hotel, booted up her computer, studied a succession of downloads, checked her watch and phoned the Director.

61

The Langham Huntington, Pasadena

He was stuck on the Shirley Highway, driving from the Hoover Building to Quantico in rush hour traffic.

"Sir, it's Gwen Harrison." She could hear the engine noise, brake squeals, and horn honks in the background.

"What have you got, Gwen?"

"I think I may have something substantial, sir," she said.

"Really? Run it down for me."

"I just spoke with Jane Appleman. Her brother was at the University of Wisconsin when the radical students there blew up Sterling Hall. They used the same types of explosives as were used to blow up Denise's Clinic. Three of the students were caught and tried; two remain at large. Appleman may have encountered one of them, who then killed him to secure his silence. The last thing the fugitive would have expected was to encounter someone from the distant past who immediately recognized him. Gwen would have seen their pictures in Bureau records. There's the *connection*, or at least a plausible connection. The assumption is that she tried to make an arrest and was killed in the process."

"Wait, Gwen. Let's back up a sec. Run down the names for me."

"They called themselves the New Year's Gang. There were two brothers—Karleton and Dwight Armstrong—and a freshman named David Fine. All three were later captured. Until recently the Armstrong brothers were operating a bakery in Madison called the *Radical Rye*;

Dwight died in 2010. A fourth individual, Leo Burt, remains at large. It's clear that Burt was involved in the bombing. A fifth individual, Harold Bucher, also remains at large, but his role is less clear. He had been Burt's roommate. Both of them were on the crew team at the university. When Burt disappeared, so did Bucher. Neither have surfaced since.

"They were very successful in blowing up Sterling Hall--the building which contained the Army Math Research Center, which they saw as a key example of university complicity in the Vietnam war. A young physics postdoc was killed in the blast; that drew a great deal of attention. Prior to that operation they had attempted to blow up the Baraboo Ammunition Works. That effort failed. They actually tried to drop aerial bombs, but they didn't explode."

"That was a long time ago, Gwen—what, late 60's or early 70's?"

"August, 1970, sir, for the bombing of Sterling Hall."

"I remember Burt being on the Bureau Top Ten list, but I don't remember Bucher being there."

"There was a BOLO on him, linked with the Burt entry. There are pictures of both of them on the Bureau site now, but since Burt was removed from the Top Ten list in the 1970's there have been fewer public reports. The most recent account recorded a sighting in Oregon."

"The distance in time is tremendous, Gwen. Denise was an exceptional person, but she would have had to have a tremendous memory to make the connection between a decades-old photograph and a contemporary individual."

"I agree, sir, but you have to look at this from another angle…"

"Yes…" he said, his skepticism evident.

"The Top Ten list was implemented in 1950. There have been 500 names recorded during that time. However, 469 of those individuals have been apprehended or located. If you're a young and ambitious agent, hoping to make a mark, you might think about arresting one of the people on that list (or one of their key accomplices). Given the fact that the vast majority are already located, the remaining number is very manageable. Denise was very studious; I can imagine her working a list like this and preparing herself for the off chance that she might actually be able to collar one of them."

"That's pretty iffy, Gwen, but it's not implausible. I know that the Burt case was handled for years by some agents who have since retired. I'll see who's working each case now and get some photos to you that have been aged in various ways. I know that the L.A. reports so far have been of a clean-shaven individual, but it doesn't hurt to have multiple examples for witnesses to examine."

"That would be very helpful, sir. I think it would also be a good idea to have someone from the Milwaukee field office check the enrollment records at Madison. I'd like to know if Burt or Bucher took courses with Professor Appleman. Any connections among the three of them would be helpful."

"Yes, good idea. The problem is that they could have been in classes of six or seven hundred."

"Yes, sir, but maybe we'll get lucky and find out that one of them took a seminar or smaller class of some kind."

"We'll also check the newspaper morgues and see what kinds of pictures appeared there that Appleman might have seen."

"Yes, sir. There are two city papers—the *Capital Times* and the *Wisconsin State Journal* and two campus papers—the *Daily Cardinal* and the *Badger Herald*."

"The university won't like us rooting around in their records, but I'll do what I can to smooth the way. I'll also keep this as quiet as I possibly can."

"Thank you, sir. I'm doing the same at this end. As far as I can see, the local Bureau office is continuing to remain on the sidelines. I've had to let a few individuals know that I'm more than a curious bystander, but they wouldn't cooperate with me without some assurance that I'm working in an official capacity and have their interests at heart, along with the resources to provide for their security."

"Good. I know that there comes a time when you need to badge people. I'm counting on you to keep those times to a minimum."

"Yes, sir, and I'm taking precautions to keep my profile as low as possible when I move about interviewing people."

Gwen then brought the Director up to speed on Charles's injuries as well as his observations.

"The reports have been pretty consistent, even if they've been pretty generic. Statistically it makes sense anyway. The likelihood of identifying a suspect with grossly different features than the average is always remote. That's what *average* means. If you're right and we *are* dealing with one or more people who were athletes it would not be unexpected that they would look like athletes now—or at least appear to be reasonably well-preserved."

"I agree, sir. How soon do you think you can get me those photographs?"

"As soon as I can, Gwen. I realize that you've got three more hours in your day left than we have here. I'll post them on the private site, hopefully in an hour or two, depending on the availability of the investigating agents. And you let me know the minute they bear fruit."

"I will sir. Just one other thing…it appears that the perp used Denise's weapon to kill Detective Dearing."

"I know," he said. "We've sealed the information flow at this end. And Gwen…"

"Yes, sir."

"I don't need to tell you to watch your back."

"No, sir. I'm doing just that."

"Check out the front and sides from time to time as well."

62

The Langham Huntington, Pasadena

Gwen was pleased now that she had taken a room with a work station that included a printer. The Director would have multiple pictures of each suspect, some with facial hair, some without, some with receding hairlines or male-pattern baldness, some with fully gray hair, some with ballcaps. There would be varying depths of facial lines and varying numbers of age spots. One likely problem was the generic appearance of each man's face. Another variable was the possibility of plastic surgery, but such procedures are far more common in the movies than on the streets, where good surgery is very expensive and bad surgery is very noticeable. With the constant tweaking of identikit systems and the constant upgrading of image retrieval systems it was far easier now for law enforcement to stay ahead of the perps attempting to elude them.

While she waited to hear from the Director she called Frank and filled him in on her meeting with the professor's sister and her request to the Director. "How's Charles doing?" she asked.

"Charles is being Charles," Frank said. "He doesn't wince and he doesn't complain. He just lays there looking very impatient and anxious to get back on the street. He's still not ready for solid food, but he just asked for an extra cup of broth. That's probably a good sign. He's also completely alert now, in part because he doesn't hit his morphine button as often as most people would."

"I'll bring the pictures over as soon as I get them," Gwen said. "Maybe he'll recognize one of them."

"We'll be here," Frank said.

"Anybody suspicious come around?" Gwen asked.

"Not that we've noticed," Frank said. "I've got a couple men watching the most likely and least likely entry points. How about with you?"

"Not yet," Gwen answered. "I've been taking the long way around whenever I walk or drive and making it as difficult as I can for anyone to follow me."

"Good," Frank said. "We'll wait to hear from you."

Figuring that she had at least an hour and possibly two to wait, Gwen ordered some food from room service. Realizing that one meal would blow her full Bureau *per diem* she went for maximum calories and protein per dollar, choosing some braised short ribs and rigatoni with meat sauce. Some beer or red wine would have been a nice complement; too bad it was out of the question under the circumstances.

The presentation was very nice, with heavy silverware, thick cotton napkins, ice water with lemon slices, and every conceivable choice of sweetener and a full creamer of half and half to use for the 6-cup pot of high-test coffee she had ordered.

She was on the second cup when the email came in from the Director:

"See new site."

The site was not new, but the material was. The site was a nondescript electronic catalogue of plumbing supplies with heavily-passworded access and multiple filter systems for enhanced security. There were twenty-four pictures of the two suspects, all in formats small enough to be carried discreetly but large enough to show key features. The Director had also included full lists of personal data on each fugitive: last-known height, weight, and hair color as well as blood types (each was B). The Bureau had seven good fingerprints for Burt and six for Bucher.

Gwen printed out the six pages that contained them and then razor-bladed them into individual images and separated the Bucher pictures from the Burt pictures. As she sorted them she studied them carefully. She had a faint recollection of the Burt picture from a class at the Academy, but none of the presumably-contemporary images—of either of the individuals—looked familiar to her. She took two complimentary hotel envelopes from the desk drawer and slipped the Bucher pictures into the first and the Burt pictures into the second.

She then opened her suitcase and removed a silk scarf and light wool cap—elements of a rudimentary disguise that she would remove as soon as she was a few blocks away from the hotel. Anything that would temporarily change her appearance could be of potential use, on the off chance that someone was observing her movements.

She called the valet parking kiosk and they told her her car would be available in five minutes. The use of the service was mandatory; street parking within several blocks of the facility was carefully monitored and pedestrian traffic that did not involve dogs and athletic gear would have drawn immediate attention.

She also checked her weapon, pausing for a few moments to remind herself of the use that had been made of Denise's. Slipping it into her purse, and verifying that she had the two envelopes of pictures, she proceeded to the elevator, slipped on her sunglasses, arrived at the lobby, greeted the parking valet and was directed to her car, which was parked at the more distant edge of the semicircle, the closer spots being reserved for the Bentleys and Porsches that provided the preferred indication of the hotel's clientele to individuals who were arriving for check-in.

The cars were parked above a tapered curb and as she pulled out there was a slight bump as the rear wheels slid onto the pavement. She drove out onto Oak Knoll and headed north. Slipping through the commercial lots of South Lake she took off her scarf and cap and headed west toward the hospital, anxiously anticipating Charles's responses to the pictures of, potentially, his niece's murderer.

63

Huntington Hospital, West California Boulevard

When Gwen entered the ICU she was stopped by a plainclothes LAPD officer. She badged him, he waved her on and she proceeded to Charles's room. "Good security," she said to Frank.

"Larry Moore," Frank said. "Good man."

As soon as she appeared in Charles's doorway he began to scoot around in his bed, hitting the button that raised him into a sitting position. "What have you brought us?" he asked.

"Two possibles," she said, "in multiple versions." Gwen cleared the drink cups from Charles's table, slid it in front of him and put as many of the pictures on it as it would hold. Charles studied them and then asked to see the rest. Gwen watched his eye movements, hoping to see an indication of recognition, but there was none. Maybe he was giving them his inscrutable side.

"What do you think, Charles? Ringing any bells or setting off any alarms?"

"I wish I could say yes," he said. "Either one of them could have been the person I saw on Vermont, but neither of them jumps out at me. Not with any certainty."

"Look carefully, Charles," Frank said. "Take your time."

Charles turned to Gwen, smiled, and said, "He says that to all of his witnesses."

"It's still good advice," Frank said.

"I know and I agree," Charles said. "There is nothing in the world that would make me happier than being able to finger one of these characters for you, but I'm just not able to do it."

"That's all right," Gwen said. "Thanks for trying. We've got some other people who might be able to identify one of them. I'll start with the History chair. Frank, could you get me his home address?"

"Of course. Name?"

"Stuart Stern."

Frank went into the hallway and got on his cell phone.

"Where's Mary?" Gwen asked Charles.

"Staying with a friend," Charles said. "I wanted her to get some decent food and a good night's sleep. She'll be back in the morning."

"An *armed* friend?"

"Yes, Charles said. "You can never be too careful."

"I agree," she answered.

Frank returned in a little less than five minutes. "I want to go with you," he said. "I've got somebody coming here to spell me in a couple minutes."

"Sounds good to me," Gwen said. It would be easier to use Frank's connections to track down potential witnesses if he were with her rather than back at the hospital.

Fifteen minutes later Frank's captain, Carl Loram, appeared at the door. Frank introduced him to Gwen. He was thick in the hands and arms and barrel-chested, with a grey/white flattop—a younger Brian Keith but with rougher edges.

"I've heard a lot about you," Gwen said.

"Don't believe either of these two," Loram said.

"I appreciate your coming, Captain," Frank said.

"It's good all around," Loram said. "This is the only way I can really guarantee that Charles will stay put and not kick off an international incident."

"I'll need a few more minutes' rest; then I'll be ready," Charles said. "It's good to see you, Carl."

Stern lived in Pomona. "His wife teaches at Harvey Mudd," Frank said. "I already called him; he's home and he'll meet with us. It won't take us too long, driving against the traffic."

The nearly-thirty miles took just over forty minutes. Stern lived in a small craftsman just below the 10. The walls were crammed with books. One of the bedrooms—near the front door—had been turned into an office with back to back tables and back to back computers. It looked like a workshop for scholarly elves. The wife was not in evidence though the house still carried noticeable cooking smells, the scents of peppers, garlic and onions predominating.

"This won't take long, Professor," Frank said. "We have some pictures we'd like you to look at. They're older pictures of two individuals that have been aged electronically. We're not certain about the person's current appearance, but the different versions will give you some choices."

Gwen spread them out on the weathered cypress coffee table in the living room. Stern studied them carefully. He picked up two or three of them and looked at them under the light of a pole lamp. "I'm very sorry," he said. "I don't see anyone in these pictures that I recognize. The features are very common ones. It might be easier if there was something more... out of the ordinary."

"You're certain?" Frank asked.

"Quite certain," Stern responded.

"We understand," Gwen said. "Thanks very much for your time."

"Where is the other gentleman," Stern asked, "the one who was with you when we met at the library?"

"He wasn't able to join us," Gwen said.

"But now you're with a policeman," Stern said.

"A friend of the other man's family," Gwen said. "He's doing this as a personal favor."

"I see," Stern said. "Anyway, I'm sorry I couldn't be of help."

As soon as they got back in the car Frank called his office and asked for the home address and phone number of the Dean of the School of Social Work at USC. "Let's try the Denise connection," he said to Gwen. "If the Clinic was under the Social Work umbrella, he should know the people who came in contact with them."

It was actually a she: Elise Cobham. She lived in Altadena. "One of Charles's neighbors," Frank said. He called and got her husband, who gave him her cell number.

"I'm still at work," she said, "but I'm about to leave."

"We're in Pomona," Frank said. "Could we meet somewhere in Pasadena?"

"Yes, good idea. We'll arrive at about the same time."

"How about at the main parking lot of the community college--at Colorado and Hill? That's right on your way home. We just need a few minutes of your time."

"That's perfect," she said. "If the traffic gods cooperate I'll be there in about thirty-five minutes. I'm driving a maroon Avalon. I'll get as close as I can to the northwest corner of the lot."

"Very organized," Frank said to Gwen, as he clicked off his cell. "Very efficient."

Dean Cobham was already there when they arrived. She was talking on her cell phone and making notes on a small pad. Frank pulled in beside her, got out of the car, badged her and introduced himself and Gwen.

"Elise Cobham," she said. "How can I help you?"

"It's very simple," Frank said. "We've got some electronically-aged photographs of two individuals. The originals are about fifty years old, so we're making some calculated guesses on what the individuals might look like today. We'd like to know if you can identify either one of them."

Gwen handed the stack to her and looked through the windshield at her eyes, again searching for any indication of recognition. She didn't have to wait long. The dean shuffled through the stack of pictures quickly and pulled out two, each of the same individual. "This is Gerry Burke," she said. "This one here is closest to what he looks like now. What's he done?"

64

Pasadena City College, Colorado at Hill

"He hasn't been charged with anything at this point," Frank said. "We consider him a person of interest on several cases."

"Oh my God," the dean said. "The Clinic bombing…the murder of the nurse there?"

"Several cases," Frank answered. "Could you tell us about his duties."

"He heads up our IT team. There's a central IT office that deals with large issues and there are separate school and college teams. The central types walk around in suits and carry clipboards. They go to a lot of meetings. The college guys get dirty. They pull wire, open boxes, set up machines, troubleshoot, show the faculty how to turn on printers… that kind of thing. Each college or school has its own needs. Operating systems differ. Software systems differ. Gerry's job is to keep everything functioning and everybody happy. He's got some PC specialists and some Mac specialists who do the majority of the work. He fronts the organization and goes to a lot of meetings with the central types."

"And he would have spent a lot of time at the Clinic," Gwen said.

"Absolutely," the dean answered. "They're one of our largest units. He was probably there at least once a week, sometimes more often than that."

"Have you noticed anything about his performance that has changed recently?" Frank asked.

"Not really. He reports to my associate dean for operations. Just a sec." The dean picked up her cell phone and punched in a number on her speed dial. "Ken…Elise. Quick question. Anything out of the ordinary happening with Gerry Burke these days? Right…right…OK, thanks."

She clicked off and said, "Nothing noteworthy. Gerry's a bit of an odd duck. He's a techie, a cybernerd. They all speak their own language, you know, but my associate dean said that nothing's happened in his shop that's out of the ordinary. He said he hasn't talked to him in several days. Ken's got his hands full with the bombing right now."

"I understand," Frank said. "I'd appreciate it if you could call him back and ask him to keep that conversation confidential."

"I understand," the dean said. "I won't say anything either. I'm not sure where Gerry lives. Ken would know…"

"We can find that," Frank said, "but I'd appreciate your associate dean's full name and number in case we have to get back to him on anything else."

"Certainly," the dean said. "His name is Ken Beston. I'll jot down his number for you." She wrote the name and number on one of the post-it notes on her console.

"I appreciate that," Frank said.

"I put my own number on there too, just below his--in case you need to reach me again."

"Thanks again," Frank said.

They returned to Frank's cruiser. "See what I mean," he said, "very efficient." He paused for a second and then spoke again. "Unless I'm misremembering," he said, "Dave Carlow mentioned that he had talked to the IT guy. The guy had seen somebody hanging around the receptionist's desk, somebody who looked more like a workman than a client. Just a second…"

Frank flipped through his notebook. It took him a minute or two to find the passage in question. "Here it is," he said. "Average height… average build. Burke says he only saw him in profile. He thought he had on a colored tee shirt. He waffled on the hair color, didn't see a baseball cap, thought he might have had a soul patch."

"That hair thingie under the lower lip."

"Right," Frank said.

"It sounds to me as if he was describing himself. Not with the soul patch thing necessarily but with everything else being so generic. "Yeah, I saw a guy, but he looked like every other guy…like me for example.""

"Maybe it's the one instance in which he's told the truth," Frank said. He pulled his cell phone from its case and speed-dialed headquarters. "Art…Frank White. I need a current address for a Gerry Burke, Gerry with a G. Information technology specialist at USC. Yes, I'll wait…"

Frank wedged the phone between his shoulder and left ear, held his notebook open with his left hand and removed his pen from his pocket. A few minutes later he wrote down the address.

"Should be good," Frank said. "He just renewed his driver's license a month ago and this is the address he gave."

"Where?" Gwen asked.

"San Fernando, small street off of Brand."

"Long commute to USC," Gwen said, "*very* long."

"Maybe he's got something to hide," Frank said. "Maybe a lot of things."

65

The 210 in La Crescenta

As Frank drove across the 210 at a steady 70 they both worked their cell phones. Gwen called the Director, taking him out of his meeting at Quantico.

"I trust this is important, Gwen," he said.

"It is, sir. It's Harold Bucher. We just got a positive i.d. from the dean of the school that houses the Clinic. He's her chief IT person."

"So he would have visited the Clinic but not worked there regularly."

"Yes, exactly. He spoke to Lieutenant Dave Carlow just before the Clinic was blown up. I'm thinking the bombing was part prevention, part subterfuge. He decided he didn't want Carlow to mention his name to anyone and he wanted the LAPD to continue to believe that there was something important in the Clinic records, which are all little more than scorched confetti now."

"Keep the focus on one of their clients and keep it off of him. Makes sense, Gwen. What alias is he using?"

"Gerry Burke."

"I'll start running our own techs through our data bases. Gerry with a J or a G?"

"A *G*. This clarifies another thing, sir."

"What's that?"

"The theft of Clemmer's car. William Clemmer; Denise's supervisor."

"Yes?"

"Bucher was driving it when he shot Detective Dearing near the Police Administration Building. We had thought that it could have been stolen by a person who had walked into the Clinic, a client perhaps. I talked to Bucher's supervisor. He always traveled in a golf cart or van—a golf cart on campus when he was delivering computer hardware or just tooling around from building to building and a van whenever he was off campus. He couldn't have followed Dearing in the van because it has bright crimson lettering and a huge picture of Tommy Trojan on the side. He would have been identified immediately. He took the nearest car available and that was Clemmer's."

"Makes sense. Where are you now, Gwen?"

"On the 210, with Lieutenant White from the LAPD. Bucher's place is in San Fernando. We just passed La Crescenta."

"Be careful, Gwen; remember--this guy likes to use bombs."

"Yes, sir."

"I'll tell you what…I'll notify the Central California field office and tell them what's what. I'll tell them that you were in the area on another assignment, that this information just broke, and that you're in charge and in pursuit. That way you can call on them for any support you might need. I realize that the LAPD wants to take this guy down, but if he gets away the Bureau can be of help in trying to follow his steps and limit his options. He may already be feeling the heat and heading for the border."

"Thank you, sir."

"Keep me posted, Gwen."

"Will do, sir," she said, and clicked off.

Frank finished his call a few seconds later and clicked off as well. "We've got a S.W.A.T. team as well as a detail from the bomb squad," he said. "I don't want any of us to step on a trip wire or pass through a motion detector and light up the sky in the East Valley. They'll be coming in by chopper and positioning themselves before we get there."

"I trust that he won't hear them overhead," Gwen said.

"No," Frank answered. "They'll swing out and around and come in the back door. This guy is not stupid and we don't want to tip him off in any way. What did *you* learn?"

"I'm no longer undercover," she answered. The Director is letting the local field office know that we've identified Bucher and that I'm in pursuit. They'll help us in any way that they can."

"Good," Frank said. "They can also run interference for us with Homeland Security. After all, this guy is a domestic terrorist. He may not be wearing a turban or kneeling on a prayer rug, but they'll still want to take him down. As you know, we've got umpty-ump airports, train and bus stations, ports, marinas, islands, and a hefty border with Mexico. If he's already left they can help cast a wider net than we can."

"He's evaded capture for fifty years," Gwen said. "That's long enough; it's time for him to start sleeping in our house."

Bucher's home in San Fernando was a ramshackle cottage in an industrial district. It sat on a lot just slightly larger than a tattered picnic blanket. The grass had been neglected and what little land there was had reverted to desert, with a lot of weeds, a predominance of grit and a collection of loose paper and trash trapped by anything green that had managed to survive in the sand. Behind the house was a single car garage. The paint was flaking off of each structure and their roofs each listed off center.

"What a dump," Frank said. "I've seen rats that wouldn't live in buildings like this."

"I wonder which one contains the bomb lab," Gwen added.

They were standing fifty yards away in the shadows cast by a warehouse security light. "The porch looks like it was ready to be replaced about twenty or thirty years ago," Frank said. "I'm afraid our people might fall through it if they all step up on it at once. He probably comes and goes through the rear door. And that's probably not a problem since it doesn't look as if he entertains very much."

"There's a mail slot in the front door," Gwen said. She was using her pair of miniature binoculars. "The porch must be strong enough to at least support the mailman."

"Right," Frank said. "Maybe he knows which sections haven't been eaten by the termites or carpenter ants yet. What we'll do is encircle both the house and the garage. I don't see any light on in either one, but that doesn't mean anything. If he's been into suspicious activities for this long he's probably smart enough to black out the windows. I want the bomb squad guys to go in first and protect everybody else. If we've got the area encircled he's not going to go anywhere."

"Can I make a suggestion?" Gwen said.

"Of course."

"I think you should have at least one person stay by your cruiser. If he does somehow slip through he might have a vehicle stashed nearby and take off. It'd be good to have someone ready to follow him and coordinate with the choppers."

"Good idea. I take it that you probably don't want to play that role."

"Oh no," Gwen said. "I want to go in right after the bomb guys."

66

Brand Boulevard, San Fernando

The S.W.A.T. team reported that they had picked up some heat sources in the house, but that they could have been caused by light bulbs or pilot lights. There were none in the garage. The bomb squad said that there were no observable motion detectors or trip wires and that their dogs were not picking up any suspicious scents.

"We've got plenty of probable cause," Frank said to Gwen. "This guy's been eyeballed by a credible witness and identified as a known fugitive. We'll start by tossing in some stun grenades and some sting grenades with CS. If he's in there I want him softened up before any of our guys go in. I also want to see some sign of his physical presence before we commit."

Both structures were encircled and the teams switched from radio contact to hand and arm signals. Frank gave the go-ahead and the sound of broken glass was quickly succeeded by the sounds of the stun grenades and the bright flash which accompanied them. The rubber projectiles of the sting grenades pinged against the walls and the smoke from the vomiting agent seeped from the broken windows. "I wouldn't have wanted to live in there before," Frank said, "but I definitely wouldn't want to be in there now."

They waited and watched for a few seconds, but no doors opened, no windows shattered, and there was no gunfire or other response from either the house or the garage. Frank signaled the teams to go in and he and Gwen followed, their flak jackets and gas masks all in place.

Each building was cleared in a matter of seconds. The dust and smoke were dense but it was clear that Bucher was gone. The windows and the front and rear door were fully opened to allow the CS to dissipate. The head of the S.W.A.T. team was in the kitchen. "He was here recently, Lieutenant," he said. "There's milk in the refrigerator with a sell-by date of next Wednesday. There's also a pizza box with the tag still attached. It was delivered last night."

"Does he have a gas range?"

"Yes, sir, and a gas hot water heater and gas furnace in the closet."

"Pilot lights all on?"

"Yes, sir."

The bed was unmade, but the sheets and blanket were cool to the touch, as were the lightbulbs that survived the sting grenades. "Post some men outside," Frank said. "He may be on his way home now. I don't want him to drive up, see this activity, and leave. Put the men about a block away at obvious entrance and exit points. His car is a 2006 Explorer. Black. California license 317 JFT."

"What do you think?" Frank said. "It's pretty basic."

"Two bedrooms and a single bath, a kitchen from the 50's, a small living room with just enough floor space for a small table and two chairs," Gwen said. "And a lot of piles of junk. What's in the garage?"

"Let's find out," Frank said.

Two S.W.A.T. team members had opened the garage door and were standing just inside. The walls were bare wood, with that scorched look that comes with age. The garage itself was tiny, with just enough room for a small car. "He would have needed a giant shoehorn to get his Explorer in here," Frank said.

Just then an officer reported that they had found his car. "Where is it?" Frank asked.

"It's parked about 75 yards behind your cruiser, Lieutenant."

"So he must have been here as we were arriving," Frank said.

"Yes, sir."

"He couldn't get his SUV in the garage anyway," Gwen said, "so he left it out on the street in an inconspicuous location in case he needed to get away quickly."

"Right," Frank said. "He must have seen or heard something and taken off without it."

"Unless he has another vehicle," Gwen said.

"Nothing of record, unless he stole one," Frank said.

"Wait a second," Gwen said. "Look at this..." She pointed to a small set of brackets on the wall of the garage.

"What, a mountain bike or something?" Frank asked.

"Yes, and he could have exited from the door at the rear of the garage, the one leading to the house."

Frank quickly directed the choppers to take off and shine their searchlights throughout the area. "That seems like a long shot to me," he said, "but we can't afford to take any chances. He can't get very far on a bicycle but, unfortunately, he doesn't have to. All he needs is a place to hide the bike and begin eluding us on foot."

"Question," Gwen said. "This guy's a techie. Where's his computer?"

"Maybe he took it with him," Frank said.

"Let's have another look inside."

Another message came in from the S.W.A.T. team. "Lieutenant, we've got something interesting in his SUV."

"What's that?"

"Carpentry tools; expensive stuff. Also some hammers and nails."

"Don't touch anything," Frank said. He turned to Gwen and said, "Carpentry tools in his Explorer."

"No room for them in the house," she said. "That garage door could be opened by an enterprising ten year-old. They're valuable to him. Maybe incriminating too, but I doubt it. He discarded both of the hammers in the two murders."

"And if there are any 16 penny finishing nails they're probably too generic to identify."

"Right," Gwen said, "but it explains why he'd use those kinds of tools as weapons. He was waiting for his victims in his car or truck."

"Yes," Frank said. "Now what about that computer?"

They went over every inch of the house, opening drawers and cabinets. Nothing. "Wait a minute," Gwen said. "There was a router on top of the fridge. With a wireless system he could use a laptop anywhere. She hurried into his bedroom, checked under his mattress and then under his bed. Nothing but dust and grit. The dining table and chairs were solid, unupholstered wood. She hurried to the couch. The cushions were attached to the frame. "Lean it back," she said to Frank. He put his hands on the arm and back of the three-cushioned couch and pushed. Gwen was on her hands and knees. "With a guy like this I don't like to just start reaching around without seeing what I'm touching" she said, as she slid out a silver MacBook Pro. "The only new thing in the house," she said. "Feel it."

"Frank slid his hand across the base of the laptop. "It's still warm; we just missed him."

67

Elbert at Brand, San Fernando

Gwen ran outside to the garage, beginning at the back door and look-ing for tread marks from Bucher's bike. There were faint traces in the dust, between the footprints of the S.W.A.T. team and bomb squad. They led to the back of the lot and the remnants of a driveway that ran behind the cottages along the street. An occasional clump of cracked blacktop survived among the encroaching weeds. She began by checking the easterly path but found no tread marks at all. She had more luck checking to the west. The faint tread lines were replaced by deeper marks. Bucher had walked the bike initially, then mounted it once he was in the driveway.

She came to the adjoining street and found some symmetrical pieces of earth in the gutter—cast-off from the tire treads when they hit the uneven pavement. There was more in the center of the street and more, again, in the gutter on the other side. Bucher had ridden across the street and onto the driveway behind the set of cottages on the other side of the intervening street. This driveway had either been carefully maintained or been resurfaced more recently. The asphalt was dark and largely free of weeds working their way through the cracks. There were some brownish stains from seeping ground water but the initial tracks of the bike were clear. The farther she went down the driveway, however, the fainter they became and by the time she reached the next intervening street they were all but gone.

She flipped open her cell, called Frank, and told him where the tracks had dead-ended. He met her there a few seconds later in his cruiser. "Good eye," he said, "but now it's going to get tough."

The neighborhood consisted of a series of small commercial operations—street after street of garages with boutique blue collar businesses: auto upholsterers, butchers' supply houses, warehouses with stack after stack of splintered skids, plumbing supply outlets, a company that specialized in valves, small motor repair shops, and, occasionally, something slightly more upscale: a store that specialized in home wine and beer-making supplies and an antique clock repair store. The addresses all had a lot of letters and numbers in them.

"This is not just a honeycomb of places in which he might hide," Frank said. "It's a neighborhood filled with commercial vehicles. If I were him I'd find a dark corner to stash the bike and then jack one of the vans or half-tons. It's 7:17 now; nobody's coming back for over twelve hours. Citizens run out for bread or milk at all hours and notice if their car or truck's missing. If he steals a commercial vehicle he buys the whole evening and night. By the time the theft is reported he's in the redwood country or a restaurant in Phoenix. Check that--or working his way through Baja."

"Commercial vehicles have markings," Gwen said. "Easier to spot. I suspect that as soon as he's out of San Fernando he'd look for something less obvious. Something more generic—just like him. You are what you drive. He'll be in a Civic or Taurus."

"We'll reduce his options," Frank said. "My people are already notifying the airports, train and bus stations and border patrols. This guy's picture is going to be seen by more people than Brad Pitt's and Tom Hanks's."

"I'll contact the Bureau," Gwen said.

"Already done," Frank said. "I called personally. They already knew that you were on the case and liaising with the LAPD."

RICHARD B. SCHWARTZ

"Maybe a BOLO on any vans or commercial vehicles on the local freeways…"

"Already done," Frank said.

"How about used car lots and new car dealerships?"

"In progress," Frank said. "Throughout the valleys and the basin."

"That's a lot of territory," Gwen said.

"Yes, but we'll concentrate all available manpower for the next couple of hours. If he's going to make a move he'll have to do it quickly. He got out of here like a bat out of hell. He's not going to slow down now, not at the time when he's most vulnerable."

Gwen looked at him skeptically.

"What? Should I have said *person*power?"

"Don't be silly," Gwen said. "We may be thinking the obvious. He could also head for the mountains and lay low for awhile. Toss his bike in the back of the stolen truck or van in case he needs it later. Tour the woods. Find some people camping in a remote area. Cut their throats, leave their bodies in their tent and trade them vehicles. The site wouldn't draw attention until the decomp smells were strong enough to be noticed at a distance. Lots of decomp in the woods. That could take days. By then he's in Chicago."

"Or on a lake in Canada," Frank said. "We'll notify the state and federal park services and ask them to keep an eye out. They can warn people at the entry points."

"I hate this," Gwen said.

"What's that," Frank asked, "the feeling of powerlessness?"

"The waiting," she said. "Until somebody reports a missing vehicle all we can do is make phone calls and pray. Anyway…we'll do both. Besides, we've got a whole set of other options to pursue."

68

The 210 Southbound Ramp at San Fernando

"He's originally from Kenosha," Gwen said. "I'll get the Milwaukee field office to check out his remaining relatives and intercept any cell or landline messages coming in to them. We'll also keep an eye on their email. He should know our technical capabilities in this area, but he's desperate and he might still make a dumb move. He was on the crew team with Leo Burt. Those guys stay pretty close. We'll keep an eye on as many of them as we can find. The Burt family is always under surveillance, so he's unlikely to try to contact them. I wonder about old girlfriends. If he's casting around for possibilities he might try to contact an old college girlfriend, maybe even a high school girlfriend. We should also check with his supervisor, Dean Beston, and see if he knows anything about his friends in L.A. The members of his IT team might give us some help as well."

Frank took out his notebook and turned to the last page. The post-it note from Elise Cobham was there, with Beston's phone number. He turned it toward Gwen, who punched in the numbers on her cell. He picked up on the third ring and she explained the reason for her call.

"Elise gave me a headsup," he said. "I've been waiting to hear from you."

"What can you tell us about Gerry Burke?" Gwen asked. "His friends...acquaintances...anything?"

"As far as I know he isn't married," Beston said, "but I don't think he's gay. I'm not sure why I say that, but I don't think he is. Maybe just his demeanor…I know that sounds homophobic, but I'm just giving you my impressions, not trying to be judgmental."

"I understand," Gwen said. "Who did he hang out with?"

"I can't really say. *I* didn't socialize with him. He's a computer expert; I'm a counseling psychologist. He lives somewhere out in the East Valley; I live in Diamond Bar. I sometimes see him with members of his IT team, but that's at work. If we've got a PC problem he brings his PC person. If it's a Mac problem he brings the woman who handles Macs. They solve the problem and then they disappear."

"Good employee?" Gwen asked.

"He gets the job done," Beston said. "He's a little quirky sometimes, but IT people often are."

"What do you mean, quirky?"

"You know how they are. They have their own language for everything. They talk in shorthand. They look at you as if you're some kind of alien for whom they have to translate. Most of the time our problems come from arcane default settings. Something happens—a change in software, a power loss, whatever—and suddenly the computers are acting funny. The techs come in and reset them. This involves going through ten or twelve different screens. It's too complicated to explain to lay people, but it's simple to the techies. They solve your problem and move on. In the meantime they don't talk; they just point and click. They don't do the kinds of things that most of us do…you know, go to meetings, look at statistics, write reports…I guess the Central IT people do a lot of that, but the school and college people don't. They're like…I don't know…a combination of meter readers and witch doctors. They come in and out, work their magic, and leave. That kind of work…it changes the way you communicate. They're *quirky*. But I think they're all more or less that way. It's not a criticism of them; it's just the way they are."

"I understand," Gwen said. "Does your school ever have receptions, picnics, that kind of thing?"

"Yes. There's a fall reception and a spring banquet."

"Who would Gerry Burke bring to such events?"

"I can't really remember. There was no one special, if that's what you mean. I think he usually just came by himself. He'd sit with the members of his team, I guess."

"Anyone in particular?"

"Not that I remember. I'm sorry; I'm not being very helpful, am I?"

"We're just gathering information at this point, Dean Beston. We won't know what's important and what's not until we get farther into the investigation. I certainly appreciate your talking to me."

"I think you should talk to Sue Wang."

"Is she a member of his team?"

"Yes, she's his Mac person. I can get her number if you'd like me to."

"That would be very helpful. Thanks."

"I'm online anyway; let me go to the school's site…OK…here's the IT team…we don't put home numbers on the site, but we list cell numbers."

"Any idea where she lives in L.A.? Wang is a common name."

"I think she's over in Culver City somewhere. I heard her mention once that she was doing some freelancing for a film company there. She does computer stuff for films, you know, computer-generated image stuff."

"Yes, I do."

He gave her the number; she thanked him and clicked off. Her cell line rolled over to a message center on the first ring. Gwen asked Frank to check on her landline. He called in and held while they got it.

"It looks like she may have a little side business going," he said, his hand covering the base of the phone. He removed it when his man continued.

"I've got two numbers, Lieutenant," the officer said, "one for her apartment and one for her company. That's probably an answering service."

"Give me each of them, Bill. Slowly. I have to repeat them to someone who's writing them down…"

When Gwen called her she didn't pick up on the home phone, but a few seconds later she connected with her using the business line. Gwen told her that she needed some information on Burke; Sue Wang told Gwen that she was busy doing a little moonlighting but that she would be happy to help.

"Can you tell me if Gerry Burke has any close friends or acquaintances…the sort of people he would call if he was in a jam?"

"Hmmm," she said, "that's tough. We're all sort of loners, you know. I mean, why would we go into a business where we sit by ourselves in front of a screen and tap keys all day? Anyway, I don't think he's got a steady girlfriend or anything like that. You know, Gerry's older than he looks. He's pushing 70, I think. At that age you're set in your ways. You have your own schedule, your own routines…your own ways of doing things. I don't think he goes out very much. He sticks to himself. I saw him have lunch once or twice with a woman in the dean's office, but she left a couple years ago. Her name was Nancy. Schneider or Schneidhorst or something. German."

"Do you know where she went?"

"No, sorry. She did a lot of heavy duty wordprocessing. She'd freelance at night for the faculty…type their books, that kind of thing. She probably just got a better job somewhere or a job with a better commute. USC's a good place to work, but nobody wants to live around there, so you're pretty much stuck with a long commute."

"I understand," Gwen said. "Thanks a lot."

She clicked off and called Beston. "Snyder," he said, "not Schneider. She moved to…let me see…Oregon, I think. Not Portland. I want to say Corvallis. University town. I think she was going to finish her baccalaureate degree. I remember her saying that she wanted to go someplace quiet."

Gwen thanked him and got on the computer in Frank's cruiser. He was talking to his office again, checking on any possible leads on the vehicle or any reports of suspicious activities in remote forest areas or nearby commercial areas. It was probably too early to get any hits, but Bucher could have been in the Angeles Forest by now or in any number of used car or new car lots.

Gwen called the Milwaukee office, explained the case, and asked them to check out possible friends and relatives of Bucher in Kenosha. She also asked them to start checking on the members of Bucher's crew team. She then called the Portland office, told them about Bucher, and asked them to check on Nancy Snyder. They reminded her that there had been an alleged sighting of Leo Burt there a few years previously, but that it had never been confirmed.

She clicked off just as Frank did. By now it was dark as they drove south in silence, watching the white headlights in the northbound lanes and the red taillights in front of them, waiting for something, anything, to break.

69

The Langham Huntington, Pasadena

The next morning the reports came in from Milwaukee and Portland. Special Agent Mike Nolan called on his cell from the road in Wauwatosa at 8:15.

"Special Agent Harrison, Mike Nolan calling from Milwaukee. The SAC asked me to check on Bucher's people and get back to you."

"I appreciate that," Gwen answered.

"Unfortunately, there's not much. The parents split in the early seventies and the father moved to Florida. He died in the late eighties. The mother stayed in Wisconsin, but moved to Green Bay about fifteen years ago. We've run periodic checks on possible communications between her and her son, but we've always come up dry. She's very religious apparently and has had trouble with the fact that the New Year's Gang killed the young physicist when they blew up the building. They also tried to bomb the Baraboo Ammunition Works. In some ways that bothered her more."

"I was aware that they had tried to do that," Gwen said. "What in particular bothered the mother?"

"First off, Baraboo's not exactly the kind of place where they assembled ICBM's. It wasn't a huge facility full of engineers and scientists in white coats carrying clipboards and drawing down huge government salaries. At Baraboo they were basically making 7.62 mm NATO rounds—putting slugs into casings, that sort of thing. You're talking about a couple shifts of blue-collar workers, many living in trailers, scratching out a living doing work that could be done anywhere and *would* be done anywhere if they were taken out. Why bomb *them*? It wouldn't stop the war effort in any way and it would have killed a lot of defenseless people. That's what his mother thought, at least.

"He has a brother, Donald Bucher, who sells insurance in Minocqua. That's way up in the boonies, four and a half hours or so north, on Lake Tomahawk."

"Is that near the old Dillinger hideout?" Gwen asked.

"That's about another half hour—Manitowish Waters," Nolan said. "I know what you're thinking. We thought so too—this would still be the perfect hideout, even for your modern-day fugitive. Loons, walleyes, deer flies, Bucher and Burt. Didn't pan out. The brother's a straight arrow. Decorated Vietnam vet. Nothing like Harold. We checked him out anyway and monitored for possible communications with his bomber brother, but we didn't turn anything.

"There was a high school girlfriend named Donna Wills. She's living in South Carolina. Teaches accounting at a community college… just about ready to retire. No contact with Bucher since the sixties. He had a couple dates in college but nothing significant as far as we could determine. His closest friend on the crew team was Burt, but each of them actually drifted away from the team when they got more interested in politics.

"We *did* find one interesting tidbit, however, and it's something that confirms one of your other suspicions."

"What's that, Mike?" Gwen asked.

"We checked on Appleman's classes at Madison. Had to dig the old enrollment and grade sheets out of the archives. He never had Leo in class but he had Harold. Twice. First for a survey course with a cast of thousands and then for an advanced course. He got an A in the first one; that may have encouraged him to try Appleman again."

"How'd he do the second time?"

"Got a WF—the semester right before the bombing of Sterling Hall."

"What's a WF, Mike?"

"Withdrew, failing."

At 10:12 she received a call from the Portland SAC, Bill Drew. He was working from the notes of Special Agent Carol Ponder, who had emailed them before responding to a local emergency.

"OK if I call you Gwen, Special Agent Harrison?"

"Absolutely."

"I'm Bill Drew. I asked one of my agents to check out Nancy Snyder and I just got her report. I'll run it down for you. I don't think you're going to need to take too many notes."

"Thanks, I appreciate it," Gwen said.

"Nancy Snyder—DOB 10/28/69, brown hair, blue eyes, approximately 135 pounds. She was working at USC, where she overlapped briefly with your suspect. Relocated to Corvallis two and a half years ago, where she completed her bachelor's degree in something called New Media Communications. From there she went to Portland to work for a company that does websites. Now she's doing communications for Ponzi."

"The winery, not the scheme?"

"Yes. Good operation. Good wine. She's been there about six months. She does some writing, some web design, graphics…that sort of thing."

"Any recent communication with Bucher that you know of?"

"No, none at all. Nada. Actually, Special Agent Ponder also had some interchanges with the Central California field office. They couldn't find *any* records of communications between the two of them when they were each at USC. Her guess was that they might have had a spontaneous lunch or two but there wasn't anything serious going on between the two. I called Ms. Snyder a few minutes ago and asked her about the relationship. She remembered the guy's first name being Gerry but she wasn't able to recall his last name. She said that he fixed her computer once and they had lunch afterwards. She paid, as a thank you because he came out right away to help her. He said he'd pay the next time. He did and there wasn't a third time. My impression is that this was all very informal. He'd drift in and out of peoples' offices, helping them with their IT issues. Everybody knew him as the IT guy, but nobody really *knew* him, if you know what I mean."

"I do," Gwen said. "That makes sense to me."

"Special Agent Ponder is going to do a face-to-face with her tomorrow. If that leads anywhere we'll certainly let you know, but at this point we're not optimistic."

"What about that Leo Burt sighting from several years ago?" Gwen asked.

"Unconfirmed," Drew said. "Not beyond the realm of possibility, of course. Lot of rain, lot of fog, lot of pine forest; lot of places to hide."

"Lot of tourists coming and going," Gwen said. "People don't pay too much attention to unfamiliar faces turning up."

"That's true," Drew said. "Especially along the ocean and through the wine country. There's kind of a circuit. People drive up and down the coast—when the fog's not too dense; they taste wine and they go to the Tillamook factory and taste cheese. Then they fly back home. Easy to be anonymous if you stay with the tourists. Otherwise you'll draw attention."

"I know you'll let me know if he surfaces there," Gwen said.

"We will indeed," Drew said. "First we'll take him down, then we'll chain him up, then we'll frog walk him to a cell. After that we'll call, first thing."

"Wish I could be there for the whole process," Gwen said.

"Me too. In the meantime I'm afraid you'll have to pursue other possibilities," Drew said.

Gwen clicked off and got a glass of ice water. She realized that she needed to make another call, but took a brief break first. As she returned to the desk near her window and reached for her cell phone there was an unexpected knock at her door. She had finished her room-service breakfast and had already returned the tray. She picked up her weapon, walked across the room and reached for the knob.

70

The Langham Huntington, Pasadena

She looked through the peephole and was surprised to see her visitor standing there. She opened the door quickly and ushered him into the room.

"Charles, I don't want to sound like your mother but you know that you should be in the hospital."

"You think so?" he asked. "I'm not able to do much good there."

"Sit down," she said, pointing to the overstuffed chair next to the desk. He was supporting himself with a cane and carrying a brown leather bag with his other hand. His face was still puffy, though some of the swelling had gone down. The stitch marks were still evident.

"I can walk without the cane," he said, "but I want to give the leg a little relief so it can heal more quickly. It's just a hairline break. The surgeon put a screw in it that seems to be working. There's very little pain."

She could see the outline of the leg brace through his slacks. "I appreciate the visit," she said. "Does anybody know that you've left the hospital?"

"Oh yes, they made me sign a few dozen forms, releasing them from liability."

"Does Mary know?"

"Yes, she knows."

"And Frank?"

"Yes."

"And do they approve?"

"I wouldn't go that far."

"And do they know that you're here?"

"I wouldn't say that either. They know that I'm doing my best to recuperate in my own way."

"And that's by helping me find Denise's killer."

"Exactly."

"And what's in the bag, Charles, a small arsenal?"

"Just a few tools that might be necessary."

She reached for the zipper on the bag. "Do you mind?" she asked.

"It's just a few things," he said. "I don't mind."

Inside was a plastic bag with several sets of underwear and socks and a minimal collection of male cosmetics—toothpaste and brush, soap, scent-free deodorant, shaving cream and razor, and some ointment to put on his incisions. Underneath the plastic bag was a .357 magnum, a .45 automatic, assorted ammunition, a roll-up canvas case with an assortment of knives, and a piece of piano wire strung between two oak handles. "How are you going to use this with one hand?" she asked, holding up the latter weapon.

"That always comes along," he said. "Think of it as something like a lucky gold piece."

"So what's the plan, Charles?"

"Very simple, Gwen, if you're comfortable with it…"

"Yes…?"

"You track this man and when we find him I'll kill him."

"Has the virtue of simplicity," Gwen said.

"I thought so too," Charles answered. "I'm sure that he's running for deep cover somewhere. That's almost surely beyond the boundaries of the LAPD, but the FBI can go places that they can't go, especially now that it's a true federal case."

"And you think I can find him?"

"I *know* you can find him. You may need a little help from your friends, but *your* friends have a very big computer and a lot of other things that could come in handy."

"I don't think it's going to happen quite that way," Gwen said. "They'll be there to help, but they're going to be occupied with a whole set of institutional protocols. They're going to be checking ingress and egress terminals; they're going to be checking borders; they may even set up some highway checkpoints. And they're very good at that. But they're not going to catch him that way. He's smart enough to know what they'll do, so all of their efforts will result in his having to find a different route and a different way. That's still important, but it's all that they're going to be able to do. They've had nearly fifty years to find him and they haven't done it. At this point what they'll be doing is simply limiting his options."

"We call it *canalizing*," Charles said, "setting things up so the only available route is in the sights of your automatic weapons, tank guns and artillery pieces."

"Not as easy when the battlefield's this big, Charles."

"I understand," he said. "That's why I came here. We've got to get inside his head. That's a complicated trip and I just know that you're the person to find the right map."

"Thanks," she said. "As a matter of fact I was just about to make a call when you appeared at the door."

"So you're willing to let me join you, then."

"I'm concerned..." Gwen said.

"About what?"

"I don't want to be the one to tell your wife and family that you won't be making it back, but..."

"But?"

"But nobody's had to make that call yet and I figure if you're along they might not have to make that call about me."

"That's a fact," Charles said. "I may be a little rag-tag at the moment, but even on a bad day I can usually hold up my end. Besides, I'm motivated on this one…"

"I know you are, Charles. So am I. We may make an odd pair, but if I was Harold Bucher I'd feel my muscles clenching up and some hot breath on the back of my neck."

"And then maybe my lucky piece around his throat…" Charles said.

V

BLOOD ON THE TALL GRASS

71

The Langham Huntington, Pasadena

As she reached for her cell phone it rang. It was Frank. "Is Charles there?" he asked.

"Yes," she said.

"And barely ambulatory?"

"Yes."

"But saying it's only a flesh wound."

"Yes, more or less."

"And he wants to tag along with you…"

"Yes."

"Does he have his little brown bag?"

"Yes."

"I wouldn't try to take it through any metal detectors."

"Right."

"This is all against my better judgment," he said.

"I understand."

"Anyway, I've got something else to tell you. We think we've got a lead on Bucher. A van was stolen from a small printing shop in San Fernando. It turned up this morning in Azusa. There were no fingerprints that matched Bucher's, but it appears to have been stolen last night. The owner drove home in his personal car yesterday at noon, and no one nearby reported any suspicious activity in the company lot during the day, so it was probably taken after dark. It's rare that a vehicle would be abandoned this quickly unless some kids had taken it to joyride and driven it until the tank was empty. The tank on the van was half full."

"Lots of car dealers in Azusa."

"Right. That's next. The Toyota dealer—the one right above the freeway--reported the theft of a new Camry."

"What color?"

"Black. Technically, 'Midnight Black Metallic'."

"It doesn't get much more generic than that," Gwen said. "Metallic silver is probably a more common color these days, but black disappears in traffic, especially at night. If I were him I'd drive it to another big dealership and trade it for the same kind of car in a different color. Those lots have hundreds of cars. So long as the markings look right and the row of cars is full the salesmen are unlikely to get suspicious. Until they're actually ready to sell they're not going to check the registration number against their inventory records. The thing he'd want to do is razor blade the dealer's sheet off of the last car stolen and glue it to the window of the car from Azusa. Small hassle, but it could buy him another day or so while we look for a black car. If the dealer's sheet included information on color he'd need to smudge that in some way."

"Good thought," Frank said. "I'll have somebody warn the local Toyota dealers that he might pull something like that."

"The double theft suggests that he's going on a road trip," Gwen said. "If he was just trying to get to a local airport or other terminal he could drive the van and leave it nearby. Was there any lettering on the side of it?"

"No. It was a simple white Econoline."

"Year?"

"2012. Showing its age, but it would have provided reliable transportation."

"He's planning a long trip, not a quick milk run. The van could draw attention. They're used for daytime pick up and delivery jobs. They'd raise suspicions if they were being used for personal transportation. How many do you see parked outside motels, for example?"

"You might see them at camp sites," Frank said.

"True, but the hardcore camper probably wants something that's a step or two up from a delivery van."

"Right."

"He's thinking reliability, gas mileage, and an inconspicuous vehicle. If I'm him I've got to go with the Camry."

"But where is he headed?"

"Harder question," Gwen said. "Let me think about it a little. I'll let you know as soon as I turn anything."

"And you're taking Charles along for the ride?"

"Yes," Gwen said.

"On balance, I probably would too."

"Against your better judgment?"

"Desperate situations call for desperate measures."

"I agree," Gwen said, and clicked off.

"He advised you to leave me here, didn't he?" Charles asked.

"Not exactly."

"Good. I'll take that as a no," Charles said. "Now let's get back to the business of getting inside this punk's head."

"My thoughts exactly," Gwen said, checking her notes and punching in a series of numbers on her cell.

"Hello, this is Special Agent Gwen Harrison; could I have the AD's executive assistant?…Thanks…Hello, this is Special Agent Gwen Harrison; I'm calling about the Harold Bucher case. Has that been assigned to the Criminal Division or the Counterterrorism Division?…Thanks. Could you bounce my call to his EA?…Thanks…Hello…is it Jeanne? Gwen Harrison. Do you know if the SAC's been briefed on my involvement in the Bucher case?…Good. I'm sure you're all over this already, but I'd appreciate anything you have on his financial records— credit cards, bank accounts, anything at all in regard to recent activity and any longer-term stuff that might give us a lead on where he might go from here. Thanks, I know it's a long shot, but you're better set up to check than I am. Here's my cell number…"

She clicked off and turned to Charles. "He can't be completely independent of public records," she said. "Not if he wants to get paid by USC. Places like that will want to wire his pay directly to a bank or checking account and they'll have to take out Social Security and Medicare as well as state and federal taxes. Obviously he's cooked up the new identity, but he'd still want to keep as low a profile as possible. I'd be surprised if he had any credit cards. He's strictly pay-as-you-go. My guess is he's got his money in the USC credit union or some other place that's a smaller target for federal auditors than a big-time bank or S&L. As I said, this is a long shot, but you have to check."

She picked up her phone again. "This is more likely to lead somewhere," she said, checking her notes and punching in a new set of numbers.

72

The Langham Huntington, Pasadena

"Mike, Gwen Harrison. How are things in Milwaukee?"

"Nothing new, Gwen. What can I do for you?"

"Bucher's on the move. We think he stole a commercial van in San Fernando and then traded it for a Camry in Azusa."

"More anonymity," Nolan said.

"Right. We figure he's off on a road trip. When people are on the run they go where they're most comfortable, some place they've been before, some place that they know will work as a hideout."

"I agree," Nolan said. "You want me to root around some more in his past, see where the family went for vacations, that sort of thing."

"Exactly. It would help if you could check with the people in Madison, too. See if he did junior year abroad or some kind of exchange program. Maybe he was out in the boonies somewhere in Latin America, for example."

"Got it," Nolan said. "I'll be back in touch."

Gwen turned to Charles. "Any ideas?"

"Not really. I agree with you about the homing instinct. He'll go somewhere he's comfortable."

"Maybe his family had a favorite spot," Gwen said. "I'm thinking something like Door County—that peninsula that goes into Lake Michigan. Sturgeon Bay, up around there."

"Crowded in the summer, mostly deserted in the winter, I'd think,"

Charles said. "I've logged a little time in Detroit visiting relatives; that's cold enough for me. Up in Wisconsin you're talking 40 below and a mountain of snow and ice. Still, he might be comfortable there."

"Right. People tend to go back to the same places. You get a feel for the geography after awhile. And the hidey-holes."

"The junior year abroad may be a long shot," Charles said. "Things were pretty heated on the campuses in those days. Somebody political would probably stick around. Afraid he might miss something if he headed off to a foreign country."

"Unless he was doing an internship with the Sandinistas," Gwen said. "Maybe he got radicalized abroad."

"Definitely worth considering as a possibility," Charles said.

"Are you still comfortable in that chair, Charles?" Gwen asked.

"I feel fine," he said. "You don't have to worry about me."

"I'm not trying to coddle you," she said, smiling. "I want you to be in top-notch shape when we're in the field."

"If you don't mind, I could move between the chair and the bed from time to time, get the leg into different positions."

"Go ahead," she said. "How about the arm?"

"It's tender," he said. "I can't count on it anytime soon, but I can do a lot of things with my left hand."

"Shoot?"

"No problem at short range."

"Use a knife?"

"Of course."

"Did you have breakfast?"

"I don't usually eat much for breakfast."

"You're supposed to be on the mend, Charles. Hospitals give you pills and bed rest, not quality calories. How about some bacon and eggs?"

"That's very thoughtful," he said.

"Here they bring it with a flower and an orange slice twisted into a fancy shape."

"Better still," he said.

"I'll get us some more coffee too."

Nolan called back in an hour and fifteen minutes. Charles was still working on his breakfast. "They weren't regular vacationers," he said. "At least not according to the mother. She said they went to Washington, D.C. once and to California and Disneyland. Their only repeat vacation was to Lake Tomahawk. Bucher's brother liked it so much that he settled there after he retired from the military, but Harold was pretty young when he was there the first time and the second—when he was around 10—he broke his leg and spent most of the vacation on a porch chair."

"How about junior year abroad?" Gwen asked.

"Nope, sorry. He'd drop in and drop out from semester to semester so he was technically what they call a rising junior at the time of the bombing."

"What did he study, besides history?" Gwen asked.

"I don't know that he studied anything in particular," Nolan said. "He wouldn't have had to pick a major until the fall of 1970 and by then he was on the run."

"Right," Gwen said. "Could you give me the phone numbers of the mother and brother and then give them a headsup that I'm going to call them."

"No problem," Nolan said. "I'd be happy to. Maybe you can pry something out of them. They're both still pretty angry."

"I understand," Gwen said. "And how about a high school and college transcript? Could they be sent to my phone?"

"I don't know about that," Nolan said, "but they could probably fax them to you. They may require a warrant. If so I'll get them one."

"Much appreciated," Gwen said, and gave him the fax number for the work station in her room. As she hung up there was a knock at the door. "I didn't ask them to pick up the tray," she said.

73

The Langham Huntington, Pasadena

Gwen looked through the peephole and saw the person standing with her index finger across her lips. She nodded in the direction of the stairs and Gwen said to Charles, "Excuse me a minute, I'll be right back."

They took the rear stairs to the lower level at the north end of the building. The empty stairwell linked with the dressing rooms and snack bar just beyond the pool.

"Elizabeth," Gwen said, "I didn't expect to see you here."

"The Director told me where you were staying and I knew that Charles White was with you. I didn't want to involve him without speaking with you first."

"How did you know I was with Charles?"

"I heard you address him," Elizabeth said. "I was standing outside the door for a few seconds before I knocked. Here, I've brought you something," she said, reaching into her purse and removing a silk-encased object. It was cylindrical in shape and approximately six inches in length.

"They're designed to look fashionable as well as functional," Elizabeth said, "the sort of thing a society lady could take to the opera as well as to the bird sanctuary."

Elizabeth untied the strings enclosing the object and unrolled the silk case. Inside was a set of fold-up binoculars, which Elizabeth opened and snapped into place.

"Chichi birding glasses," Elizabeth said. "Standard *Leica* Ultravid, at least in appearance. Lightweight, 8X, waterproof, leather-clad rather than rubber-coated. Very upscale, with a list price around $1900. This set's been modified. If you put your finger over the *Leica* logo and apply pressure you access its additional features. There's no special feel; it doesn't click or depress, so you're not aware of the capability or the modification unless you've been briefed. After you've applied pressure for approximately six seconds the features become available. The choices appear as you look through the lenses and you push on the top or bottom of the logo to make selections. The range increases dramatically; you have night-vision capability and you can use the binoculars as you would a parabolic microphone to pick up distant sounds. It's like a super hearing aid. You should practice with it before you use it in the field. It also includes a homing device. If you open the binoculars without holding your finger on the logo the device emits a new signal."

"So if they fall into someone else's hands and they check them out, you would know," Gwen said.

"Yes, exactly. With the homer we'll know where you are at all times and if they fall into someone else's hands we'll know that something's wrong. They're new to the Bureau inventory, but the Director authorized us to let you have a pair. We know you may find yourself in a difficult situation and we want you to know that we'll be able to pick up the trail if you're unable to continue."

"I appreciate the euphemisms, Elizabeth," Gwen said. "And I appreciate the help. These could come in handy. Any new developments on your terrorism case?"

"No. There's still every indication that our subject is unaware of our tag. He continues to plot and scheme but there's still no evidence of any connection between his activities and Denise's death. We intercepted some email traffic that indicates that his group sees her death as random violence—the sort of thing that's common in our infidel culture."

"So they're paying attention to it."

"Oh yes, they're always very jumpy and suspicious. They know that she provided one of them with medical services and they immediately sat up and took notice when her death was reported. Our read is that they had nothing to do with her death, but that their take is that if she was not their friend whoever killed her *is*. Anyway, they're not—to our knowledge—pursuing it, so we believe that you're on the right track in your investigation. And Gwen," she said, changing her tone slightly, "you know that we want you to succeed."

"Thanks," Gwen said. "And I appreciate your keeping an eye on me."

"With satellite support we can locate the binoculars to within a few square meters. Getting somebody there quickly, should you need them, would depend on your location. It would vary between a few minutes and, approximately, three quarters of an hour at the outside."

"That's reassuring," Gwen said.

Elizabeth took her through the uses of the device one more time and then left, walking behind the pool in the direction of the main building. Gwen returned to her room and briefed Charles.

"Nice tool," he said. "Could have used it on a number of occasions."

"Right," Gwen said. "Now I've got to call the Buchers."

The older brother, Donald, confirmed what she'd learned from Mike Nolan. The Buchers were not big vacationers. "We'd have an outing every now and then," Donald said. "We went to a Packers game every couple years. My brother was very young and usually bored, frozen, or both. We didn't have a lot of money and we weren't into large family affairs. A big deal for us was a dinner at *Karl Ratzsch's*, the German restaurant in Milwaukee. My brother would complain about the menu and want a hamburger. My father would get drunk. This wasn't the world according to Currier and Ives or Thomas Kinkade."

"I understand," Gwen said. "How about closer to home? Was there any place that your brother used to play that was private or remote—someplace wooded, e.g., or someplace that was abandoned?"

"You mean like an old quarry for swimming or something like that?"

"Right. Any place that he might return to now. A place where he'd feel comfortable, a place where he knew his surroundings and could settle in for a while."

"I really don't know of any," Donald said. "As you know, I'm older than my brother. By the time he was old enough to go anywhere beyond our backyard I had already left. When he was 12, I was in Basic Training at Ft. Benning. My mother might know."

Gwen thanked him, clicked off, and called Mrs. Bucher. Her number was busy, so Gwen had a cup of lukewarm coffee and waited. Charles was lying across the bed; his eyes were closed and he appeared to be resting comfortably.

Ten minutes later Gwen tried again and connected. She introduced herself to Mrs. Bucher and asked her the same questions she had asked Donald. The responses were brief but they squared with those she had received from him.

"How about any local places where Harold might have played, Mrs. Bucher? Woods? Quarries? Remote sites of one kind or another?"

"He and his friends used to play on some property south of us. It was an old dairy farm. The main house and barn had been bulldozed, but there was a farm pond. Kids would swim in it in the summer and slide on it when it was frozen in the winter. I told him not to go there, but I know that he did."

"Were there any woods nearby, or anything that would provide cover and concealment?"

"I think there were some trees," she said, "but none of that's there anymore. I go back every now and then. It's all changed. There's a discount store, a strip mall and a motel. A couple fast food places. They've been there for years."

"Would your son know that?"

"I don't have any idea what he knows," she answered. "If he can use the internet he could figure it out."

"True," Gwen said. "Was there any place, any place at all that we haven't discussed, a place that he might be familiar with and return to—some place where you might have vacationed, some place that you might have visited? Maybe a relative's place or a friend's?"

"I'm sorry, but no. You've got to realize…"

"What's that, ma'am?"

"It's not that I wish him any physical harm, but my son…I hate to have to say this…he's been dead to me for years. I don't understand what he did and I don't understand why he hasn't taken responsibility for it. He's a criminal. That's terrible to say about your youngest child, but that's what he is. He's a criminal."

"Thanks, Mrs. Bucher. I appreciate your talking to me."

"I'd like to ask you not to hurt him if you can help it," she said, "but the wages of sin are death and I know that you have to do what you have to do. He's committed crimes, then and now, I assume, or the FBI wouldn't be calling me like this. It's all a great shame. At the time there was a lot of talk about the boys who blew up that building. Local people thought it was done by outsiders, radicals, that sort of thing. Everybody was surprised to find out it was done by local kids and nobody could figure out why. We couldn't understand. *I* still can't understand. Our family wasn't anything to write home about, but how many are? One thing's for sure; we never brought up our kids to blow up buildings and kill people."

"I don't think you should blame yourself, Mrs. Bucher," Gwen said.

"I don't, Agent Harrison," she said. "I just don't understand it. At his age he should be enjoying his grandchildren, not hiding from the FBI. But I guess he's got reason to, and it's sad."

74

The Langham Huntington, Pasadena

Forty minutes later she got a call from Mike Nolan. "The transcripts should be here soon," he said. "They're scanning them and sending them as email attachments. I've given them a secure address. As soon as I get them I'll bounce them to you."

"Much appreciated, Mike," Gwen said.

"I don't expect to see any good conduct certificates," he said.

"No, me either. Back then they'd probably call it *deportment*," she said.

"Yes, well, his was probably bad. Or at least it didn't improve over the years."

"Right. I'll sit tight. Thanks again."

She clicked off and asked Charles if he needed anything. He said no.

"How are you feeling?"

"Better by the minute," he answered.

"*Better's* a relative term. You didn't have anywhere to go but up."

"That's a fact," he said, "but I *do* feel better. Look here." He raised his right arm, not wincing despite the weight of the cast. "And how about this?" He wiggled the fingers of his right hand and then made a fist. "The good thing about the cast is that I could use it as a club, if needs be. I don't have a whole lot of mobility with it, but it's deceptive. A man sees somebody in a cast, he figures that the person's incapacitated, an easy mark. He doesn't think about catching that cast across the bridge of his nose or the elbow point in his mouth or eye. I could be seriously *misunderestimated.*"

Gwen smiled.

Fifteen minutes later her laptop beeped and she opened her email. The transcripts came as separate attachments. She opened the high school document first.

"Interesting," she said. "He went to a Catholic High School. Somebody there should have slapped some sense into him. Standard college prep curriculum. Two years of Latin. Wow, the good old days. Then he switched to French. A lot less Spanish in those days. Algebra I and II, Trig, Plane and Solid Geometry, no Calculus. A lot less common then than now, I think. English, History, Civics. Religion (probably didn't pay attention in those classes), Chemistry and Physics, but he dodged Biology. He took Typing instead."

"Practical," Charles said. "If you could type you could always get a job. If you could type in the Army you'd spend your time in the day room rather than in the field. Had to type a lot of forms but didn't have to walk through as many swamps."

"Grades are pretty good. Not like he'd be bound for Caltech or Princeton, but respectable enough. There's also a notation about extracurricular activities. He was on the Student Council. Fancy that."

"Political," Charles said. "Probably went to Boy's State, pretended to run the government. Made him want to do it full time later."

"Doesn't say so," Gwen said, "but I wouldn't be surprised if you were right. Nothing about Crew. Most high schools wouldn't have that, even if they were sitting on one of the great lakes. It says he ran Track and Field for three years and played basketball for two."

"Could help us," Charles said. "He might have blown out his knees and switched to Crew as a result. He'd still need leg strength, but he wouldn't need to pivot and stretch in the same ways. He's kept the weight off over the years, but sometimes athletes' bodies have taken a lot of early abuse that comes back to haunt them later. Whereas, an old infantryman...a real gravel agitator...he has the advantage because walking is the best exercise after swimming."

Gwen smiled again. "Let's check out his days as Joe College," she said, clicking out of the first attachment and opening the second.

"Well," she said, "he just keeps surprising me. He actually went to the University of Wisconsin-Parkside for a semester and then transferred to Madison. Generic curriculum at Parkside: English, History, College Algebra, Sociology, and more French. All of the credits transferred. Then more of the same at Madison. English, History, Sociology, still more French...French was the language of diplomacy once upon a time—not part of *his* career path."

"He'd rather blow things up than talk," Charles said.

"Right. He finally took Calculus at Madison. Got a C+. Then it looks as if he got off track. He took a course in film and a course in Comp Lit."

"What's that?" Charles asked.

"I'm not sure," Gwen said. "I don't think they've figured it out for themselves yet. Well, this is odd..."

"What's that?"

"He took something called Physics for Poets and then Geology."

"That *is* odd," Charles said, "the hippie course, then the hard science."

"Very hard," Gwen said, "with all those rocks. He must have really liked it though."

"How so?" Charles asked.

"Because he took a second course in it and then went off for the summer to a field camp run by the University of Wyoming. That's *very* interesting."

75

The Langham Huntington, Pasadena

"Geography was my thing," Gwen said, "but I took a sequence in Geology. Wyoming is about as interesting as it gets, geologically speaking."

"That's your land too," Charles said.

"Well, my grandparents' more than my immediate family's," Gwen said, "but it's not unfamiliar to me. Let me check on this some more."

She googled the University of Wyoming and their program in Geology, now Geology *and Geophysics*. Charles rested his arms across his chest and waited while she worked.

"These are old programs," she said. "There were people at the University of Missouri's site in Wyoming in 1911. The geologists keep returning to the scene every year. The rocks keep getting older; they like it that way. The pictures are fun. Old duffers in boots and leggings; women in long dresses. And always one constant *there*: the snow."

"*It* always looks the same," Charles said. "And up in those mountains…never leaves. You get a lot of melt but they still close roads as late as June."

"Right," Gwen said. "This was probably quite a course he took. I can't imagine that it's changed all that much since he was there. He got six credits then and they're still giving that many today. The students enrolled in the program study geologic phenomena, learn different methods of mapping those phenomena, and interpret the data they collect in the process. There are a lot of individual and special projects. The students are on their own a lot."

"Helps young people develop self-confidence," Charles said. "Nowadays they don't spend the time in 4H and scouting the way they once did. An experience like this…it's a kind of substitute for that. Changes their lives."

"Exactly," Gwen said. "They're not sitting in a classroom falling asleep over a desk, hoping somebody else will raise his hand; here they have to produce. When they find out that they actually can, they begin to grow up. It makes everything special…helps create the memories."

She checked some more sites and said, "Good lord, they really get the grand tour. They're not just in Wyoming. They're all over Utah, checking rivers and gorges and thrust faults. They're even in the Sangre de Cristos near Taos and at the Anasazi ruins in Frijoles Canyon."

"Lot of wilderness," Charles said. "A lot of places to hide."

"Places he already knows," Gwen said, "or at least he thinks he does. I'm sure they made a big impression at the time, but an interval of fifty years creates a lot of distance. We think we remember things vividly because they hit us hard at the time, but as we turn them around in our memories we're thinking about *our impressions* of them rather than of the things themselves. It's like an old girlfriend or boyfriend. You remember those bright blue eyes that lit up a summer afternoon. When you see them now and they're all lined and bloodshot behind thick glasses you feel as if something's gone radically wrong. Why aren't the realities keeping up with the memories? Of course the rocks wouldn't change all that much, but you might be surprised to find a Burger King casting a shadow over some of them."

"Where do they go in Wyoming proper?" Charles asked.

"The Owl Creek Mountains, the Wind River Basin, the Bighorn Basin, and the Bighorn Mountains."

"Those last two have a familiar ring," Charles said.

"Yes," Gwen answered. "The Owl Creeks are a subrange of the

Rockies, the boundary between the Bighorn Basin to the north and the Shoshone Basin to the south. The Wind River passes through the gap between the Owl Creeks and the Bridger Mountains to the east. It becomes the Bighorn River on the north side of the mountains. The range is entirely within the Wind River Indian Reservation."

"Which tribe?" Charles asked. "Anybody you know?"

Gwen smiled. "Two, actually--the Eastern Shoshone and Northern Arapaho."

"I suspect he'd stand out pretty clearly if he tried to hang out with one of them."

"I think you're right," Gwen said.

"Where *would* he go?"

"That's the big question," Gwen said. "Look at it this way...he's familiar (more or less) with all of these areas. He'd pick the one that came closest to meeting his needs. For one thing he'd need cover and concealment. Open areas won't help him. It wouldn't hurt to have some cabins or caves or rock shelters in the area—some place to get in out of the rain and snow and sleet. It can't be in the absolute middle of nowhere, because he'd need supplies from time to time, but he doesn't want to be in the middle of a busy tourist or camping site either. He'll know that his picture will be spread all over the place, so he'll want to be near civilization but not smack in the middle of it. He'll also need a food supply. He can't go into the Safeway every day to pick up his provisions and after a couple of decades in L.A. it'll be hard for him to eat like an old mountain man or desert rat. He'll want deer rather than creepie crawlies, or at least something on four legs that he's at least heard of before and stands a fair chance of being able to kill. All in all it'll take just the right combination of elements to satisfy him, especially if he plans to be there for several weeks or months before he makes a run for the north or south border."

"Probably the north," Charles said. "Didn't the New Year's Gang go to Canada for awhile?"

"Yes, the Armstrong brothers were both arrested in Toronto, though David Fine was caught in San Rafael, California. There were reports of Leo Burt being in Canada…"

"There might still be some friendlies there," Charles said. "Again, you go where you're comfortable."

Gwen was tapping incessantly on her keyboard, leaning into the screen of her laptop. "So, Harold," she said, "where would *you* be most comfortable? Don't be shy now, because we're going to be visiting you very, very soon."

76

The Langham Huntington, Pasadena

"It's only a guess, but it's as educated a guess as I can make," Gwen said. "I think he'll head for Wyoming, probably the Wind River area."

"Then let's go," Charles said.

"One problem," Gwen said.

"What's that?"

"You remember your comment about Harold trying to look inconspicuous on an Indian reservation?"

"Yes," Charles said. "Oh…OK…I see what you mean…there aren't too many black men tooling around in Wyoming."

"There aren't too many *people* in Wyoming," Gwen said. "Less than a third as many as you'd find in the San Fernando Valley, except that in Wyoming they're spread across a space of about 100,000 square miles."

"Not a problem," Charles said. "I've got the perfect solution. Works every time."

"What's that?" Gwen asked.

"Simple. It's all in what you wear. If a white man walks into a mall in old clothes they figure he's been working in his yard. If a black man walks into a mall in old clothes they figure he's getting ready to rob the jewelry store."

"That's true," Gwen said.

"But if the black man is wearing a coat and tie they figure he's there to shop or report for work in his sales job. These days…he might even be reporting for work in his job as a store manager."

"That's right."

"So you've got to dress up if you don't want to be hassled."

"Unfortunately," Gwen said.

"But there aren't going to be any malls where we're going."

"No," Gwen said, "there won't be."

"So I've got to wear something that will make the locals feel comfortable."

"Exactly."

"Not a problem; I've got just the thing," Charles said.

"What's that?"

He reached inside his bag and pulled out a small leather box with his name inscribed in tiny gold letters. "The best form of i.d.," he said, "as long as you can convince people they're yours." He opened it and showed her its contents: a folded copy of his DD-214 and lapel versions of Army medals. There were three--a Silver Star, Distinguished Service Medal, and the one you seldom see in real life, the one with the blue background and array of small stars.

"The problem is," Charles said, "that most people don't recognize the DSM. They might think it's some kind of lodge pin. And the Medal of Honor is pretty rare, so they might think it's not really yours. I could wear them to a military event, but not to some place in the boondocks populated mostly by civilians. The Silver Star will work, though. It's a meaningful award, but not so rare that people won't recognize it."

"Perfect," Gwen said. "If we find that our law-enforcement role is raising too many eyebrows that'll be our story--we're looking for the father of a medal recipient. I'm a long-lost cousin and you're a representative from the DOD. Retired military type. We want to present the father with the medals that his son was awarded before his untimely death."

"Works for me," Charles said.

"In Wyoming," Gwen said, "you flash that Silver Star and they'll hug you. Excellent idea, Charles."

"When do we leave?" Charles asked.

"Just a second," Gwen said, and got back on her computer. She worked for about fifteen minutes, then picked up her cell phone and called the Director.

Clicking off her phone she said, "We're all set, Charles. It's something of a tossup. About 300 miles from Salt Lake and about 370 from Denver. The flights to Denver are more convenient, so we'll catch a United flight out of Ontario. The Denver field office will set us up with a fully-equipped vehicle and we'll drive north."

"And where are we headed?" Charles asked.

"Lander, Wyoming," Gwen answered. "A large metropolis by Wyoming standards, with a booming population of about 8,000 people. We've got rooms at the Best Western and we're booked for late arrival. Today we travel; tomorrow we search."

"Sounds good," Charles said. He was already rearranging the things in his bag and putting his Silver Star pin in the lapel of his poplin jacket. It was a struggle for him, using his left hand with a little awkward movement from his right. Gwen thought about volunteering her help but knew that Charles would want to do it himself. She put her own things together, most of which were already folded neatly in her single piece of luggage. She folded up her laptop and packed her weapons and ammunition. "I'll check your bag as mine," she said. "With my Bureau i.d. they won't worry as much about the arsenal."

"Sounds good," Charles said. "Eight thousand people, huh?"

"Right. Maybe a few hundred less."

"I'm thinking about the person who increased that number by 1," Charles said.

"If he's there," Gwen added.

"I'm thinking about him wherever he is," Charles said.

"Then let's go find him," Gwen said.

77

Denver International Airport

"My first time flying that far in a plane that small," Charles said, as they left the jetway and headed toward the baggage area. "You're giving me a wonderful lesson in contemporary airline travel."

"It's usually survivable," Gwen said.

Their luggage had been taken off separately by security personnel and locked in an office closet. Gwen retrieved it from the baggage claim officer after first presenting her credentials and then engaging in some small talk about the two bags' obvious 'weight'. Charles remained in the baggage claim area, talking to the special agent from the Denver field office who had earlier greeted them at the luggage carousel with a sign that read:

A. HARRISON

Gwen had seen him at a distance. "The A is for Agent," she whispered. "You wouldn't think that with the formal script."

"Clever," Charles said. "Also having a guy actually dressed like a driver with the black suit and black tie."

"Right. That's a departure from standard Bureau gray. Agents are supposed to disappear into the wallpaper, not stand out. This guy would stand out *as an agent* but *not* as a limo driver. It's always in the details…"

Gwen returned with the two bags and the agent introduced himself to her as Bill Davidson. No '*Special Agent* Bill Davidson' in an enclosed space with potential lip readers or high tech microphones. He took the bags from Gwen and asked them to follow him. He took them to the nearest visitor's lot, popped the trunk on a new Bureau sedan, put the bags in the trunk, closed it, and handed Gwen the keys. He also handed her a card. "The SAC's number and cell number, with my number and cell number on the back. Call us if we can be of any assistance," he said.

"Thanks very much," Gwen said. "We won't hesitate to do that."

Davidson then turned to Charles and shook his hand. It was awkward, with the cast, but Davidson figured he wouldn't want to use his left hand. "A real privilege to meet you, Sergeant," he said, and got in the passenger side of the already-occupied adjoining car.

"His partner," Gwen said, "keeping an eye on the Bureau car, just in case."

"How did he know my name?" Charles asked.

"Your reputation precedes you," Gwen answered.

"I wouldn't expect it to in Denver," Charles replied.

"The Director briefed the Denver SAC; he spread the word. In the world of law enforcement you're a celebrity, Charles."

"More like a suspicious character," Charles answered.

"Maybe," she answered, smiling, "but on our side."

A few minutes later they were on E-470. "Where is everybody?" Charles asked.

"It's a toll road," Gwen said. "Great road. Horrible tolls. They scare everybody away. That means it's always available and quick."

When they got on 25 Charles asked Gwen how much of a lead Bucher had. "Depends on how wired or how distracted he was," she answered. "From San Fernando to Lander (assuming he's there) it's about a thousand miles. L.A. to San Berdoo, into the desert, across Nevada and Utah…maybe 16 or 17 hours. He had to stop in Azusa to switch cars and he may have switched again, maybe several times. The Lander PD is checking on new black Camrys in the area—as inconspicuously as possible—but they haven't found *his* yet. At least the Director hasn't told me if they have. We're trying to lowkey that. All that the locals know is that a car might have been stolen and might have been driven there. We don't want a small town police department knocking on doors and setting off alarms. In part it's for their own safety; we don't want them to get ambushed or blown up.

"So if you figure that he left last night he's probably already there. We're less than a hundred miles from Cheyenne and from Cheyenne to Lander it's another 275 miles or so. Conservatively we're six hours behind if he just got there. Not a big deal. If he's driven a thousand miles to get to the Wind River Valley he's probably planning to be there a little while. His getting there first works to our advantage in some ways. It gives him time to buy some things before he digs in. That gives us a possible group of people to show his picture to and ask some questions that could help us pick up his trail."

"Right," Charles said. "I wasn't thinking that we needed to rush. You know I can be very patient when I have to be."

"That's what I hear," Gwen said.

After they crossed the Wyoming border they pulled into a rest stop off of 25, just below the junction with 80 at Cheyenne, which would take them west to Laramie and, eventually, to Lander. The rest stop was huge, with several parking lots above an extended plain with multiple prospect points affording travelers views of the animals below: bison, antelope, mule deer, bighorn sheep, elk and other species from the indigenous population.

"It's a little staged, but still nice," Gwen said. "The message that they're trying to convey is that you're not in Kansas anymore. Nor in

Colorado, for that matter. This is the real west now. This is where the deer and the antelope play. Also the bears, we should remember."

"I hope none of them have eaten him yet," Charles said.

"You've got your own plans, don't you?" Gwen asked.

"I do for a fact," he answered.

78

The Best Western, Lander

The Best Western was on Grandview Drive, just off 287. It was all rustic timbering and Frederic Remington reproductions, each larger than the original. The rusticity combined with the simplicity of the appointments and modesty of price—about a third of what it had cost Gwen to stay in Pasadena. "The people in the Hoover Building who count the pennies will be very happy," she said.

The weather was cool for late spring and the snowmelt was increasing each day, with thousands of gallons of mountain water rushing down the canyon rivers. "You can hear the waters churn through the granite and almost taste the trout," Charles said.

Several roads along the mountain crests were still closed to vehicular traffic, but the hikers were undeterred and the few sites at the camp grounds in Sinks Canyon, six miles south of Lander, had all been claimed earlier that morning. The cool clear air was a nice break from its yellow counterpart in the San Gabriel Valley. Charles's and Gwen's twill slacks, turtlenecks and poplin jackets offered sufficient warmth and comfort; after checking into their rooms and stowing some of their weapons they went to work.

Route 287 ran through town from the south to the northwest, with 789 splitting off to the northeast, just beyond the motel. They began with service stations on the main highways within reasonable driving distance of Lander. "I can see where he might want to keep a low profile by buying outside of town," Gwen said, "but when you're on the run the natural impulse is to refuel at the first opportunity, so that you'll be ready, with a full tank, if you have to make a quick departure. He's not going to depend on a vehicle that only has a half tank of gas."

"I agree," Charles said, and they confined their search—for the moment—to nearby stations. When Gwen approached the counter clerks there, Charles stood behind her with a modified parade-rest posture. On duty, but in reserve if he was needed. Gwen introduced herself in different ways, depending on the clerk, with more-official titles for likely owners and more-familiar ones for hourly help. She didn't want the gossip mill to grind any more quickly or loudly than necessary and characterized the questions as *routine.*

"Good evening," she told the clerk at the Sinclair station. "This gas comes from right here in the state, doesn't it?"

"Yes, it sure does," he said. "Nothing but the best. How can I help you?"

"I'd just like to ask you a question or two," she said. "I'm Officer Harrison and this is Sergeant White. We're doing a routine check on a stolen vehicle. I've got a picture here of a person of interest and I'd like you to take a look and see if he looks familiar to you."

"I can do that," the clerk said. His clip-on name tag read *Kyle.* Gwen showed him the picture of Bucher. "Remember," she said, "he could have some facial hair, sunglasses or even a wig of some kind, so focus on the key features."

"Yes, ma'am," the clerk said. "Can I hold it?"

"Of course," Gwen answered.

He took the picture, holding it carefully by the edges, and put it under the reading light illuminating the keys of the cash register. He stared at it for at least twenty seconds. "I'd certainly like to be of help, ma'am," he said, "but I can't say as I've seen this person."

"I appreciate your looking at it," she said. "When did you come on?"

His face lit up at that. Anxious to help, he said, "Right, ma'am, I just came on an hour and a half ago. You should come back first thing in the morning and talk to Estelle. She and her husband Dave actually own the station. She was on all day and she's got a wonderful memory for names and faces."

"We'll do just that," Gwen said. "Thanks again."

None of the other night clerks recognized the picture. They tried two restaurants, one in town and one just outside on 789. The first was a fern bar in training, with salads, wraps, flavored teas, and other things they hadn't expected to find in a small town in Wyoming. The second was a mom-and-pop comfort-food stop, with the emphasis on beef, pie, and a hot and active deep fryer. Neither the head waiter at the fern bar, a man named Terry, nor the waitress at the mom-and-pop, a woman named May, recognized the man in the picture. "He looks a little like my sister's brother-in-law," May said, "but they live in Ohio and don't get out here too much anymore."

"I don't recognize him," Terry said, "but if you'll leave me your card I'll be happy to call you if he comes in. I'll be discreet, of course."

At 11:00 most of the lights were going out along the main streets, but they made it into a food mart just before the door was locked for the night. The manager's name was Craig Fellowes. He was in his mid-30's, neatly dressed and attentive to detail. The day's records were stacked on the counter before him; the cash register had already been emptied and the receipts locked in a thick canvas bag, ready to be taken to the night depository at a nearby bank.

"I'm terribly sorry," he said, "but we've just closed."

"I understand," Gwen said. "We're law enforcement, not customers."

"Oh," the manager said.

"No problems with your store," she said. "We'd just like you to look at a picture and tell us if the person in the photograph has been in."

"Could I please see some identification?" the manager asked.

"Certainly," Gwen answered, and badged him.

"Oh my," he said, "FBI."

"Standard interstate vehicular theft case," she said. "This is the person of interest."

The manager adjusted his glasses, then moved slightly to the left to catch more of the light from the overhead fixture. "Height and weight?" he asked.

"Right around six feet and 185 pounds," Gwen answered. "Brown hair and blue eyes. The blue eyes are very light in color, nearly gray. He appears to be about 60, but he's actually older, nearly 10 years older."

"Pouchy eyes," the manager said. "We see a lot of that. People drive all night. They squint into the sun, push themselves, push their bodies. A good night's sleep helps. Not with him, though. The eyes were lined. There's history there. And anger."

"Then you've seen him," Gwen said.

"Yes, I've seen him. Earlier today..."

79

The Stop-N-Shop, Route 287, Lander

"It was mid-afternoon when he came in, right around 3:00, maybe quarter of or quarter after, but close to 3:00. I know, because I get my milk around 3:00 o'clock every day and the delivery man was stocking the case when he came in."

"Do you remember what he bought?"

"Oh yes," the manager said. "Standard camping sale, but in larger quantities. He bought two cases of bottled water, at least five pounds of jerky, three pounds of dried apricots, three pounds of dried pineapple, and four large bags of trail mix. Usually people buy enough for a couple days. You can stay in the Canyon for a maximum of 14 days in any 30-day period, but most people don't. They're usually on a circuit—the Tetons, Devil's Tower, the Black Hills, that sort of thing. The tourists spend more time in the Black Hills, the diehard climbers at Devil's Tower. This is a good place for hikers but the Canyon Trail is only a 4-mile loop and the Nature Trail only a mile. Most people…they take a couple hikes, see the Sinks and the Rise, and then move on.

"The people who come here for a longer period are the geologists, but they're usually part of a class or study group and their meals are catered. They might buy some snacks, but they're not going to buy enough to subsist on."

"Did he buy anything else?" Gwen asked.

"Yes, he bought some batteries. D's, probably for a flashlight. He also bought some toothpaste."

"You've got a great memory, Mr. Fellowes," Charles said.

"Oh, I have the sales receipt right here," he said, holding it up by the edges for Charles to see. "Would you like me to make a copy for you?"

"That would be very helpful," Charles said.

"Oh yes, I nearly forgot. He also bought some band-aids and a collapsible drinking cup. He bought the stainless steel one, not the plastic."

Fellowes took the receipt to the copying machine, dropped in a quarter, and copied it. "Tell you what," he said, "I'll give you the original and keep the Xerox. Just in case you need it as evidence. Unfortunately, there's no signature or credit card number, because he paid cash. And the fingerprints would be on his copy, not mine."

"Thanks very much," Gwen said. "Was there anyone with him?"

"No, not that I could see. Actually, I wouldn't have expected anyone to be with *him*."

"Why is that?" Gwen asked.

"Because he was so unpleasant. People who come here are usually in a good mood. The air is clear; the scenery is beautiful. It's not crowded or noisy or smoggy like so many cities. It's real *nature*, the kind of thing you see in travel magazines. That didn't seem to make any impression on him. He was in a foul mood, complaining about the brands I carried, complaining about the prices. He said something about the town being *godforsaken*. Who would want to travel with somebody like that? If I'm on vacation I want to enjoy myself, not listen to somebody who complains about everything…but I guess maybe he's not on vacation… otherwise, you wouldn't be looking for him…you wouldn't be showing me his picture and asking questions about him."

Gwen nodded affirmatively. Charles asked if the manager had seen his car.

"Standard camper," he answered. "You can get a pretty big rig into some of the Canyon sites…I mean like up to 40'…but this was a small vehicle, one of those little trucks with a tent on the back that can be opened up so that you sleep off of the ground. You know what I don't understand?"

"What's that, Mr. Fellowes?" Gwen asked.

"He didn't buy anything to cook or season the fish with. I guess he could have brought it with him, but he didn't bring any other supplies, so I'd be surprised if he had brought the fish gear but no water, for example. I mean…I understand that we have to set our prices so that we can stay in business…anybody who was planning ahead even a little bit would buy things like water or dried fruit and jerky at Wal-Mart and use the local convenience stores as a last resort. He bought all that other stuff but nothing for the fish. The Rainbows and the Browns out there are fantastic. You can't fish in the Rise, of course, but you can fish down around the Sawmill Campground. These are some of the best trout in the world, some up to 12 pounds or so. I guess he'd rather eat the packaged stuff that he bought than go to the trouble…"

Gwen and Charles remained silent.

"Or, of course, he may not want to go out where he could be seen," Fellowes said. "He's probably trying to lay low…maybe even stay moving…so you all can't find him."

Gwen nodded again. "You've been very, very helpful, Mr. Fellowes. If you think of anything else—anything at all--we're staying at the Best Western, here in Lander. Give us a call. And Mr. Fellowes…"

"Don't worry," he said. "I won't say anything to anybody about this and if he comes back I'll call you right away."

"We'd appreciate that," she said.

It was 11:30 when they got back in their car. "I'm going to call the Director," Gwen said. "He'd rather be awakened than be uninformed."

He answered on the second ring. "I was working late," he said, "and needed to talk to you anyway. You go first…"

She brought him up to speed on the most recent developments. "I'll notify Denver," he said. "You can notify Lieutenant White. The Camry hasn't turned up yet, but I'll let the locals know that he's since stolen a camper. They can go over any reports of missing vehicles and look for the Camry in that area. I hope they don't find the camper owner in the trunk of the sedan."

"Thank you, sir," Gwen said. "We're going to continue our search at first light. I don't want to signal our approach by using flashlights and I don't want to work our way through rough terrain in the dark--not when there's a good chance of trip wires or other booby traps."

"I agree," the Director said. "There's something else you should know. It just came in; I bounced it to your in-box. Not that there's anything you can do about it now, but it's important that you're aware of it."

"Yes, sir…?"

"There was a leak in either the Field Office or the LAPD. If the leaker is in the Bureau his or her career is about to come to a very quick close. If it came from the LAPD I'm sure Lieutenant White wasn't responsible, though he may have an idea who the source was. Either way, it's something we'll want to run down quickly, because I don't like leaks, particularly when they impede investigations and put agents at risk…"

"Yes, sir…?"

"The leak revealed that the Bureau has been brought into the Denise White case. Burke is not explicitly named, but the leak states that the key person of interest is a USC staff member. You *are* named and so is Sergeant White. The leak talks about your experience with earlier cases and your personal family background. It portrays Sergeant White as a potentially violent person and questions the decision to allow a civilian to participate in an investigation, particularly a civilian with a personal relationship with the victim. It portrays him as a vigilante and snipes at both the Bureau and the LAPD. I'm not worried about the adverse publicity, because Sergeant White is an eye witness—the only one to survive the bombing of the Clinic. I can spin his involvement as that of a public-spirited citizen. He's not on the Bureau payroll and there's no law against an interested civilian's desire to be of help to law enforcement."

"Who's running the story, sir?"

"The *L.A. Times*. It already hit their website."

80

The Best Western, Lander

Gwen was up at 4:00, with first light at 5:02 and sunrise at 5:38. She checked her weapons, dressed, and knocked on the connecting door to Charles's room at 4:40. When he opened it he was holding a knife and a small sharpening stone. She wondered how he was sharpening the knife with only one good hand. "Ready?" he asked.

"Yes," she said. "I figured we'd drive to the picnic area at around 7,100 feet and then work our way back down the canyon, looking for truck campers and anything that looks suspicious."

"Sounds good," Charles said, "let's do it."

The Bruces Picnic Area was deserted except for two couples at a single table, drinking coffee from a thermos and sharing a box of Krispy Kreme donuts. "Sunrise watchers," Charles said. "They just drove up."

"Right," Gwen said, and continued down the canyon. The separate habitats were clear, even at first light. The north-facing slope was heavily forested, the south-facing slope drier, with sagebrush and juniper predominating. "There are only about thirty campsites in the area," Gwen said, "so if we're going to see anything obvious we'll see it quickly."

"Look," Charles said, as a golden eagle flew above and over them. "Tell me about the area," he said. "Why is it called Sinks Canyon?"

"The river is called the Popo Agie," she said. "The second word is spelled A-g-i-e, but the two words together are pronounced *po-po-shuh*. It's Crow for Tall Grass River. 'Agie' means river and 'PoPo' means tall rye grass or simply tall grass. They called it that because of the flora that grow along the banks of the river in the valley.

"The Popo Agie flows out of the Wind River Mountains and down through the Canyon. This is actually the middle fork of the Popo Agie. About halfway down the Canyon the river takes an abrupt turn into a limestone cavern and sinks into the cracks and fissures at the back of the cave. It then flows underground for a quarter of a mile and emerges farther down the Canyon in a quiet, large pond called 'The Rise'. The cave and the underground passages are unexplorable because of the log and rock jams.

"This time of year, with the snowmelt, there's probably five hundred cubic feet of water rushing down the channel every second. What's amazing is that the water is so calm when it re-emerges at the Rise. What's even more amazing is that it takes more than two hours for that churning, white water to make the quarter-mile trip. And there's more of it in the Rise than there was above the Sinks."

"So there are underground springs of some kind," Charles said.

"Right. That's the theory."

"And the water is taking a roundabout route underground. Maybe through other caves and seepage points."

"Right. Has to be. The glaciers carved the Canyon and exposed the softer limestone below the granite. The Native People knew of the Sinks for generations; the white fur trappers didn't see them until the early 1800's."

"How do they know that the water in the Rise originated in the Sinks?" Charles asked.

"Dye tests," Gwen answered. "Geologists' delight, huh?"

"Yes, I can see that," Charles said. "When this is all over…"

"Yes?"

"I'd like to come back, try to catch some of those trout."

"You can't fish in the Rise," Gwen said. "The tourists feed the fish there—big ones, like the convenience store manager said--but they don't catch them."

"I could do that," Charles said.

At the Sinks and Popo Agie Campgrounds every site was taken, most of them right along the river amid lodgepole pines, aspens, and huge granite boulders that had been turned and jumbled over thousands of years. "I see what he meant when he talked about real *nature*," Charles said.

The tents were expensive and elaborate, with interior space for multiple cots. There was occasional but faint lantern glow through the webbing of some of the tents. No truck campers, only vans and SUV's, including some Lexus LX's. The license plates were from as far away as Louisiana, with Colorado predominating. At the Popo Agie Campground they caught the smell of bacon and saw a heavy set man presiding over a large portable grill. "How do you want your eggs?" they heard him say.

"You could probably count on some skillet-fried potatoes too," Gwen said. "That guy's done this before."

Charles nodded approvingly as they continued to look and drive. They drove past the Visitors Center, which didn't open until 9:00, saw the sign for the Rise, and continued down the Canyon to the Sawmill Campground, where there were only five campsites and a fishing pier for the river. All five of the sites were taken. With the exception of a tent capable of holding at least eight cots, most were smaller than those at the campsites at the higher elevations. "We're still above 6,000 feet," Gwen said, "but this is the last of the campgrounds." There were two vans, an SUV, an old Ford Country Squire and a small Winnebago. All of the tents were dark except for the large one, where the sounds of young voices were audible. No one was cooking yet.

Gwen's phone twitched in her jacket pocket. It was the Director.

"No, sir," she said, "nothing yet. Unless he's changed vehicles again, there's nothing close to the description of the vehicle which we got from the convenience store manager."

"And you consider him reliable," the Director said.

"Yes, sir, very reliable."

"We got a report on the Camry," he said.

"Where, Sir?" she asked.

"Ontario, at the airport."

"So he flew here," she said, "evaded the officers."

"Yes, and probably picked up the new vehicle in the airport parking lot at Denver or Salt Lake. Those are the logical entry points to that part of Wyoming. Out there there are people who keep their campers ready all the time, just like the people who leave their ski racks on year-round. Nobody's reported a stolen vehicle, but if it was in long-term parking the owner could still be off on a Mediterranean cruise or an extended trip to Maui."

"Right," Gwen said.

"What's your next step?" the Director asked.

Gwen paused. She didn't have a ready answer.

81

The Sawmill Campground on the Popo Agie

"We'll go farther up in the mountains and we'll check trails and dirt roads—anyplace off the beaten track where he could be hiding. It was probably too optimistic to expect him to be sitting out in plain sight."

"Not necessarily," the Director said. "He stole a camper, not a jeep or an all-terrain vehicle. That doesn't mean that his plans haven't changed, but that *was* the vehicle he brought to town. And it's a small town. It's one thing to boost a car in southern California, quite another to try that in a rural town in Wyoming. Whatever he brought he's likely to keep, at least for awhile. And remember another thing about that small town—it's one in which every one is likely to be armed."

"I agree," Gwen said. "He may well be using his camper, but in some unofficial site."

"What would you think of my calling in the people from Denver and surrounding the area? There aren't that many highways in Wyoming. We could draw a circle around the immediate area of Lander. If he got past you he wouldn't get past them."

"Could they do it without local law enforcement?" Gwen asked.

"No, probably not."

"Then we're back to the problem of leaks. When the *Times* runs their piece today the story will pick up momentum. Local papers will want to get in on the action. The next step will be the reports of roadblocks in Wyoming. Before you know it we'll be surrounded by reporters and rubberneckers. Our hand may already be tipped if he's checked the internet, but if we create a major incident it could really spook him. He could try to work his way through our barriers; that could put more civilians at risk. He might also think about taking hostages. We don't need that. In some ways I'd rather we keep the situation compartmentalized—to the extent that that's possible."

"I thought you might say that," the Director said. "And you know how much I trust your instincts. I just don't want this character to get away again."

"I understand," Gwen said. "Give us a day."

"He can drive back to California in a day, Gwen, or even further if he pushes it."

"I know, but he's gone to a lot of trouble to come *here*. And he doesn't know yet that we're here, only that he's a person of interest in Denise's death and that two people are looking for him."

"Not just two people," the Director said, "the Bureau's top tracker and the kind of soldier who would make Rambo pee down his pants leg. Pardon the vernacular."

"Thanks for the compliment," she said, somewhat surprised at the expressions, which were stronger than any she had heard from the usually circumspect Director.

"Take a few hours," he said, "and then check back with me. If you see anything noteworthy in the meantime, *anything*, call me right away."

"Will do, Sir," she said and clicked off.

"Is he getting cold feet?" Charles asked.

"A little," Gwen answered.

"I agree with you," Charles said. "The park is open from Memorial Day to Labor Day. The tourist and camper traffic help him to a degree. If it was completely deserted or at least covered with snow he'd be much easier to find. Heat sensors would pick him up immediately. On the other hand, the tourists and campers all have cell phones and nearly all of them have internet access. News travels fast these days and it travels everywhere. If the word gets out that there's a fugitive in their midst with armed people in pursuit we've suddenly got a situation, a situation that he could exploit. For the moment there could be a small window of opportunity. If he *doesn't* know that we're here the FBI and the locals could set up a noose and start tightening it, while we poke around inside the circle, looking for him, and doing what we can to keep the civilians out of the line of fire, but that's a big *if.*"

"Right," Gwen said. "He's also a techie, so whatever you *could* have he probably *does* have, particularly if he's worried that he's being followed. He will be scanning police radio frequencies, possibly even doing some elementary data mining, certainly surfing the web on his smart phone… you name it. At first I thought we could try to get a story planted that would locate us in Wisconsin or someplace else a long way from here, but one of the things my father always says is that if you live by the media you die by the media. If a planted story's identified as such, the press is suddenly chewing on raw meat and turning up the spotlights. Right now all he has is a report that smells like something between a leak and a rumor. Instead of giving him Part II and raising his suspicions I'd rather give him silence or white noise."

They drove back up to the Bruces Picnic Area and caught what is termed The Long Road that runs to route 28. In the 30+ mile course there was nothing out of the ordinary except for some college kids with heavy backpacks and expensive cameras trying to take pictures of a publicity-shy moose. There was a rumor on the radio to the effect that a bear had been sighted in the area and tourists were advised to keep a due distance. Instead, it drew rubberneckers. There was one truck camper parked on the side of the road, but it was owned by a young family that had pulled over to check out the scenery and take some pictures: the husband, wife, and two sons, with no one remaining in the vehicle.

They drove back to the Popo Agie, parked at the Sinks Campground, and explored the 4 mile loop, Canyon Trail. Then they drove down to the Popo Agie Campground and explored the 1 mile loop, the Popo Agie Nature Trail. Each of them had secured broken limbs that could function as walking sticks and Gwen had provided Charles with a ballcap, so that they might look more like civilians than law enforcement personnel.

By now the park staff were in place at The Visitor Center, but there were no vehicles in the parking area that could be even remotely described as suspicious. The campgrounds were all largely unchanged, except that the donut eaters at the Bruces Picnic Area had left and two of the campsites had been vacated at the Sinks and one at the Popo Agie. The five sites at the Sawmill Campground were still occupied and this time there was movement and the smells of breakfast food. A group of kids were standing on the pier, trying to catch breakfast but not showing any evident signs of success. There was more mild pushing and shoving than serious fishing.

Gwen called the Director, updated him on their efforts and promised to call back soon. He did not ask her about their next steps. Neither did Charles. At this point all that they could do was explore the entire park on foot or return to Lander and start questioning service station operators and convenience store managers. There was little likelihood that he would be staying at a motel or in one of the town's handful of Bed and Breakfasts. If he wanted to try to sustain his anonymity in that way he'd be far safer in a large metropolitan area with fleabags and flop houses.

"Well, Charles," she said, the only other installation in the area is Camp Branson, the University of Missouri site, and while its field camp is on hiatus before the summer there's still a resident staff. They would have noticed if someone had suddenly moved into one of their dormitories and then shown up to try to mooch breakfast from their cafeteria. We could check in with them, but I think that's a long shot. I figure we drive back into Lander. It's a small town. We can cover most of the streets in less than an hour. Maybe he's left his vehicle there, gathered up his supplies and then walked into the park. If so, we can check out the vehicle, estimate his most likely entry point into the park and follow on foot."

"Sounds good," Charles said. "Let's do it."

Driving through the parking lot at the entrance to the park, Gwen suddenly stopped. "Well my oh my," she said, "a modified Ford pickup with a tent camper in the payload bed. Check out the license plate, Sergeant White."

"*Ski* Utah!" Charles said, "GREATEST SNOW ON EARTH. That's with an exclamation point after the *Utah*. And not a moment too soon."

"I'd say it's time to take a closer look," she added.

82

Sinks Canyon State Park

The vehicle was empty except for a discarded water bottle and some wrapping material that had encased a packet of beef jerky. Both were sitting on the floor of the front passenger seat. The vehicle itself had a coating of dust and slabs of mud adhering to the tire wells. "He's been off road," Charles said. "That may be why we missed him the first time."

Gwen called the Director and read him the registration number, so that the owner could be notified and report the vehicle's last known location. "Be careful," the Director said. "If he parked in a public lot and he's still in the area, it's probably for a short time. He could appear at any moment and he won't be happy to find you there."

As soon as Gwen clicked off, Charles asked if he should remove the plug wires and disable the car.

"I think not," Gwen said. "He could always just steal another one; he seems to be good at that. I'd rather him not suspect that we're onto him. It's clear that he feels comfortable enough in the area to park his vehicle in an obvious location. Let's let him keep that false sense of security."

"OK," Charles said. "How about if I just let a little air out of one of his tires. Not enough that he'd notice, but enough that it'd wear down quickly if he had to make a run for it."

"Sounds good," Gwen said. "That's much less likely to make him suspicious. Go for the right rear; that's the one he's least likely to look at automatically."

"You got it," Charles said.

In the far corner of the lot there was a break in the asphalt, revealing an ingress/egress point for a narrow dirt road. The earth was tightly packed with scattered vegetation, large rocks, and the elbows of tree and shrub roots. There were fresh tire tracks in the thin layer of dust that blanketed the road.

"What do you make of this?" Charles asked.

"It goes someplace that cars can negotiate, even if they're not made to feel particularly welcome."

"The locals would know the soft spots and the hard," Charles said. "An outsider wouldn't. Safer to park in the surfaced lot and go the rest of the way on foot. Maybe he started to drive in and then thought better of it."

"Let's do the same," Gwen answered.

Less than a half mile into the forest and brush Gwen saw a cabin. It was substantial, not just a shed or lean-to. There were curls of smoke wisping off the stone chimney and an Explorer with an Oklahoma license plate parked beside the wooden porch. Charles slipped around the back and positioned himself behind a stand of blue spruce as Gwen approached the front door.

She had to knock three times to attract the occupant's attention. He unlocked the interior door and stood facing her, behind the screen. "Good morning," he said. "Are you lost?"

He was wearing corduroy slacks, a plaid flannel shirt, and the kind of camp boots sold by L.L. Bean. The smells of eggs and sausages made their way through the house and to the porch. There were two cats standing behind the man's legs. They looked as if they had just left the warmth of the hearth to satisfy their curiosity.

"No, actually I'm not," Gwen said, "but I'd like to come in and talk to you if I could."

"Suit yourself," the man said, opening the screen door and pointing toward the kitchen. "My breakfast is just about finished cooking; care to share it?"

"No thank you," Gwen said.

"How about some coffee then?"

"Coffee would be great," she said. "I've got a partner still outside. Would you mind if I invited him in?"

"No, of course not. You do that while I make sure my food's still edible."

When Charles came in the man showed a hint of surprise around his eyes and mouth, but didn't say anything. "Have a seat," he said. "Your friend's already turned down breakfast; how about you?"

"No, thanks," Charles said. "I will take some coffee though if there's enough to go around."

They sat down at the kitchen table, a circular oak antique. "I don't mean any offense by this, but you two are sort of an odd couple."

"I understand," Gwen said, and badged him. She then introduced Charles and told him that they were looking for a fugitive.

"My name's Staunton," the man said. "Don Staunton. I should say, Don Staunton, Petroleum Geologist. That's what I called myself for forty-two years. My wife died a couple years ago. Now it's just me and the cats. We spend the winters in Oklahoma City and the summers here. I couldn't always get away for that long when I was working, but now that I'm retired, I can. The cats like it too. Lot of mice around here, at least until they arrive. You can have a cat or you can have mice. Not many other choices in these cabins."

"I wasn't aware that there *were* cabins in the area," Gwen said. "Do you rent from the park service?"

"Oh no, we own them," Staunton said. "They don't permit private cabins in the park anymore, but so long as you're already here and you maintain your cabin you're allowed to keep it. It can be inherited, but it can't be sold. There are six of them. Several are owned by people like me—old geologists who came to the Wind River Valley and fell in love. There's one academic—a geologist from California who teaches in the Missouri program every May and June. The rest of the time he's in Riverside."

"And are all of them occupied now?" Charles asked.

"All but one at the moment. The professor and his wife are here—along with their terriers—and I got in a week ago. The professor's field camp teaching is finished, but he'll stay here until mid August or so and do his research. Two of the other cabins are occupied, one by a man named Maris, another by two brothers, named Lawrence. Bill and Ed Lawrence. Bill's the geologist; Ed was an accountant or something, but he's an amateur naturalist. The cabin just above mine was inherited by Carl Wallace's son Jim. He's there with his wife and daughter. The last cabin is still boarded up. It's owned by a man from Dallas named Stimson. Dave Stimson. I call him Davey, because I've known him for thirty years. Unfortunately, he's been ailing and doesn't expect to make it here this summer. He'll be here next year. As you can see, getting here's not all that easy. It's a deal at our age, and for that matter it's pretty rustic--not everybody's cup of tea. Some people like the beach; some like the big city; and some of us like old rocks, fresh snow, and an occasional moose or bear. Davey loves it, of course. He used to be the chief geologist for Mobil Oil, before John Marshall got that job. Bill Lawrence worked for Standard Oil, like Carl Wallace. Ours is a pretty small world."

"And what is the professor's name, Mr. Staunton?"

"Richard Connell; his wife's name is Edna. The terriers are called Calvin and Hobbes—after those cartoon characters. If you go near Richard's cabin you'll meet them first. This is a paradise for dogs, as you can imagine."

"And do they bark and fuss whenever anybody new comes around?"

"They do, but only right around their own house. They're trained to stay within about 50 yards of the cabin. Otherwise they could be eaten."

"I understand," Gwen said. "And you haven't seen anyone around Mr. Stimson's cabin."

"I haven't, but I wouldn't," Staunton said. "Of all of them here it's the most remote—about a quarter of a mile past the professor's. I know Davey's not here, because I talked to him last week. He was in the hospital, the place that they took JFK to. Except Davey was having his hip replaced. For the second time. How about another cup of that coffee?"

"It's delicious, and thanks very much for all your help," Gwen said, "but we better get back to work. By the way, have you seen this person anywhere around these parts?"

She showed him the picture of Bucher. He took his glasses out of his pocket, stared at it, and said, "Sorry, I haven't."

"Thanks," Gwen said, "and thanks again for the coffee. If you happen to see him, call me right away." She wrote her cell number on a piece of the motel's stationery.

"If I *do* see that fella…"

"Yes?" Gwen answered.

"I'll let you know right away. In the meantime I'll keep one of my shotguns handy."

"Good idea," Gwen said.

83

The Staunton Cabin, Sinks Canyon State Park

Staunton gave them directions to the Stimson cabin. "The professor's is surrounded by junipers," he said, "and they have a couple flags on their porch. Davey's is just beyond it, about a five or ten minute walk, depending on how fast you're going. You'll see a dirt and gravel path. Just follow that."

They thanked him and took off. As soon as they were thirty or forty yards past the rear of his cabin and shielded by trees they checked their weapons to make sure that they were loaded. The wind began to pick up and they could hear its distinct sounds whistling in the trees and shrubs. Gwen thought she could hear the river in the distance, coursing over the rocks and roots along its edges.

A few minutes later they saw the Wallace cabin. The drapes were pulled and there was no smoke emerging from the chimney. A dusty Suburban was parked beside it. The cabin was slightly smaller than Staunton's but it had been given a recent coat of stain. The Lawrence cabin was nearby, a twin to the Wallace structure. Charles thought they might have been constructed simultaneously for the branches of a large family and then sold off separately when that was still permitted. Each had industrial-strength doorlocks and there were no signs of attempted entry.

According to Staunton's directions the professor's cabin should be next. Charles had gone off the path, in order to guard against the possibility of an ambush, while Gwen was examining the earth, step by step. There were a number of footprints remaining in the dust. The light rain the evening before had thickened it and the wind off the mountain was not yet so strong, nor the sun so warm as to dry the earth and erase the marks left by those who had recently used the path. There were some marks from a pair of small tennis shoes, the Wallace's daughter's in all probability, prints from larger shoes, mostly indistinct with regard to tread or waffling, and the occasional prints of animals. She had seen fresh deer pellets near the Lawrence cabin and the outline of what had probably been a moose was still perceptible in some tall grass just beyond Staunton's. There was also what she took to be moose scat, larger and rounder than the deer's, but it was drier as well and at least several days old.

As she got closer to the professor's cabin Charles emerged from the trees and signaled her to stop. Then he waved her toward him and pointed to his left. She joined him at the edge of a clearing and saw the subject of his attention: it was one of the professor's terriers, a male Scottie. It had been stabbed repeatedly, its thick, wiry coat matted with blackish-red blood.

"The other one is back in the grass behind me," Charles whispered. "Its throat was cut but it was stabbed as well."

Gwen reached down to touch it.

"No need to do that," Charles said. "It's not warm, but rigor hasn't set in yet. It was killed recently. We should approach the professor's cabin very carefully."

The juniper afforded them a significant degree of concealment. "The dogs came out to check on him and he killed them," Charles whispered. "Then he probably made the same approach to the cabin that we're using."

They saw a Yukon SUV on the side of the cabin and the flags on the porch, one Danish (Edna?) and one British (Richard?). Gwen took out her earbuds and the modified binoculars that Elizabeth had given her and set them to access sound. Aside from some humming noises--some insect, some from the cabin's appliances--there was nothing else.

They approached the cabin from opposite sides, listening at windows and trying to catch a glimpse of anything that indicated activity or movement. Neither heard or saw anything. "You guard the front," Gwen said. "I'll go in the back. I don't want to knock and give him a chance to prepare. I'll go in quickly and then see if there's any response." Charles nodded and circled around to the front of the cabin, beneath the porch.

Gwen approached the back door. There was an unlocked screen and then a panel door with a window. She looked through it and saw the kitchen sinkboard, but nothing else. She tried the doorknob, but it wouldn't turn. Then she took a single, deep breath, struck the glass with the heel of her automatic, hit the remaining jagged shards to clear the way, reached through and turned the knob from the inside, entered, and moved through the house as quickly as she could. The range and sinkboard were clear. The dining porch beyond the kitchen was empty. The table had not been set and there were no food smells in either room. She hurried into the living room, her weapon aimed at chest level. The room was empty, but there was blood on the carpet and on the wide-plank pine floor at its edges. The shade of a floor lamp was slightly askew. She opened the front door, unlatched the screen, and waited for Charles to emerge from the side of the porch.

The bathroom in the hallway was empty, but there were blood smears along the floor in the hallway as well as on the wall just above the quarter-round molding. The smaller bedroom was on the left. It appeared to be a combination den and sewing room; it was unoccupied.

Both of the bodies were in the master bedroom, on the floor, between the bed and the far wall. The copper-penny smell of blood filled the room. Each of the victims had been bludgeoned and each had been stabbed. The wife's throat was sliced evenly, the husband's much more abruptly, though the results were the same in each case. The wounds from the blunt instrument were small and round. "It looks like he used a hammer," Charles said. "At least he's consistent."

"He probably dragged the bodies in here and shoved them between the bed and wall so they couldn't be seen from the windows," Gwen said. "He's in a hurry though. Otherwise he would have cleaned up the blood and straightened things up a little, then removed the bodies, along with the car. This is a slapdash job. The dogs heard him, so he killed them. Then he worried that the professor and his wife might have heard the dogs so he killed them too."

They checked the kitchen drawers; the knives were still in place and none was obviously bloodied. The tool kit in the kitchen cupboard contained a hammer that appeared new and free of any bloodstains. The refrigerator was filled with things that a fugitive might steal—cold bottled water, some leftover pot roast, packaged cheese, fresh juice, and imported beer.

"This was just an intermediate stop," Gwen said. "If he was looking for something, it was something they didn't have."

"So he killed them anyway," Charles said.

"Yes," Gwen said. "That's what he does."

84

The Connell Cabin, Sinks Canyon State Park

They hurried toward the Stimson cabin. Charles was holding his weapon in his left hand, but steadying it with the fingertips of his right. His gait was unnatural but he told Gwen that he was not in pain and that she should keep up the pace. "I think we're close," he said, "and we can't afford to lose him now."

The Stimson cabin was the largest of all, with a porch that covered the front of the structure and wrapped around both sides. It too had been freshly stained. It sat in a bright clearing and the roof was free of moss and pine needles. It was less rustic than the other structures, with dark plantation shutters, brass door fittings, and a rock garden with a small, stone Celtic cross.

"Civilization," Gwen whispered. "Not the sort of place where you should see the likes of Harold Bucher."

She took out the modified binoculars again and listened. There was the insect hum and the sound of rushing water. Aiming directly at the cabin she could hear the sounds of appliance motors. There was also the sound of a faucet dripping, probably against the base of an aluminum sink.

They went through their previous step—listening at windows and trying to detect any indication of movement or life within. Again Charles took the front and Gwen the rear door, but when she walked up the two steps to the kitchen porch and opened the screen door she saw that the solid door was loose against the jamb and the lock and strike were gouged, probably by a large screw driver. She stepped to her left in case Bucher was on the other side, waiting for her silently, and pushed at the center of the door. It swung open and she was greeted by the musty smell of a home that had sat vacant through a long cold winter and damp spring.

She checked the rooms quickly and then opened the front door for Charles. "He's gone," she said, "but he was here. The back door had been jimmied and it was open when I got there."

Gwen went back to the kitchen and inspected the dripping faucet. It was a single-handled Moen. She picked up a pencil from the counter and pushed the handle near its base. The dripping stopped. "Look," she said to Charles when he entered the room. There were red droplets in the corner of the sink. "He noticed that he had some blood on his hands and tried to rinse it off. He probably tried to shut off the faucet using his wrist or elbow, since he didn't want to leave any prints. He didn't shut it off completely."

"He left in a hurry," Charles said. "He must have planned to be seen if he was so worried about bloodstains. There's plenty of water out there, both at the campsites and with the river itself. He could have washed his hands anywhere."

"So why did he come in here?" Gwen asked. "Why did he take the time to jimmy the back door?"

Charles didn't answer. Instead they both began a search of the house. The refrigerator was empty except for a box of baking soda to absorb smells. There were some canned goods in the cupboards and some spices, but all appeared to be untouched. Like the professor, Stimson kept his tool kit in his kitchen cupboard, but the tools did not appear to have been disturbed and there were some potential weapons there—an awl, for example, and what was likely to have been Bucher's tool of preference, a large clawhammer.

There was a wideband, battery-operated radio on the kitchen

counter, next to the refrigerator. He could have used this, Gwen thought to herself, and he already has the D batteries. She went into the master bedroom and checked Stimson's closet. Perhaps Bucher wanted some fresh clothes, particularly if the clothes he had been wearing were covered in blood splatter. The wardrobe was minimal—several pairs of wool socks, some cotton underwear, flannel shirts and twill slacks. Everything was neatly folded. The cabinetry smelled of cedar and while there were few clothes there, each of the compartments where they were stored was filled. On the floor inside the cupboard was a pair of rubber boots and a pair of camp shoes.

Just then Charles appeared at the door. "Gwen…" he said.

She followed him into the second bedroom. Inside the cupboard was a steel cabinet. There were deep scratch marks around the padlock site, but no lock in place or on the floor. Charles was holding a handkerchief and he opened the cabinet along the edge, near the top, where there was less likelihood of any latent prints that might be disturbed.

"Stimson's gun safe," Charles said. One rifle was missing. On a shelf above the weapons were slots for ammunition. "He took as much as he could carry," Charles said. "There's still a box at the back."

Gwen got up on her toes to look. "A .30-30," she said. "Your classic deer rifle and one that's easy to load. Not the most accurate necessarily and not as much firepower as he might have liked, but it's the sort of thing that would draw little or no attention in the woods of Wyoming."

"It's also a weapon that can be carried comfortably," Charles said. "He may be planning for a long stand as well as the need to eventually have to hunt for his dinner."

"I'm not so sure," Gwen said. "He left his car in the lot and came in here looking for a weapon. I'm thinking he'll hurry back to his vehicle and take off. He started here because he knew there were remote cabins that were likely to contain weapons. Maybe now he heads for Utah or Colorado."

"I'll go back to the parking lot," Charles said. "If the truck's still there I'll let you know. If it's not we can alert the Bureau and local cavalry."

Gwen didn't comment on Charles's physical condition, but she knew that if Bucher was heading to one of the campsites to steal another vehicle she would have a better chance of following him and negotiating the terrain than Charles.

"Don't worry," Charles said. "If he comes near the truck I'll make sure he doesn't leave in it."

"I'll try to pick up his trail here and then check the campsites or wherever it is he's going," Gwen said. "Go. We don't have a second to lose."

85

The Stimson Cabin, Sinks Canyon State Park

As Charles made his way along the trail he checked his cell phone to make sure it was set to vibrate rather than ring. It was the third time that day that he had done so—a nervous gesture that helped divert his anger at his inability to move with his usual speed and dexterity. Neither his leg nor his right arm were in great pain—the percocet had seen to that—but he desperately wished that he could function at full capacity. He did not doubt his ability to take Bucher down; he simply wanted to be able to do it on his own, precise terms.

As he avoided turning his ankle on rocks and roots he understood Bucher's decision to walk rather than to drive to the Stimson cabin. A single false turn or bit of inattention and the tires and undercarriage of his vehicle could be destroyed. Beautiful at a distance, the terrain was treacherous at ground level.

As soon as Gwen left the building she began examining the surrounding dust for tracks. The footprints she had seen earlier were noticeably larger than Charles's, who wore a 9 ½ and much larger than her own size 7. For a moment she thought that the open back door could have been designed to mislead her and that Bucher actually left by the front, though there was no hard reason to suggest that he was aware of the fact that he was being followed. Nevertheless, she checked the front porch just to be certain, but saw no prints other than faint ones left by Charles. She also carefully lifted the porous fiber mat in front of the door. If Bucher had cleaned his shoes carefully to avoid leaving prints the dust beneath the mat would have been disturbed in some way, but it was not. The grit and moisture from the fall, winter, and spring had left a greenish imprint on the porch that remained completely intact.

She returned quickly to the rear of the cabin. Just beyond the back porch was a gravel walkway with a thin blanket of brown pine needles. Beyond it there were no obvious marks, but the earth there was as dense as hardpan, perhaps from tamping or perhaps because of wind currents that kept it clear of dust. She walked further and eventually found a toe print, then a full footprint.

The print was large, probably at least an 11 and possibly a 12. Bucher had been an athlete, she remembered. The stride was long for an individual of his height. He was walking briskly. She called Charles.

"I think I've got his track," she said, "but I wanted to check in with you."

"I'm just coming up on the parking lot," he said. "I can't see the vehicle yet, because there are larger ones parked in spaces that were vacant when we drove in. Give me a second."

A few moments later he spoke again. "It's still here. I figure he's heading in your direction rather than returning to this vehicle, but he might be off the trail, taking a more cautious route. I'll find a good vantage point and keep an eye out for him. If anybody else appears I'll ask them if they saw him. In the meantime I'll guard the area and join you as soon as you actually see him…or a new victim. If I don't hear from you in thirty minutes I'll start walking in your direction."

"Sounds good," she said, clicking off and verifying that *her* phone was set to twitch rather than ring. The breeze came up again and there were swirls of dust in the open areas, frustrating her attempts to follow his tracks. The sun was warm now, the sky a cloudless ice-blue.

Eventually she found his tracks again; a hundred yards through the brush they merged with the main trail leading to the Sawmill Campground. When she reached the pier and campsites there the kids were no longer fishing from the pier and there were only two remaining groups of campers. She approached them, gathered them together, badged them, showed them the reconstructed photograph of Bucher, and asked if anyone had seen him.

The first group was a husband and wife with their 9 or 10 year-old son, the second a pair of middle-aged men. The family said that they had not seen him, but that they had been in town until just a few minutes before. "We were getting some stuff for lunch," the mother said. "We're driving into Lander for dinner and just staying one night. I'm not big on camping, but my men are, so we kind of compromise this way."

The two middle-aged men were both tall and thick, with faded, unbuttoned shirts and baseball caps with torn bills. "Can I see that picture again?" one of them said.

"Of course," Gwen said, and took it from the mother and handed it to him.

"I think I did see this fella," the man said. "He was mostly turned away from me but he came through about eight or ten minutes ago. At least a guy who looked something like this did. He was standing by my truck, looking in the window. I asked him if I could help him with something and I think I startled him. He said, 'No, I was just admiring it.' I thought that was a little strange because that truck's twelve years old and it's got 163,000 miles on it, but maybe it looked special to him. Anyway, he just tipped his cap to me, wished me a nice day, and took off."

"Was there anything special about his appearance" Gwen asked, "something different from the way he looks in the picture?"

"Well," the man said, "keep in mind that I'm not certain that that was him. He had on a cap and sunglasses and he hadn't shaved in awhile, so I'm just trying to figure out how close he was to the guy in your picture."

"How about height and weight?" Gwen asked.

"Little guy, skinny," the man said.

"Compared with you?" Gwen asked.

"Yeah, I'm 6'3", 260 and my cousin Bill here's 6'4", 270 and change. This guy wasn't but about 6' and less than 200 pounds, maybe no more than 175."

"Was he carrying a weapon?" Gwen asked.

"A *weapon*?" the man said. "He was carrying a deer rifle. I don't know what he was going to do with it, maybe try to take a black bear. He couldn't be going after deer, moose, antelope, elk, or bighorn sheep. Those seasons don't start in any but a few areas until September and the peaks of the seasons are in October and November. Unless he plans to just walk around for two or three months first, he better not get caught shooting at anything or he'll get his ass fined big-time."

"And where did he go from here?" Gwen asked.

"Straight up toward the Rise," the man said.

"Thanks, you've been very helpful," she said. "That man is wanted in connection with several violent crimes. I suggest you all get in your vehicles and clear this area."

The family said thanks and got right in their SUV. The other men continued to stand there. "Do we *have* to leave?" the smaller of the two asked.

"For your own safety," Gwen said, "I think it's best."

"I think we're pretty safe," the man said, "at least from him. My AK-47 shoots a lot faster than that .30-30."

"How about your cousin, Bill there?" Gwen said.

Bill smiled and said, "Shi-i-t, Cletus is right. That old AK'll get the job done. I ain't got anything with me except for my Desert Eagle. Mine's a new one, a Mark XIX. I got the .44 Mag. Seemed like the right size, you know, for *my* hand. Jews know how to make guns, don't you think? Mine'll stop a black bear and it'd sure as hell put that skinny boy on his back."

"Maybe you two *should* stay here," Gwen said. "If he does come back I'd be very grateful if you would detain him."

"That'd be our pleasure, ma'am," Cletus said. "Asswipes are always in season, especially the kind that would steal your truck…sorry…I shouldn't of said that."

"No problem," Gwen said, and hurried up the trail.

86

The Rise Trail, Sinks Canyon State Park

As she hurried beside the river, Gwen called Charles, briefed him on what had happened, and asked him to close with them. "I'll try to get ahead of him," she said, "and you come behind him, blocking his escape route. I'm afraid he's either going to the Rise to take a hostage or to the Visitor Center at the Sinks to steal a vehicle."

"I'll be there," Charles said.

"I'll keep my cell on," Gwen said, "so that you can hear anything I say if I find him."

"Good idea," Charles said. "I'll keep mine on too."

There were at least fifteen people at the Rise, including a half dozen children, several of whom were feeding the trout. The convenience store manager was right; the fish were huge and getting larger with every bite. There was no sign of Bucher, either at the water side or in the surrounding area, so she continued toward the Visitor Center, a quarter-mile walk that would take her past the overflow channel. When she got there, she saw him. He was walking among the parked cars, looking for one to steal.

She wanted to flush him out of the lot, because as long as he was there he could take advantage of the cover and concealment afforded by the parked cars. At the same time she didn't want to give him enough leeway to break into a car and force her to choose between letting him escape and firing at him in the presence of bystanders. She also wanted to position herself above him, between him and the Popo Agie Campground, so that Charles could come in from the lower elevation and together they could squeeze him.

Unfortunately, what she *wanted* and what she *could have* were two different things. She hurried around to the far end of the parking lot and then came in on him, her weapon raised and aimed at his heart.

"Freeze, Bucher, or I'll drop you where you stand."

"Princess Summerfall Winterspring," he said. "I've been expecting you. Where's that over-the-hill spook you've been hanging out with?"

"Close," Gwen said, "ready to help me take you out of here in either cuffs or a body bag."

"Somehow I doubt that," Bucher said. "Besides, I've got a lot more to lose than you and I'm ready to take a round or two from that toy gun of yours while I cap a few gawking tourists. I don't think you'd want a career-killer like that, not somebody as ambitious as you are. And I don't think the boogie cavalry is going to arrive anytime soon. He's too fucked up from the boom boom at the Clinic."

Gwen let him run on; every moment he took would give Charles a chance to move closer. Then she saw what she had most feared—not just a potential hostage, but a helpless one. There was a baby in a car seat in the vehicle where Bucher was standing. Keeping her gun aimed at him, she changed position so that from the corner of her eye she could see the tourists standing above the Sinks. They were all looking at her and one in particular—doubtless the child's mother—had stepped forward, urged on by the fear for her child's safety, but frozen in place by the sight of Bucher's rifle and Gwen's handgun.

The car door was locked and the window slightly cracked at the top. The air was cool and the child was comfortable. The mother had probably wanted to take a look at the Sinks but didn't want to awaken her sleeping child, so she had secured the car and walked over to the river, keeping her eyes on the vehicle every few steps. Gwen couldn't take her eyes off of Bucher, but she could sense the woman's panic and see her shaking at the edge of her visual field.

"What are you doing? Who are you? You're endangering my baby!" the woman said.

"What do you think, Princess?" Bucher said to Gwen. "You want to take the risk of shooting up this woman's kid? I can see the headlines now and they don't look pretty."

All the while he spoke he was smiling, enjoying Gwen's dilemma and the woman's fear. The one thing in her favor was the fact that Stimson's .30-30 was slung over Bucher's back. Walking through the crowd with the rifle in his hands would have aroused too much suspicion. Now it would take him several seconds to pull it around and aim it.

She couldn't fire at his head or chest when he was standing next to the car window and she couldn't let him escape, so she did the best under the circumstances—she fell to the ground to give the mother some slight bit of reassurance, braced her elbow and then shot Bucher in the right leg. She could see the plume of red vapor as the round went through his thigh. As he fell to the ground he tried to reach around for the rifle.

"Don't even think about it," Gwen said. "The next one's going between your eyes."

Suddenly the woman ran forward and screamed, "I'm getting my baby out of there!"

"Stay where you are," Gwen said, but the woman ran to the opposite side of the car. The momentary distraction was all Bucher needed and he quickly scooted around to the front of the adjoining car, dragging his leg and marking the white gravel with red smears.

"My turn now, bitch," he said, positioning himself with Stimson's rifle. "Which one do you want me to kill first, the mother, the kid, or you?"

Just then a truck pulled into the parking lot. It looked like Cletus' but Charles was behind the wheel. He hit the brake, the dust and pebbles flew, and he rolled out of the driver's seat and onto the lot. Then he began to make his way around behind Bucher.

Gwen didn't speak. She knew that Bucher was alert and intelligent enough to know that the doors were starting to close and that his only chance was to try something rash. She didn't have to wait long for him to act.

87

The Sinks Parking Lot, Sinks Canyon State Park

Charles didn't hesitate. He fired four rounds in quick succession. Bucher had positioned himself behind the vehicle's left front tire, which was struck by the first round. The second two sliced through the car's front bumper and the fourth pinged through the fender of an adjoining vehicle, missing Bucher by a few inches. While Gwen was moving closer under Charles's covering fire, Bucher suddenly rose, aimed, and shot back at Charles. The sound of the projectile striking metal was heard, and then, all at once, there was silence and Gwen's heart began to sink.

Now Bucher was moving quickly between the cars, balancing himself with his free hand. He was limping badly but the adrenalin was winning out over the loss of blood and the throbbing pain. Positioning himself between Gwen and the tourists he knew that she would hesitate to fire. She also knew that he would exploit that hesitation and fire at her.

She also knew his intention—to move across the Popo Agie, using the ceiling of limestone that covered the Sinks, forming a natural bridge over the river. Once on the other side he would have a clear field of fire when Gwen attempted to follow. Unless he lost consciousness from the bullet wound he would put more and more distance between himself and the roads, paths and other markers of civilization along the river and disappear into the wilderness.

She yelled at the tourists, "Get down, you're in the line of fire," and several did, but some ran down river and one simply sat down, paralyzed with fear, her upper body sitting yoga-like, silhouetted against the surrounding sand and rocks. Gwen opened fire on Bucher, but he hit the ground, rolled rapidly to the side and shot indiscriminately in her direction before he could assume a conventional prone position and get off a shot that was properly aimed. She went down as well and aimed for the center of his face, but with all of his movement the round caught the edge of his shoulder. She saw his reaction, but he continued to fire, the next round striking the gravel just before her face and pinking her cheeks and forehead.

Instinctively she closed her eyes and then opened them immediately as he squeezed the trigger again and the rifle simply clicked. She jumped to her feet and approached him, hoping that there was another round left in her magazine. He reached in his pocket in order to reload and she promptly aimed and squeezed the trigger of the Sig, but it was empty.

She knew she only had a second or two before he could fire, so she ran toward him, planted her left foot and kicked him in the center of his face with her right. His nose snapped and he loosened the grip on his rifle. With the blood coursing over his mouth and chin, she pulled the rifle out of his hand and swung the butt at his head. He rolled to the side and the butt struck his shoulder but he continued to move.

On his feet now and bracing his leg with his right hand and arm he hobbled closer to the river and the limestone bridge above it. Gwen pulled her throwing knife from the sheath strapped to her right leg, followed him for a few yards, gripped it, positioned herself, and threw it, striking him squarely in the right shoulder.

He stopped and turned toward her, his eyes glaring with rage and pain and reached for the handle with his left hand. He couldn't get a good grip on it, but he was able to work the blade loose. She was moving closer to him as it fell to the ground, but as she got close enough to strike him he bent over, picked it up, and held it in the air, pointing it at her eyes.

"You think you could take me out with some campfire-girl piece of shit like this?" he said. "I don't kill easily, and I'm damned sure you're not going to do it. You want to try? You want to find out how it'd feel to have this stuck in your eye?"

Gwen stepped back so that Bucher could not lunge at her with the throwing knife. He smiled and said, "That's what I thought, little girl. You're in the wrong business. Now why don't you just get the fuck out of here and leave me to mine."

Gwen stood there, staring at him, slipped off her jacket without moving her head or eyes, and removed her Buck knife from the sheath that was slung between her shoulder blades.

Bucher laughed. "So what the fuck do you think you are, some kind of Rambo?"

Gwen didn't respond. She just held the knife in her hand and let him look at it for a moment. It was a Strider Solution, just under ten inches in length, with a contoured handle and grip ridges on top of the drop-point blade.

"I'll just say this once," she said. "You're bleeding from the face, leg and shoulder and you're forty years older than me. I can follow you across this land and watch you bleed out or I can get you medical attention and let you have ten years of appeals before they execute you. Pick one."

"Fuck you," he said, and lunged at her, stabbing at her face with the throwing knife. She pivoted to the side and stuck her Buck knife in his left cheek. He screamed in pain, dropped the throwing knife, grabbed at the wound, fell to his knee, and then started crawling toward the river.

He fell across the rocks at the river's edge, clutching at roots and shrubs as the white water coursed over his legs, pulling him toward the Sinks. His face was a mask of hate and rage. Gwen stared at him, raised her knife, said "This is for Denise," and then did something that she feared she might come to regret forever. Then she stood and watched the river as it pulled his helpless body along the white water, through the edges of the rocks, over the exposed roots and into the limestone cave.

88

The Sinks, Sinks Canyon State Park

She completed what she needed to do and then turned to walk toward the parking area. When she did she saw the dark silhouette of a man limping toward her. As she got closer she saw that it was Charles. His face was bloodied and his right eye was swollen shut.

"Charles, are you all right?" she asked.

"Yes, did you get him?"

"Yes," she said.

"His shot took the side mirror off of the truck I was using for cover. The mirror protected me from the round, but then I caught the whole assembly in the middle of the forehead. I wasn't aware of it at the time. I simply blacked out, but when I came to I saw it lying on the ground beside me and tasted the blood running down my face. Where's Bucher? What happened?"

"He went into the Sinks."

"Dead?"

"He will be," Gwen said.

"I don't understand," Charles said.

"I know. Listen, I need a little time. Let me borrow Cletus' truck. I'll meet you at the Rise in an hour or so. You go in the Visitor's Center, get some medical attention…bandages…whatever they have…and then meet me down river. OK?"

"OK," he said.

They actually had a full first-aid kit and were able to clean Charles's wounds, put some butterfly bandages over the slice in his forehead, and offer him some aspirin and cold juice.

"Thanks, but I've got my own," Charles said, taking the vial of percocet from his jacket pocket and washing two tablets down with the juice. "That tastes good," he said, smiling appreciatively. As the three Lander PD cruisers arrived he slipped out of the building and began making his way down river to the Rise.

Along the way he saw some of the tourists who had fled from the Sinks when the shooting started. He told them that everything was over and that it was safe for them to return. They wanted to continue talking to him, but he told them that he had an appointment and had to leave.

When he got to the Rise he sat down on a broad slab of granite and felt the warmth of the sun on his face and shoulders. Thirty minutes later Gwen arrived with Cletus and Bill. She got out of the truck, said a few words to them and then walked over to Charles.

"He's lucky he didn't get past you," Charles said. "Those old boys would have had him for lunch."

"Almost like angels," she said.

"Yes, could be," Charles said. "Wings and all are nice, but in this case a .44 magnum and an AK-47 can be of more help."

They walked over to the Rise. "Do you want to tell me what happened?" Charles asked.

"He bled out, just like Denise," she said. "He was shot through his leg, shot in his shoulder, his face was crushed and he had multiple knife wounds. Nothing comes out of the Sinks once it goes in, so his body is churning in the cave, turning into food for fish and whatever lives in those underground caves and tunnels and streams."

"Where did you just go?" Charles asked. "If you don't want to tell me, I'll understand."

She waited a full thirty seconds before responding. "I didn't want questions raised," she said.

"Questions?" he asked.

"Without a body. There are plenty of witnesses who can testify that we had a fugitive, but probably none who can testify convincingly that it was *him*, not beyond any doubt. *We* know it was him and *we* know what he did, but there's no significant forensic evidence to quiet the kind of endless speculation and second-guessing that we could be facing."

"I don't understand," he said.

"I know," she said. "I just wanted to make sure that we had… closure."

He didn't respond at first. Then he said, "You wanted to check with Cletus and Bill and make sure that they could verify the identification."

"They really couldn't," she said, "so I needed to follow up further."

She paused and then continued. "Fortunately there were prints on the driver's side door handle of their truck. There were also prints on the kitchen counter and bedroom wall of the professor's cabin. That will satisfy even the most skeptical people in the press or the Bureau."

"So you went to check on them," Charles said.

"Yes," she said, glancing at her watch.

A few minutes later she checked her watch again and approached the edge of the Rise. "Look," she said.

They stared into the clear water, filled with trout, hitting the surface, waiting to be fed. "They get lazy," she said. "It's too easy for them. Somehow they know they won't be hooked or netted here. All they need to do is look cute for the tourists."

"Not a bad trade-off," Charles said. "They get fed and the tourists get entertained as a reward for all their hiking. Especially the tourists today, getting themselves caught in a crossfire between a fugitive and law enforcement. That's a real day's work for them. They deserve to get back to the theme park and have some fun."

"Right," Gwen said. "Look…"

The difference was slight, but the water was edged with a tinge of pink as the first current of blood entered the pool. The trout seemed to respond to it, swimming toward it, their senses alert, their tails churning the water.

About fifty yards up river were a group of tourists, approaching the Rise. "See if you can hold them back for a little while," Gwen said. Charles nodded and walked toward them.

When he turned away and took a few steps Gwen slipped her hand in her jacket pocket and removed two bloodied, plastic evidence bags. She emptied their contents into the pool and watched the trout seize the eight severed fingertips and thumbs and devour them hungrily. "Be patient," she said. "There will be more eventually."

After a few minutes she walked over to Charles and the tourists. "It's all clear now," she said. "You can check out those trout."

When the tourists walked toward the Rise she said, "What did you tell them?"

"I told them that this was a potential crime scene and that we just wanted to make sure that all of the evidence had been secured."

"Just so," Gwen said.

Epilogue

Since Denise had not been assigned to the local field office, Gwen was asked to represent the Bureau at her memorial service, rather than the Detroit SAC. She talked about the difficulties of working under deep cover, particularly for a new agent. She fudged the timing and location of the actual assignment, suggesting that Denise was being prepared for a new assignment in southern California when she ran into Harold Bucher.

She talked about Denise's unique skills as both an agent and a nurse practitioner and recounted several anecdotes from their time together at Quantico. She read a letter from the Director, praising Denise's work and urging the family to take pride in all that she had been able to accomplish in her all-too-brief life.

Gwen reassured Denise's family and friends that Denise's murderer had been brought to justice for his many crimes, including the murders of Professor Appleman and Professor and Mrs. Connell. "Some people teach, some people heal," she said, "and some people destroy. Denise was with the angels—then as well as now. She healed all who came to her and she taught many lessons to all of us who were blessed enough to know her."

Charles resisted speaking but finally agreed to say a few words. He spoke of the thin line between civilization and savagery. He said that it was a line that man had walked for centuries and that Denise and Gwen were among those who had helped protect us from those who somehow felt the need to cross it. "It breaks our hearts to see someone so young, so beautiful, and so sweet fall in this battle," he said, "but without people willing to stand guard along that line there would be little hope for the rest of us, who love them and who depend on them."

A week later there was an informal gathering at Charles's house. By then he was wearing a small brace rather than a cast; his leg was functioning at near 90% capacity and the swelling around his eye had gone down and the cut across his forehead had largely healed. Mary had prepared steaks and baked potatoes and a salad that contained some ingredients from her own garden. Frank was there, along with his captain, his med tech, Jerry Dailey, and a PI friend named Grant. The men were drinking expensive scotch in Denise's honor and telling stories.

Carl Loram, Frank's captain, asked Gwen if it was true (as reported by one of the witnesses at the scene) that Bucher had referred to her and Charles using racial epithets. "The reason I ask," he said, "is that it wouldn't have made any difference to Charles, because he's an equal opportunity avenger."

Gwen smiled and said it was probably just as well that he hadn't gotten closer to Bucher, because she knew that what he would have done might have shocked the tourists and perhaps even shocked her.

"Shock and awe are not my specialty," Charles said. "My plan is always to do my thing, move on, and then have people wonder why they aren't being shot at anymore."

Loram turned to Gwen and said, "I heard he called you Princess Summerfall Winterspring."

"Yes, apparently he had an internet device of some sort because he was able to download material and find out that Charles and I were following him. We know that he didn't use the Connells' computer because it hadn't been turned on that day."

"The princess was from the Tinka Tonka tribe," Grant said. "I don't think that was part of the Sioux nation."

"Not that I can remember," Gwen said, smiling.

"She was very beautiful, though," Grant said. "She was later played by a live actress."

"Judy Tyler," Dailey said.

"They're a fountain of trivia," Mary said. "Every time they get together we get a tour of the fifties."

"Judy died in a car accident," Dailey said. "Very young. Very tragic."

"See?" Mary said.

"There are lessons there," Dailey said.

"Of course," Mary said. "And we're very happy that you're all telling us about them, because it shows that your brains are functioning in the face of all of that alcohol."

"Mary always looks after us," Charles said. "That's why we love her so much. She's always outnumbered by men around here but she always seems to end up in charge of things."

"Which suits you fine, Charles White," Mary said, "because you can then all keep drinking, knowing there's at least one sober hand on the wheel."

"That's a fact," Charles said.

"I think I'd rather be surrounded by this crowd, drunk, than by most commando units," Gwen said.

"That sounds like a toast," Frank said, filling Gwen's glass and then lifting his.

"Just one more thing," Charles said, tilting his head toward Gwen.

"What's that?" she asked.

"We don't want you to be a stranger now."

"Not a chance," Gwen said.

ߪߪߪ

Author's Note

Karl Armstrong and his brother Dwight returned to Madison after their incarceration. Karl is reported as saying that there were few opportunities open to him except for 'shit jobs' like driving a cab, so he and his brother acquired a State Street eatery called the *Radical Rye*, which was reputed to have excellent BLT's. When the property was taken over for the *Overture Center* Karl operated a juice cart called *Loose Juice*. Dwight died in 2010.

David Fine attended law school and passed the Oregon bar exam, but he was denied access to the bar by the Oregon Supreme Court, because of his participation in the bombing and his lack of remorse for his actions. Leo Burt remains at large though there are occasional reports of sightings, including one in Oregon. Harold Bucher is, of course, a fictional character.

I arrived in Madison in the summer of 1969, missing the Dow demonstrations and riots that had apparently affected Karl Armstrong deeply, but I was there for the bombing (awakened from sleep in our apartment on the other side of Lake Monona) and many of the events that formed the aftermath. When the film *The War At Home* attracted student attention in the late 70's and 80's and I mentioned in passing that I had been there for the events, my students' reaction was one of astonishment, as if I had somehow been present for the discovery of fire. The memories are still fresh; they were the subject of a chapter in a different book, my memoir, *Accidental Soldier: A Reserve Officer at West Point in the Vietnam Era*.

www.ingramcontent.com/pod-product-compliance
Lightning Source LLC
Chambersburg PA
CBHW032048020426
42335CB00011B/236